# SHOCK POINT

THE ENNEAGRAM IN **BURNOUT AND STRESS**

CHAD PREVOST, PH.D.

"*Shock Point* is precisely what we need in these times. It's more than a helpful understanding of the enneagram as a map to better understanding ourselves—and our relationships. It's a blueprint for how we might rise above the distress of our times. It's essential reading for recovering our hearts, our minds, our souls."

**JERRY COLONNA**

Author of *Reboot: Leadership and the Art of Growing Up*


"Well-written by someone well-versed in the Enneagram, Chad's new book weaves a mosaic taken from Enneagram theory and practice that is grounded in the work of profound thinkers such as George Gurdjieff, Oscar Ichazo, Claudio Naranjo and Gregory Bateson. He navigates Centers of Intelligence, subtypes, and psychological and spiritual Enneagram work in a comprehensive, complex, yet easy to understand, way that illuminates the paradoxes each type faces in their journey of growth."

**GINGER LAPID-BOGDA**

PhD, author of *Bringing Out the Best in Yourself at Work, The Art of Typing, and Transform You Team with the Enneagram*


"Curing burnout will require an all hands on deck approach. This means knowing what is in our power to fix. In his insightful new book, *Shock Point,* Prevost leverages the enneagram system of analysis to determine how different personalities experience stress and motivation. *Shock Point* helps us to pinpoint what we can control in a world of uncertainties for a higher-performing experience of life."

**JENNIFER MOSS**

Author of *The Burnout Epidemic and Unlocking Happiness at Work*

"*Shock Point* is well researched and extremely well-written. Chad deep dives into the ancient personality system giving the reader a short yet impactful history and overview of the Enneagram. In a reader-friendly way, Chad educates on each type, subtype, and characteristic. He describes each type's psychological roots and stress patterns, yet provides a "way out" from burnout by guiding each type through practices that decrease stress and ultimately processing the burnout to move you closer to the essence of your type."

**SHARON K. BALL LPC-MHSP**

Founder of 9Paths and co-author of *Reclaiming YOU: Using the Enneagram to Move from Trauma to Resilience*


"*Shock Point* blends Enneagram wisdom with practical application. As a coach and consultant, burnout and stress are near-constant topics of conversation as our society often rewards our tendency to push ourselves to the brink. This book offers a synopsis of how we fall into this trap and succinct ways to use the Enneagram as a path back to health and wholeness. If you've found yourself in burnout yet again, sensing that there *must* be a better way, this book is for you."

**STEPHANIE BARRON HALL**

Creator of @NineTypesCo, author of *The Enneagram in Love*


"Chad has done a profound job tackling burnout and stress with the intersection of the enneagram. *Shock Point* also intertwines the nuances of subtypes which will be a gift for all readers. This book helps to bridge the gap from stress to growth with practical wisdom."

**MILTON STEWART**

Enneagram coach, facilitator, and podcaster of *Do It For The Gram: An Enneagram Podcast*

"Chad Prevost draws from many sources to bring together perennial and contemporary wisdom around three timely topics: burnout, stress, and the Enneagram. Who hasn't experienced the first two? And the latter is attracting much warranted interest these days. Dr. Prevost suggests how each Enneagram style might deal with stress and what we all can learn from each of the Enneatypes."

**JEROME WAGNER**

PhD, author of *The Enneagram Spectrum of Personality Styles, Nine Lenses on the World: the Enneagram Perspective,* and creator of Wagner Enneagram Personality Style Scales (WEPSS)

# FOREWORD

In a world where the anxieties of living and working were already becoming unbearable for most people most of the time, the recent global pandemic introduced even more sources of stress and fear—and unveiled those that had been simmering for a long time just under the surface. With lockdowns and the threat of contracting a potentially deadly virus compounded the pre-existing anxieties of living in the world today, many of us were pushed past our breaking points. In my over 20 years of practice as a psychotherapist, I never saw a time like the last years, in which every good therapist I know had a completely full practice. It's rare for any of my therapist friends to have vacancies for new clients. It was never like this before.

We are all stressed these days. And now it's not an option to hide from all the pressures we experience or to evade the psychological and emotional consequences.

It is in this context that Chad Prevost has written this book, *Shock Point: The Enneagram in Burnout and Stress,* a useful and timely guide to addressing one of the key challenges of our world today—how to cope with and minimize stress in our lives. In this book, Chad wisely draws on the Enneagram of personality, a uniquely effective tool for increasing self-awareness and emotional intelligence, to provide ways of understanding and dealing with the crisis of overwork and overwhelm that is currently plaguing so much of our world and our daily experience of being alive.

Chad first provides important information about stress and burnout—the increasingly frequent consequence of ignoring symptoms of stress until they result in some sort of breakdown of the human system—and then offers the Enneagram as an important source for the solution. *Shock Point* is an approachable book that shows you exactly why you are stressed out and what you can do about it. It highlights the fact that the central aspects of stress can be addressed through a greater understanding of your individual stressors, blind spots, and habitual patterns. After all, an inability to recognize and reduce stress, particularly when it gets to the point of burnout, is really a problem that stems from a lack of self-awareness and an inability to consciously recognize and change one's self-destructive habits. Very often these habits are related to working too much or not knowing how to cope with anxiety. And the reasons for working excessively and not dealing well with anxieties tend to be related to personality type—and the often unconscious adaptive strategies that define the personality.

By summarizing and integrating different strands of thinking about stress with the Enneagram map, Chad provides much-needed pathways for dealing with the stresses that affect us in ways that can be seen to be individual, according to your specific personality type. What stresses you out may not stress out your partner or your friend. And the ways you automatically cope with stress may contribute to increasing your stress. By bringing together theory and data about the nature of stress itself with the Enneagram types, this book provides a useful approach to dealing with the pressures of life and work in a way that is tailored for people based on their specific stressors and inadequate coping mechanisms.

In doing this, Chad has met the moment—showing how we can use the Enneagram's age-old wisdom to do a better job of coping with all the modern pressures our 21st-century, technological world imposes on us. *Shock Point* helps us see the way we fall asleep to ourselves and the activity of our everyday lives in a way that can endanger our health and threaten our very existence. And it shows how understanding our personalities can help us increase our chances of becoming conscious enough to avoid devolving into mindless, perpetually overwhelmed automatons.

We've had the great pleasure of having Chad and his lovely wife and business partner, Shelley, in our professional Enneagram courses. Between them, they bring a diverse range of experience to working with the Enneagram through their Big Self School and coaching practice. This book supports the good work they do by clarifying the intersection of burnout and the Enneagram system so that hard-working professionals have a substantive guide to performing well and accomplishing things in life without losing themselves in the process.

By explaining the ways we can get burned out by overdoing the biases and propensities embedded in our personalities, Chad helps people understand the choices and patterns of behavior that can get us into trouble—and the things to know about ourselves that can help us cultivate a more conscious and intentional capacity for self-care and self-support. In writing this book, he has provided something that many people need in a way that perhaps we humans never have before—a way to see what stress is, what generates it, and what it does to us if we don't apply ourselves to our own path of inner growth.

If you are in danger of overdoing, overworking, or overperforming, this threat may be related to some hard-to-change features of your personality as well as your external life circumstances. If this is the case, you owe it to yourself to read this book carefully—as you will likely find real answers to your problems in these pages.

As the most powerful tool available to help humankind wake up at a time when we desperately need to awaken, the Enneagram provides a sense-making framework for addressing the causes of our individual and collective stress and anxiety. Some students of the Enneagram system believe it has emerged in the last 50 years in the West after being transmitted in secret for many centuries because we need it now as a means of transformation if we are to survive. This book supports that idea. Becoming more conscious of our habitual ways of wearing ourselves down may be the only way to truly address the physiological and psychological warning signs of stress we continue to ignore at our peril.

**BEATRICE CHESTNUT AND URANIO PAES**

Enneagram teachers, business consultants, former International Enneagram Association Presidents, co-authors of *The Guide to Waking Up: Find Your Path, Face Your Shadow, and Discover Your True Self*, and co-founders of CP Enneagram Academy

**BSB**

© 2023 Chad Prevost

All rights reserved. No portion of this book may be reproduced, stored in a retrieval system, or transmitted in any form or by any means—electronic, mechanical, photocopy, recording, scanning, or other—except for brief quotations in critical reviews or articles, without the prior written permission of the publisher.

Published by Big Self Books, an affiliate of Big Self School, LLC

Paperback ISBN: 978-1-945064-15-9

Ebook ISBN: 978-1-945064-14-2

LCCN: Available upon request

Set in Arno Pro with Work Sans
Book design by Catherine Dionne at Goodboy Creative Co.

Printed in the United States of America

*"We have to learn to trust our hearts like that.
We have to learn the desperate faith of sleepwalkers who rise out of their calm beds*

*and walk through the skin of another life.
We have to drink the stupefying cup of darkness
and wake up to ourselves, nourished and surprised."*

—from "For the Sleepwalkers" by Edward Hirsch

# CONTENTS

## PART ONE. THE BURNOUT PARADIGM

| | |
|---|---|
| How to Use the Enneagram and a Very Brief History | 27 |
| Living in Double-Bind Times | 34 |
| The Burnout Paradigm | 42 |
| The Convergence of Burnout and the Enneagram | 45 |

## PART TWO. THE SHOCK POINT OF STRESS

| | |
|---|---|
| What Stress Is and Why This Book Is for You | 59 |
| The Introspection Illusion | 75 |
| What Do We Know And How Do We Know it? | 83 |
| The Paradox of Others | 87 |

## PART THREE. THE ENNEAGRAM IN GROWTH

| | |
|---|---|
| How Our Instincts Become Subtypes | 95 |
| Eights: Yawp: Too Much and Not Enough | 109 |
| Nines: Ahhh: Waking Up to What You Want | 129 |
| Ones: Firm: Good Enough Perfection | 149 |
| Twos: Use: Deflating the Pride Balloon | 167 |
| Threes: Do: Who You Are When You're Not Succeeding | 189 |
| Fours: Match: Endless Comparing and Introjecting | 215 |
| Fives: Keep: The Walls that Hold You Inside | 241 |
| Sixes: Fret: Trusting Without Testing | 265 |
| Sevens: More: A Little of This, A Little of That (a Lot) | 289 |

| | |
|---|---|
| Afterword: Dangerous People | 311 |
| Acknowledgments | 315 |
| Bibliography | 317 |

# WHAT YOU CAN EXPECT FROM THIS BOOK

I first came across the Enneagram in the mid-90s when I was in the middle of my Seminary studies at Baylor University's Truett Seminary. It was a copy of Riso and Hudson's bestselling *Wisdom of the Enneagram* that I pulled off a Barnes and Nobles' shelf and sat down with an iced Americano from Starbucks in Waco, Texas. Money was especially tight then and I had to make a choice between that book and Julia Cameron's *The Artist's Way*. I went with the latter. My desires and calling were leading in a different direction at that point in my life. It was also hard to know what to make of the Enneagram. The symbol was a little suspect. This was also more or less pre-internet and there was no way to explore or verify what to make of the Enneagram the way everything changed just a few years later.

Fast forward 20 years. My wife, Shelley, picked up a few copies on the Enneagram around 2016 during a time when she was coming to the end of the worst burnout she had ever experienced. It culminated in her losing the tech company she'd been leading, and it was a time of soul-searching for both of us. I began to shift in my own interests and vocational aspirations and together we both began engaging with a variety of sources on the subject.

The light really went off when I discovered G.I. Gurdjieff's work in *The Fourth Way* and *In Search of the Miraculous*. There were plenty of interesting and well-conceived primers, but another light on the path was the work of making the subtypes more clearly understood through Beatrice Chestnut's work especially.

Our dream of forming Big Self School couldn't have come at a better *and* worse time. We launched in March of 2020 right as the world was shuttering its doors and turning on its Zoom cameras. We've had a lot of time since then to do our own work. We've met many wonderful and amazing people on our podcast, in the organization's we've worked with, and through the courses and programs we've joined.

There are plenty of books covering the Enneagram basics. There is a lot of repetition. In our estimation, there isn't a great deal addressing the cultural malaise of our *zeitgeist*. That is, we are stressed. Far and wide in big and small ways we are under constant pressures, anxieties, and stressors.

Similarly, we are seeing a critical level of workplace stress result in what we have come to call burnout. As a result of a perfect storm of individual and collective stress, we are seeing several important confluences. Beginning post-World War 2, but perhaps most clearly for about the past 50 years, we have seen the emergence of the term burnout, an explosion in stress research, and the introduction of the Enneagram into Western culture with a psychological overlay.

In the following pages, I lay out the situation. Why and how we are burning out at such alarming rates, and what—if anything—we can do about it (other than quitting one job and jumping into another). Also, what the latest stress research is telling us about ourselves and our environments. Finally, and perhaps most importantly, what the very best and latest approaches to the Enneagram can do to aid in our stress recovery and prevention.

The Enneagram as a system has the potential to direct your growth path unlike anything you're ever likely to discover. It contains what we call a perennial wisdom. If you are a skeptic you will find hope and room for growth through the science and psychology. If you are a spiritual or religious person you will also find hope and room for growth through the above, as well as pathways for self-discovery that are soulful and genuine and connect to source.

There is no perfectly laid out path we can follow in order to change our lives radically for the better, but we can say this: All of our great contemplative traditions focus on transformation work with the understanding that what we want and desire in our outer lives at the deepest level must exist within us for us to even recognize its essence in the outer world. In fact, that very concept lies behind the work we commit to on a daily basis at Big Self. Do the inner work to see the benefits in the outer world.

Please note that I refer to almost all of the books listed in the bibliography in the back. Specific citations with page numbers are almost always included with reference to the given book in the body of the text. Only when citing Naranjo is this not the case. I refer to his work in *Character and Neurosis* primarily.

Finally, I encourage you to read about all the types. At first, it may feel like a "seek and find" if you have no idea what your type is. But really understanding the spectrum of personality styles gives you intimate knowledge into understanding all the others in your life. Similarly, for your own growth path—as you expand into your wings and then consider the more advanced arrow work—you will want to fully understand the high sides of these conscious shifts. You can't know what the benefits are to your self-awareness and personal development in these other areas without understanding the types outside of the box you currently live in.

I came back to the Enneagram when the time was right for me. May the time be right for you in your own journey here. This book is meant to be read all the way through, but it is also meant to serve as a reference guide. You can pick it up and recognize yourself and others through the descriptions. You can also pick it up at any time and try different activities to assist you in your work.

# PART ONE.
# THE BURNOUT PARADIGM

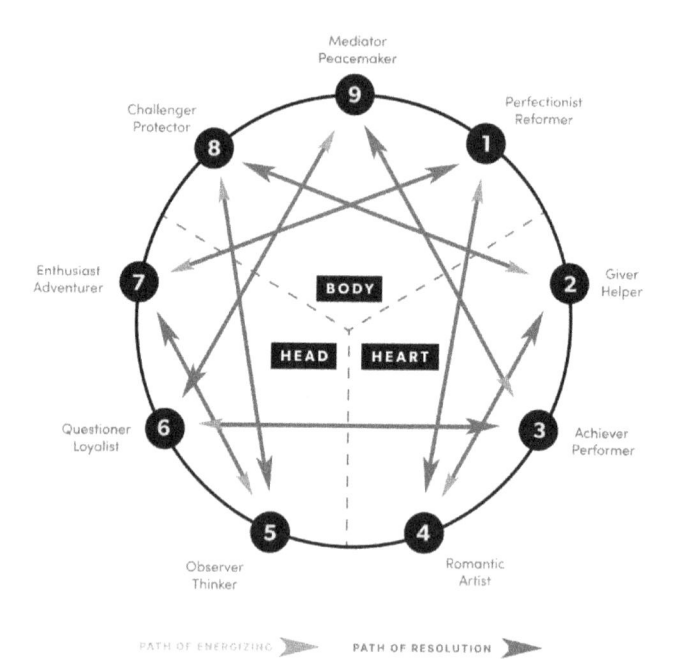

## Enneagram

- **9** Mediator / Peacemaker
- **1** Perfectionist / Reformer
- **2** Giver / Helper
- **3** Achiever / Performer
- **4** Romantic / Artist
- **5** Observer / Thinker
- **6** Questioner / Loyalist
- **7** Enthusiast / Adventurer
- **8** Challenger / Protector

**BODY** — **HEAD** — **HEART**

PATH OF ENERGIZING ▶   PATH OF RESOLUTION ▶

# 1

# HOW TO USE THE ENNEAGRAM AND A VERY BRIEF HISTORY

*"The evidence is in, and you are the verdict."*
—Anne Lamott

This book is complex enough for the advanced practitioner, but newcomers please don't be put off by the know-it-alls. The Enneagram is a tool. Powerful as it is, let us not make it out to be more than it is. The real work is not scalable. It is individual, and it is personal. This book, small as it is, contains multitudes. Democratic impulses run through its veins. Come with an open mind all you experts *and* novices. Something here may well beckon you on.

This book is for everyone who wants to understand themselves better, especially in relation to others, and in relation to your stress responses. Change in the individual is rarely easy, and when it does happen, it is usually slow. So be patient and compassionate with yourself as you by degrees become more who you are and less what others want you to be or believe you should be.

When one of us decides it is time to open awareness and

put learning into practice, it creates pressure on dynamics. It creates unrest when people change. When one person shifts their seat on a small boat, everyone has to shift their seat. Uncomfortable as the new positions may be at first, we also believe that as we do the work, everyone around us benefits. But it is yet another reason that change is hard, and we should not look at this work through rose-colored glasses.

The Enneagram gives you a container to build trust in with your people and to have hard conversations, to be self reflective, and to live out your values. There may be no true shortcut to growing yourself up. When used well and with discretion, the Enneagram provides you direction. It's more than a mirror, merely reflecting who you are. It shows you who others are. It's more like a compass, pointing to more incisive ways of interpreting your own motivations and behaviors, and reveals how you can expand into a fuller and more joyful experience of who you are and who you are meant to be.

You don't need to take a test to know your type. The best way is to read, learn, and self-observe. Still, does it come as any surprise that more people search for "Enneagram test" than for "Enneagram" on the internet?

People resistant to the very idea of self-evaluative tests often point out that it's not scientific when there's no way to verify the test's "validity." They rightly point out that if the idea of self-evaluative tests is to bring forth a greater awareness or insight into one's behavior in the first place, how are one's own subjective biases capable of leading to the necessary insight? Or, perhaps more plainly, if you're blind to yourself, you're blind. As Donald Rumsfeld famously once said when searching for "weapons of mass destruction": "There's what we know we know, what we don't know we know, what we know we don't know, and what we don't know we don't know."

Fair enough. And truth be told, many people do mistype themselves. In fact, if you haven't worked with a coach to learn and discern your type, you probably have mistyped. Bring a curious mind.

Many people follow their initial resistance with another familiar barrier to entry. "I don't want to be put in a box," or "I don't want to be labeled," they say. The Enneagram was created for the opposite, to break you out of the box you don't even know you're in. That is a more important concept about the application of the Enneagram than may at first meet the eye. We are trained to understand typologies as revealing "who we are" and using those data points to confirm or deny (or merely accept) many of our behaviors. The brilliance of the Enneagram, used as a system, shows us so much more. It brings us to source: who we are in our essence, who we are not, where certain pain or traumas still have a hold, as well as a deeper awareness of how and why our ego jumps in to block us or protect us. And in aggregate it does even more. It brings us fundamentally into a deeper and clearer connection to ourselves, and through that integration, it brings us into a deeper and clearer connection with one another. In that way, with consistent work, it contains revelatory potential.

For many, the box they're in is pretty comfortable, or the lies they have always told themselves are convincing. They may or may not be aware of how they're trapped within their personality's operating system, but it's gotten them *this* far. Many stop right there, not curious about themselves, not curious about others. People are strange, sure, but what are you going to do about it? Many are too afraid to confront their pain. For some types, pain is the very thing they've constructed their entire ego's around to avoid. In some cases, the pain is so terrific and overwhelming that it seems best just to let the sleeping dog lie. For a lot of men, the very idea isn't masculine. We aren't supposed to cry and it seems weak to "get in touch with your feelings."

Many people are fractionally curious. They'll take a test, read a few blog posts, maybe listen to a podcast on the Enneagram. Maybe they'll go so far as to read a popular book on the subject. They'll "find" themselves, or think they have, and now they're equipped with the language to discuss their "type." Much like the Myers-Briggs has been used for the better part of a century, it becomes mere typology. Many stop here, especially as the Enneagram now explodes from the trenches of the niches and enters into a far wider western popularity than ever before.

But if we stop there, we miss the real power of the Enneagram, which is explicitly about *transforming* ourselves into more authentic and connected personalities. Simply put, the Enneagram does in fact possess a rich and ancient history. It is, as Helen Palmer once wrote in an introduction for her colleague Ginger Lapida-Bogda, "arguably the oldest human development system on the planet, and like all authentic maps of consciousness, it finds new life in the conceptual world view of each succeeding generation."

Many have documented the various directions of these ancient sources as systematically as the hard evidence yields, as well as pointing in directions where research is bound to harvest new discoveries. And I have compiled a bibliography of such sources for the curious. The Enneagram's historic reach, however, is not the goal of this book. The point here is that the Enneagram is no mere typology. The Enneagram is a *system of universal knowledge*.

Scholar Fatima Fernandez Christlieb's thoroughly researched book delving systematically into the history up until 2016, is a particularly excellent source for those seeking early sources. It is a justifiable curiosity, especially as the Enneagram grows in popularity and is still often associated with the "New Age" movement, and all its corresponding baggage and lack of scientific and research rigor.

G.I. Gurdjieff brought the Enneagram out of the shadows of esoteric traditions and into the light of our western consciousness about 100 years ago. It is hard to summarize the significance, and importance of, the charismatic and enigmatic Gurdjieff. He was an author, choreographer, and you could say one of the most original spiritual teachers of the modern West. Perhaps because he was much maligned after his death by the intellectual mainstream his reputation suffered, and his name didn't reach the same level of discourse as many other psychologists and authors of the first half of the 20th century, such as Carl Jung and Joseph Campbell. Some say his "tragedy" is that he didn't decide until too late to adequately document his own teachings, and left that in the hands of others. Gurdjieff is a subject unto himself and we document a number of excellent books for further study in our bibliography.

One of the chief biographers and stylists of Gurdjieff's ideas was P.D. Ouspensky, who defined the Enneagram as a "schematic diagram of perpetual motion, that is, of a machine of eternal movement." The Enneagram is not a static symbol, but a representation of life itself in constant process.

Oscar Ichazo is credited with his brilliant arrangement of the personality fixations on the Enneagram, and Claudio Naranjo brought them to the United States (specifically Berkley, California) in 1971, with an emphasis on how the psychological and spiritual elements within a person cohabitate. If this cohabitation seems obvious to us now, it was an innovation at the time. Jerome Wagner, a student of Robert Ochs, one of Naranjo's earliest students, described the Enneagram in his 1998 book as: "A psychological/spiritual typology with roots that trace back through many traditions of perennial wisdom and tendrils that spread across many schools of modern psychology." So, while we argue the Enneagram is more than a typology, it may also be seen as a typology system with the overriding point that it is meant—and has always been meant—to be used as an instrument for growth.

Perhaps the most important point from Wagner's definition is the idea of perennial wisdom. Perennial wisdom is the kind that cuts across religions, as well as scientific and philosophical constructs, and adds to and advances our understanding of the world. You could add that this universal quality is the result, not of being above the world religions, but *because* of its syncretistic nature, the fact that it was born out of secret and secreted knowledge passed on from generation to generation.

I would also add that if you had to name one person who is the most important figure in the history of the Enneagram leading up to the 20th century, it would have to be Raymond Lull, born in 1232 in Palma de Mallorca. He broke barriers between Christianity and Islam in a way that was atypical (some would argue heretical) for his time (perhaps of any time). Beyond that, his many travels and brilliant mathematical and prolific written contributions form an Arab-Sufi-Christian bridge to the perennial legacy of the Enneagram. His significance is probably understated.

Ichazo claims to have first been influenced by his knowledge of Lull before learning of Gurdjieff. (Ichazo was also immersed in the works of Plotinus, the early Christian Desert Fathers, as well as the symbol of the Tree of Life, or Sephirot, from the Qabalah.) And, interestingly enough, many of his travels and the sects he would learn from and communicate with were in the very Armenian region where, six and a half centuries later, in 1866 (or 1872 depending on which sources you ascribe to), Gurdjieff would be born, live, and travel.

One important takeaway you get right from the start

with Gurdjieff was his recognition that we have to make this kind of work available to the vast majority of humanity who can't live in retreat from the world. That is, there have been three other ways that people have aspired to what we call "enlightenment" broadly. The "body" way of the fakir, the "heart" way of the monk, or the "head" way of the yogi. The Fourth Way seeks to integrate these centers within each of us. Also, we are to do this lifetime's worth of work in our ordinary daily activities.

While the direct line of influence remains murky to this day, there is no doubt that Gurdjieff brought the symbol of the Enneagram to the West, around 1920 when he opened his school in Paris. His Enneagram, however, was not the psychological typology we are familiar with today. As Riso and Hudson wrote in 1999:

> The system that Gurdjieff taught was a vast and complex study of psychology, spirituality, and cosmology that aimed at helping students understand their place in the universe and their objective purpose in life. Gurdjieff also taught that the Enneagram was the central and most important symbol in his philosophy.

Gurdjieff didn't reveal all his sources straightforwardly, but he should be credited with having brought it forth as an ancient symbol, and for deeper understanding of humans and our place within the operating principles of the universe. Gurdjieff also wanted to provide access to the Enneagram and Fourth Way teachings as a kind of assistance to humanity at large, especially for times when we were at a major crossroads, such as the time in which he lived. He called this collective crisis a "shock point," and it is our belief that we face another point of crisis now. His legacy lives on today in numerous manifestations, not the least of which is through the varied work of his direct followers, such as Ouspensky, Maurice Nicoll, John G. Bennett, Alfred Richard Orage, Charles Stanley Nott, Willem A. Nyland; and disciples of the disciples, Rodney Collin, A.G.E. Blake, A.H. Almaas, and Richard J. Defouw. Today, you can find active Fourth Way centers across the globe.

For all the depth and breadth of the Enneagram as a tool, as a map, as a method of inquiry, many of us need a reason and an application for why we should spend our time and energy here. We need a purpose. The purpose here is to use this tool as a means of bringing you out of your burnout and chronic stress. This book is yours. It represents one step of many on your journey into a healthier and more complete picture of who you are, what makes you tick, and why you are here. It is a guidepost to your blindspots. It will shine a light on your shadows. You will learn things about others they don't even know about themselves. Most of all, it will grow you out of the habitual place you've been stuck in for quite some time now.

**LIVING IN DOUBLE-BIND TIMES**

Philosophers and political scientists, among others, have contended for some time now that humanity is in a steady state of decline. Some date this back to only the past 70 years or so, while others hearken back centuries. Others still, like notably Ichazo, saw a Golden Age thousands of years ago. While it is fascinating to consider the cultural ramifications of our context, the case for this book is, modestly enough, to do what you can and from where you can, and to start with the self.

Nevertheless, we must at least consider the cultural milieu we find ourselves ensconced in. The scope of our malaise is not merely the collective "shock points" from a few years of Pandemic disruption, as much as the disruption has left an indelible mark on millions of lives. Neither do we face simply a "workplace issue" in which we need to address issues of toxicity, boundaries, the need for increased listening and empathy, or anything like surface self-care techniques. Yes, we need better boundaries, and workplaces are often toxic. What we need is a more expansive understanding of how the stresses and anxieties of our time manifests. We need to see a greater part of the whole in order to see how we fit in, and what we can do to break free from its underlying unhealthy ideologies and assumptions.

For the broader marketplace this book categorizes itself in the self-help or personal development category, but I fully recognize that "self-help" is part of the very cultural issue I seek to address in writing and researching and breaking new ground on the subject of burnout. The trend shows up as a constant refrain to do or to be better. We begin to believe there is something not quite right with us. We need to become what those Top Sellers and Trendsetters and Influencers and Thought Leaders are saying we need to do differently. Whether it's hustling more or working smarter, whether it's "being" somehow better or more, the general point is the same: *You are not where or who you want to be.* You are "on the grid" and in the system and yet your life is being measured out in coffee beans and commutes, quarterly meetings and nagging chores that *someone* has to do.

It's not even a trend, but more of a new form of the same monster that's pervaded our culture for well over a century. Advertisers have long since understood that in order to move the client to purchase, the client must feel as if they are lacking something unless they purchase the item. As Don Draper famously tells us in Season One of *Mad Men* (a series based on an advertising firm from the 1960s):

> Advertising is based on one thing: happiness. And you know what happiness is? Happiness is the smell

of a new car. It's freedom from fear. It's a billboard on the side of the road that screams with reassurance that whatever you're doing, it's okay. You are okay.

You are okay if you achieve the illusion the product purports to sell. In the grand scheme of things related to loneliness and the complex subject of burnout, this is perhaps a minor point. I make it, however, to illustrate on a micro level, just how sick our entire value system is. It is fundamentally entrenched in our culture. And there is no easy fix. There is no pill to swallow to feel better. As an entire culture we are crushed with inadequacy. We lack. We are not enough. Or, the inverse, whatever problem you're having is a *you* problem. And while it is true that we—like all the ancient philosophers before us—say to start with the self, we must recognize the sources of strain that we are constantly under. And so much of the pressure comes from a distortion of who the "self" is in the communal fabric and in relation to the whole. It has a tremendous effect on our sense of well-being, on our levels of stress, and the lack of control we often feel in our work lives.

Author and researcher, Johann Hari, in his book *Lost Connections: Why You're Depressed and How to Find Hope*, poses this question:

> What if depression is, in fact, a form of grief—for our own lives not being as they should? What if it is a form of grief for the connections we have lost, yet still need? (54)

Hari cites one of the earliest systematic and longitudinal studies on depression from researchers George W. Brown and Tirril Harris called "The Social Origins of Depression." After thousands of hours collecting and analyzing data, they came to the conclusion that two things make depression much more likely—"having a severe negative event, and having long-term sources of stress and insecurity in your life (62)." What was further illuminating about the results of their findings was that the underlying reasons were true for everyone regardless of class.

Whenever we're subjected to severe stress, or when terrible things happen to us, we all lose a little optimism. It's when the events take place over a long period of time that you get a "generalization of hopelessness," writes Hari, and it spreads over your whole life.

Many of us experience both. Certainly millions of us experience long-term sources of stress. Cultural anthropologist, Gregory Bateson and his colleagues, coined the term "double bind" in the 1950s. Bateson and his colleagues defined the double bind as follows:

1. The situation involves two or more people, one of whom (for the purpose of the definition), is designated as the "subject." The others are people who are considered the subject's superiors: figures of authority (such as parents), whom the subject respects.
2. Repeated experience: the double bind is a recurrent theme in the experience of the subject, and as such, cannot be resolved as a single traumatic experience.
3. A 'primary injunction' is imposed on the subject by the others generally in one of two forms: (a) "Do X, or I will punish you"; (b) "Do not do X, or I will punish you."
4. The punishment may include the withdrawing of love, the expression of hate and anger, or abandonment resulting from the authority figure's expression of helplessness.

The complexity of the psychological double-bind situations can grow exponentially, but the essential characteristic is two conflicting demands, *each on a different logical level,* neither of which can be ignored or escaped. This leaves the subject torn both ways, so that whichever demand they try to meet, the other demand cannot be met. "I must do it, but I can't do it" is a typical description of the double-bind experience. The subject must be unable to confront or resolve the conflict between the demand placed by the primary injunction and that of the secondary injunction.

Importantly, the double bind differentiates itself from a simple contradiction to a more inexpressible internal conflict, where the subject *really* wants to meet the demands of the primary injunction, but fails each time through an inability to address the situation's incompatibility with the demands of the secondary injunction. Through repeated experience, this leads to extreme anxiety.

I use this concept to consider that in many respects we live in times where we find ourselves frequently exposed to double bind situations both individually and collectively. As cultural critic, Ted Gioia writes:

> The double bind crisis of the present day is unprecedented, at least in the context of free democracies, which depend so much on truth-telling to function properly…The first thing you learn about the double bind is that the evidence is always indirect: the participants won't (or can't) admit its influence. But to the outsider, the signs are clear: the main symptom of the double bind is a persistent and structural insistence on saying things that every disinterested party can see are simply untrue…
>
> …[T]hese structural forces are everywhere today. People may complain about fake news, disinformation campaigns, political correctness, junk science, fabricated grassroots movements, spin, and dozens of other manifestations of the same structural phenomenon. But it's not a question of lies anymore, rather an

issue of pervasive double bind contexts beyond any individual person's power to disrupt or change.

Perhaps equally disturbing is that we can barely describe what has happened, and that it has become so normalized. Gioia longs for another counter-cultural movement, such as the kind we saw in the '60s, but which didn't have the lasting impact many expected (or at least hoped for).

The double-bind concept mainly gives a framework for understanding how long term stress happens to us in normal situations. For as often as these may be "growing up" issues and those related to what our parents wanted us to do or not do, they can just as readily show up in our professional lives. The question becomes not only how do you recognize burnout as it takes hold in your life (beneath the layers of denial and subtle dissatisfactions), but what to do about it once we've been able to make it more conscious.

There are plenty of inspiring stories we could share about how "you learn the most through failures" and how we need resistance to develop resilience. But when you're spiraling toward a low point—failing or burned out—you aren't thinking about getting stronger. That process involves many series of small steps over time. We don't want to fail in the first place. We don't want to suffer, to experience hardships, and certainly wishing for them isn't natural either. But this does bring up a question we are sometimes asked in our coaching or in seminars and trainings.

*Do you have to burnout before you realize that you need to grow or that a major life change is necessary?*

The answer is complicated. As one podcast guest and burnout author, Nataly Kogan tells us, "You don't have to burnout the way I did, but most people probably do have to get moved from their inertia." What she means by inertia is that our brains have a way of habituating, of staying in the same motion (as objects do) until or unless another object of equal or greater motion forces a change to the motion. *Duris dura franguntur.* Hard things are broken by hard things.

In Greek mythology, characters often experience katabasis, or "a going down." In some stories they are forced to retreat, to surrender, to experience a depression, or even descend into the underworld. And also nearly every time, when they emerge they come to a heightened realization or understanding of self and others. How much better would it be if we could always succeed without failure? How much easier would it be if we could become humble without also being humiliated?

If there is one thing you can say about us humans, we are adaptive. Not only have we continually evolved into the complex and dynamic species that we are, within our individual selves (and cells) we can adapt. And we have. And we do. But just because we can, doesn't mean we should, or that it's good for us. The idiom, *What doesn't kill you makes you stronger* suggests we can do it. It's a good mantra for working out, or getting through a difficult time. It can be encouraging. It is also patently false. There are many things that don't kill you, *and* that make you weaker and beat you down.

So many of us find ourselves sleepwalking through life, especially when it comes to work. If nothing else, it's a coping mechanism. It helps us, we believe, to get through another day full of all the accompanying necessary evils. Unfortunately, this thing we have to do that we so often feel like sleepwalking through takes up an enormous amount of our waking time, and often kills our best energy day after day, week after week, month after month, and on it goes.

A Gallup poll between 2011 and 2012 conducted the most detailed study ever carried out of how people across the world feel about the work they do. The study looked at millions of people across 142 countries. They found that a mere 13% of us are "engaged" in our jobs. Engaged is defined as "enthusiastic about, and committed to their work and contribute to their organization in a positive manner." Meanwhile, 63% said they are "not engaged." This was defined as "sleepwalking through their workday, putting time—but not energy or passion—into their work." As if that weren't distressing enough, another 24% said they were "actively disengaged." Not only were they not happy, they were acting out their unhappiness in damaging or passive-aggressive ways. And unfortunately, the boundaries between work and home have further blurred. Email checks often start hours before the official working day begins and extend far into the evening.

In his book, *Reasons to Stay Alive,* Matt Haig coined the term "derealization." The term describes a common symptom of depression where you feel like nothing you do is authentic or real. This idea connects to the very idea of sleepwalking through life, and sleepwalking in the confines of our personalities. People in burnout often deny it, just as they often deny themselves the freedom to embrace a more authentic and connected life. People in burnout are often disconnected from meaningful work. They don't feel what they do matters. And, more often than not, they feel a lack of control. It may be that they are forced to attend meaningless meetings, or that their ideas don't matter, or that they simply have no voice. There are many ways to feel out of control, or a lack of control. They have a big impact on shaping how you feel about work, how you relate to work, which impacts how you feel about yourself, and how you relate to others and the world around you.

And that is the very place where the idea of the shock

point comes in. At different times in your life, for different reasons, and from different levels of awareness, you will hit such a point—or the point hits you. You lose a loved one. You break from a long-term relationship. You move out of the house. You become an empty-nester. You lose a job. You break down. You realize you've lost your sense of purpose or identity. Or you aren't even sure what's wrong just that you're not happy and you aren't sure what to do about it.

It is at this point of vulnerability, of some degree of discomfort and struggle and possibly grief, that opportunity comes knocking. The truth is, however, that just because failures, shock points, humiliations, setbacks and burnout happen to us, doesn't also mean that we will emerge from them stronger and better. Our egos, so functional for us throughout, especially the first mountain of our lives, resist growing. Your experiences can show you bare-knuckled truths, but no one is forcing you to accept them or to do anything with them other than keep on keeping on.

As a young man, Hemingway had his own insights into this very idea as he expresses so brilliantly in *A Farewell to Arms:* "The world breaks every one and afterward many are strong at the broken places. But those that will not break it kills." A threatened ego will not go down without a fight.

**THE BURNOUT PARADIGM**

Burnout is also nothing new. It has arguably been a part of the Industrial Age condition, but we didn't have language for it until 50 years ago. But in spite of the striking parallels between the conditions of the past five decades, when the term first appeared, and now, little has changed when it comes to understanding burnout and addressing it. We will look at why in a moment. One thing is clear: burnout was already a major issue in Western industrialized cultures, and the pandemic forced the panic button.

Burnout as a subject could no longer be ignored. Burnout emerged from the shadows of shame and into the light of the common vernacular. You may be "burned out" on hearing about burnout, but when you take it in context, it is a moment in time worth celebrating.

For the first roughly two decades of the 21st century the so-called Self-Help category of nonfiction was deluged with Happiness studies. Everywhere from the idea of wishing your dreams into reality to the "hustle porn" paradigm, the drumbeat was to discover the ever-elusive happiness. Only in very recent years did some of those very researchers pivot and discover the boots-on-the-ground reality of how much *unhappiness* there actually is. No wonder those happiness books kept selling. The vast majority of workers wanted what the less-than-one-percent seemed to possess—not to mention they also had the "secrets" to how they arrived at their success and happiness.

Even some of these very researchers admit now that they, like so many of us, saw burnout as an excuse, a weakness, a fixed mindset as opposed to a growth mindset, or perhaps even a generational malaise (those whiny Millennials!). For better or worse, the dam has broken open. We also recognize things may get a little messy in the short term.

In 2019, burnout "made the list" as a "syndrome," in the World Health Organization's (WHO) main compendium of diagnoses, the International Classification of Diseases (ICD). Burn-out is defined in the ICD-11 as "a syndrome conceptualized as resulting from chronic workplace stress that has not been successfully managed."

It is characterized by:
→ feelings of energy depletion or exhaustion;

→ increased mental distance from one's job, or feelings of negativism or cynicism related to one's job; and

→ reduced professional efficacy.

The emphasis focuses specifically on "phenomena in the occupational context and should not be applied to describe experiences in other areas of life."

Burnout and stress are not synonymous. There are critical differences. Both are complex. We are going to summarize and synthesize the terms, and then with these working definitions in mind, we are going to examine how each Enneagram type and even more specifically—subtype—handle stress in general, and the measures they can take to prevent burnout, and dig out or recover from it, as the case may be.

Not everyone who is burned out, or is well down the road to burning out, is aware that it may be happening to them too. We are not here to overdraw the symptoms and create a crisis where none exists. Rather, we are creating the parameters for greater individual and collective awareness.

And, by the way, when it comes to the Enneagram there are informative tests which are helpful. (We include the best options in the back pages.) But with that said, the best ingredients to truly understand and discern your starting point on the Enneagram is to read from a variety of sources, join communities, and work with a mentor, guide, or coach.

We need to say this right out of the gate. There are systemic issues—organizational, cultural, racial, gender to name a few that are contributing to our collective burnout in many ways. We continue to partner with those working to change these phenomena in critical ways. There are untold stressors in our environment where we have very little actual control over or that have little to do with our personalities. We acknowledge this and are not blind to significant inequities that we must contend with if we are to make real changes in the burnout epidemic. For the sake of our working hypothesis in this book, we will not be addressing them out right. And we realize that this in itself is a privileged position. What we will address is how your distinct personality type reacts to stressors, and work to build healthier pathways to overcome them.

The world is not lacking for books on how to manage your stress, or even on dealing with the macro and micro issues related to burnout. There is a need for channeling these issues through the lens of personality and specifically, through the application of the Enneagram. This book will help you deepen your self-awareness, and perhaps also differentiate between good and bad stress. It will also provide you with tools for continual growth and recovery from acute and chronic stress.

## THE CONVERGENCE OF BURNOUT AND THE ENNEAGRAM

Turbulence happens when contrasting weather systems meet, cold and warm conditions disrupting weather patterns. In the United States, the late '60s and early '70s were a culturally turbulent time. The Vietnam war was in full throttle with no end in sight. By contrast with the political turmoil, there were still glimmers of optimism. There was hope for a new humanity, the promise of a new social and economic order. It was during this very time that "burn out" was first used in print as a phenomenon, and that the Enneagram of Personality was introduced.

Interestingly enough, the Enneagram such as we know and understand it, was effectively introduced to North America by Naranjo in Berkley at virtually the same time that the term "burn-out" was first used by Herbert

Freudenberger in New York. Also in parallel, Christina Maslach soon began studying a similar phenomenon of burnout in human-services work. Maslach is one of the leading experts on burnout today.

As Jonathan Malesic, author of *The End of Burnout: Why Work Drains Us and How to Build Better Lives,* points out, the broken idealism of the '60s may have played a role. The counterculturalmovement had imagined ways of living that did not place standardized workforce careerism at the center of their identity. But as the '70s marched on, the establishment remained intransigent. A generation of optimistic and well-educated people went into human-service careers, motivated by idealistic values such as winning the "War on Poverty" or "Universal Education" only "to discover how intractable society's problems were, and how much time they would spend ensnared in bureaucracy," writes Malesic.

Workplaces have always been high centers for stress in individuals' lives. This isn't a study in history, but we could at least trace working conditions back over the past 150 years or so. A significant moment on the charged issue of working conditions can be traced to May 4, 1886 in Chicago, Illinois called the Chicago Haymarket Affair.

It was commonplace for the employed to work a minimum of 10 hours a day, six days a week. Working conditions were poor and there was far less job security than anything we can probably relate to today.

Workers all over the industrial world were at a breaking point. Conditions in Chicago had boiled over. A protest began on May 3. The police broke it up, killing two of the protestors. The following day, the protestors reorganized, and just as a heavy rain began to fall and the demonstrators' numbers were dwindling, someone threw a bomb that killed eight policemen and injured some 60 more. No one knows exactly how many protestors had been killed or injured throughout the course of events by the police. The following day martial law was declared, not only in Chicago but nationwide.

According to historian Dr. William J. Adelman of the University of Illinois-Chicago, there is no more defining single event in the U.S. and even throughout the world than this singular moment when it comes to work conditions as they progressed throughout the 20th century. Still, change came about very slowly when it came to workers' rights.

It wasn't until another 40 years until a more commonly known event occurred. With the goal of increasing productivity, Henry Ford announced on May 1, 1926: "It is high time to rid ourselves of the notion that leisure for workmen is either 'lost time' or a class privilege." Thus began a march toward recognizing the five-day workweek. But what Ford's innovations also represented was another legacy of the Industrial Revolution we deal with today: automation.

For all the powerful and effective gains this revolution brought civilization, it also brought an emphasis on productivity and efficiency. Housewives might be the first to have reported how automating the house didn't come to mean doing less. The Faustian bargain with technology always promises to make our lives easier, and virtually always leads us to doing more (and often wasting more). We lived with this legacy, without giving it much thought, for at least the next 80 years. We may be giving it more thought now, but how much has really changed?

Then, starting at the top of 2020, COVID-19 happened. Generally speaking, we have climbed out of the pandemic chaos. The great pause has led to what has been dubbed "the great resignation" (with many ensuing iterations). People have a lot more options with where they work from, and real estate is in a tizzy catching up to the full implications of what it means when people can live anywhere there is an internet connection.

Technology, specifically the ability to telecommunicate, revealed that when it comes to the "thought economy" anyway, we can be just as effective at home as opposed to running a commuting gauntlet full of other stressors and distractions. As Joe Sanok, author of *Thursday is the New Friday,* writes: "The Industrialists were a step forward in a number of ways, but their fingerprint is no longer helping humanity." We find ourselves in a time of transition.

Leading up to the pandemic, numerous studies and research indicated that stress and burnout in the workplace were on the rise between 2015 and 2020. According to global consulting firm, Korn Ferry, who released a survey in February 2020:

> The vast majority of professionals (88%) said that compared to five years ago, the stress level in their workplace is higher, with 51% saying it is much higher. Ninety percent of respondents said they've lost sleep because of work stressors; more than a third (34%) said stress has gotten so bad that they have called in sick; and even more serious, 34% said they've had to quit due to stress on the job.

The American Institute of Stress documents the 2022 reality. "Stress at work comes in all shapes and sizes," they write. Regardless of industry or career, after extensive research, their data analysis team concluded:

→ 83% of US workers suffer from work-related stress, with 25% saying their job is the number one stressor in their lives.
→ About one million Americans miss work each day because of stress.
→ 76% of US workers report that workplace stress affects their personal relationships.

→ Depression-induced absenteeism costs US businesses $51 billion a year, as well as an additional $26 billion in treatment costs.

→ Middle-aged participants had a 27% increase in the belief that their financial status would be affected by stress in the 2010s compared to the 1990s.

→ More than 50% of workers are not engaged at work as a result of stress, leading to a loss of productivity.

→ Companies spend around 75% of a worker's annual salary to cover lost productivity or to replace workers.

→ The main causes of workplace stress are workload (39% of workers), interpersonal issues (31%), juggling work and personal life (19%), and job security (6%).

Jennifer Moss, a leading burnout researcher and author, conducted a survey for her book, *The Burnout Epidemic* in partnership with *Harvard Business Review,* during the pandemic. The findings were similar to the above. Among them, 89% of the respondents said their work life was getting worse; 85% said their well-being had declined; and 56% reported having increased job demands. This survey cut across all levels of seniority and tracked people from 46 countries.

The issue of burnout is anything but over regardless of whether we are sitting in the office or telecommuting from home. The *Oxford English Dictionary* credits Freudenberger with first using burnout in his 1974 book, *Burnout: The High Cost of High Achievement.* In sum, he defined burnout as "the extinction of motivation or incentive, especially where one's devotion to a cause or relationship fails to produce the desired results." In particular, he used three terms to describe this condition:

1. Emotional exhaustion—fatigue from caring too much for too long;
2. Depersonalization—depletion of empathy and

compassion;

3. Decreased sense of accomplishment—futility and feeling that nothing you do makes any difference.

Like Freudenberger, Maslach found that "detached concern" is a crucial mode for caregivers, though different professions approach it in different ways. While the norms of health-care work demand an attitude that combines sympathetic concern with clinical objectivity, human-service workers typically engage emotionally with their clients, only to find that the work drains them over time.

Maslach was married to Philip Zimbardo, author of the infamous Stanford Prison Experiment. She saw first-hand the appalling way that the "guards" of the experiment were treating the "prisoners" and how each set of participants identified with their roles so readily. She demanded Zimbardo stop the experiment, which he did after some initial resistance.

The point is, besides her own experiences as a clinical psychologist, Maslach bore witness to the ways we begin to function when we carry out dictated roles. She was an early witness and documentor of burnout. She wrote: "How people who are responsible for the care and treatment of others can come to view those they care for in object-like ways."

For what it's worth, Freudenberger's was no ordinary life. He was a Jewish-German, born in 1926, who fled Germany (with his parent's approval and using his father's passport) at an early age. He meandered through Amsterdam and Paris before finally arriving at New York and staying with an aunt who took him in for a brief stint until she became angry that she wasn't going to receive payment from Freudenberger's father. She forced him to stay in the attic and even sleep in an upright chair. He fled to live on the streets at the age of 14 before a cousin took him in.

Eventually, his parents arrived in New York, but rather than go to high school at first, he helped the family with their business endeavors. He managed to end up attending high school enough to graduate. A family doctor advised him to go to college. He began attending night classes at Brooklyn College where he would meet Abraham Maslow, who took him under his wing, mentoring him, and advising him to go into psychiatry.

He came to know burnout so intimately due to the intensity in which he threw himself into his purpose-filled work. At the same time, in the fullness of time you might say, there was a growing and overwhelming need for mental health services in New York in the late '60s. He would die at the age of 73 in 1999, having continued to work, as his son said, 14-15 hours a day, six days a week, until three weeks before his death, in spite of years of failing health.

As Malesic documents, the term "burn-out" was already being used in Freudenberg's professional world. An official at a rehabilitation center for young adult offenders in Southern California mentioned it as a "phenomenon" among treatment staff in a 1969 paper. St. Mark's Free Clinic workers did use the term to describe themselves, but they may have picked it up from the East Village streets. People used it to describe heroin users' veins: Inject into a spot long enough, and it becomes useless, burned out.

To understand what had happened to him, Freudenberger turned his psychoanalytic training on himself. He spoke into a tape recorder, then played the tape back, as if he were his own patient. In 1974, he published a paper titled "Staff Burn-Out" in an academic journal. In the paper, Freudenberger asked, "Who is prone to burn-out?"

His answer was pretty surprising: "The dedicated and

the committed." Free Clinic staff offered "our talents, our skills, we put in long hours with a bare minimum of financial compensation," Freudenberger wrote. "But it is precisely because we are dedicated that we walk into a burnout trap. We work too long and too intensely. We feel a pressure from within to work and help and we feel a pressure from the outside to give."

Freudenberger's analysis of burnout wasn't particularly scientific. He didn't have a survey or a scale for measuring burnout, only limited observations that people typically burned out after about a year working at the clinic. Burnout remains complex and while there is no scientifically validated approach, burnout assessments proliferate the internet.

Interestingly, the World Health Organization's definition of burnout sounds virtually identical to Freudenberger's original definition. For all the decades that have passed has the understanding of burnout actually progressed much? Burnout still has no status as a disorder in the American Psychiatric Association's Diagnostic and Statistical Manual (DSM). There are no scientifically validated methods to diagnose it, much less do anything about it.

It might be noted that in a few more "progessive" (and homogenous) European countries, such as Sweden, burnout is an official diagnosis that affords its sufferers paid time off and other sickness benefits. In Finland, burned-out workers can qualify for paid rehabilitation workshops that feature 10 days of intensive individual and group activities, including counseling, exercise and nutrition classes.

What is to be done? Authors like Moss have grown tired of starting with the individual. This is a collective issue, we need to change the culture. We don't disagree. Paula Davis, author of *Beating Burnout at Work,* argues that it begins with teams in the organization. Change starts at the top, but when the top all too often fails to lead, change can happen at the group level.

At Big Self, we love the mission and points of emphasis of these and so many other authors, researchers, and coaches. We are all doing what we can to make a difference, although it sometimes feels like lone cries in the wilderness.

But for all the cultural import of this issue, we choose to focus on you, the individual. We hope our culture shifts in directions that recognize more of our humanity. That cultural change begins first with the self. Burnout isn't always a work crisis. But burnout is *always* a soul crisis.

> *How can you say that burnout is an individual's soul crisis when it's clearly the result of an environment that's gone awry and is no longer healthy?*

We get asked a version of this question regularly. It's a great question. How can we move from the micro to the macro when talking about and treating burnout? While it's diagnosed as an individual "work condition" and infects us personally, it is far from an individual phenomenon. It bubbles up and circulates through a *system.* It's a condition of the collective and can only partially be treated at the individual level.

We have to understand the system in order to work well within it. I think we have to acknowledge injustices produced by patriarchy and sicknesses like systemic racism, misogyny, hetero-normative expectations that erode trust and psychological safety for many. But we can't let that be the period at the end of the sentence. I believe we have to dip into grief and anger and really feel the pain that comes with injustice. These are all conditions that we swim in and they will beat us down. They will beat the life out of us. They will douse us with unrelenting stress, this is true.

But it doesn't have to be the final stop.

I learned about the "self" in systems first through my study and research and real-life experiences working Internal Family Systems. If you want to change the family dynamics, start with yourself (and not the "identified patient"). Also, the first step toward real change and transformation begins with self-awareness.

And when it comes to self-awareness, let's just say, "Rome wasn't built in a day." If you're like most of us, you have work to do in those very areas that you probably don't think you have any time for. As Victor Frankl said, "When we are no longer able to change a situation, we are challenged to change ourselves."

The work mapped out in the following pages are literally guideposts, signs that will direct you toward the growth work ready for you. Most likely for you to set out on this adventure you are feeling the pain points. Stress is showing up in your life in one form or another. The only other part of the process for you is to have the courage to begin.

# PART TWO.
# THE SHOCK POINT OF STRESS

**2**

# WHAT STRESS IS
# AND WHY THIS BOOK IS FOR YOU

*"The best way out is through."*
—Robert Frost, "Servant of Servants"

You probably haven't been bitten by a snake or chased by a jaguar through the rain forest or had to trek alone for days with little or no water. You're probably laughing at how remote and extreme such experiences sound. Not so long ago—and for a very long time—our bodies were programmed to "survive and advance" above all. We're adaptive, incredibly complex organisms, and we are now the lone species to colonize the earth. (Ants come close, but they haven't yet penetrated Antarctica.)

Now, as of the publication of this book, some 8 billion of us occupy the planet, the vast majority live in densely populated urban epicenters. While we're highly adaptive, you could also say our bodies are prone to reactions that may be distortions to the "reality" surrounding us. It becomes hard not to "sweat the small stuff" because that "stuff" bombards us on many levels all the time.

In everyday life, situations that can elicit an acute stress response of varying degrees might occur on a daily basis. More realistically than running from wild animals, this includes everything from public speaking, to getting stuck in traffic, to not getting the garbage to the curb in time, to discovering there is not enough money in your bank account. The physiological response is immediate. Your heart rate and blood pressure noticeably increase. The general research attests that these reactions aim to preserve "homeostasis," defined as the maintenance of a steady state of body fluids, circulation, blood pressure, among other things.

Acute stress reactions are not life-threatening generally speaking because of the body's physiological ability to cope. The personality structure itself is a defense mechanism intended to help us deal with stress and the multitude of situations we may be thrown in at any given moment. More on the personality's purpose and how the "cage becomes a prison" later.

Acute stress as ordinary "one-offs" is one thing. What we are finding in modern life, however, due to a litany of factors too numerous to name here, is that the stressful situations can recur with increasing frequency and over longer periods of time than what our systems evolved us for. Long-term stress we call chronic stress.

When chronic stress happens, our systems don't have a chance to recover, and the risk of deteriorating health increases. We discuss the "burnout culture" in order to recognize a widespread and collective endemic context that we find ourselves living in. The kind of changes necessary to implement cultural changes that are so entrenched and recalcitrant is not the aim of this book. The purpose of this book is to focus on the acute stress reaction. In other words, I aim to help you discover your key patterns so as to reach insights to increase your ability to be aware of your reactivity as a starting point.

Through self-knowledge and observation, with a little time and effort, you will quickly recognize your strengths and blind spots, and then what to do about them. That is, how do you recognize, value, and maximize your gifts. And on the flip side, how do you recognize your blind spots (that are likely quite visible to others), and address them. No other system points you more accurately in the direction of self-understanding. This book is a tool in your arsenal to help you develop the resiliency to proactively prevent and treat the effects of long-term stress by recognizing and understanding how you respond to short-term acute stress.

On top of everything else, there are many things that don't "kill" you that you don't even recognize as a threat. The kind of stress most of us experience in our day-to-day lives means a kind of anxiety or nervous agitation or irritability when we are under excessive demands. Usually this is what we mean after a difficult commute or day at work or when we tell others how "busy" we are. No doubt, we live in wildly different times than anything that our ancestors for vast amounts of time ever encountered. It is a different kind of wildness than living in the wild looking out for hyenas and giant cats of prey.

Many of us are probably under some kind of nervous agitation quite often. As documented from physician and researcher Gabor Mate in his best-selling book *When the Body Says No,* here are two fascinating findings about stress:

1. Stress is not always a "subjective feeling"; and
2. stress is not always felt even when we are under stress.

The research also identifies three factors that universally lead to stress: uncertainty, lack of information, and loss of control.

Why is all this fascinating? Because it has now been scientifically proven that humans can be under stress without even knowing it. I say "now," but the research has been developed over many decades. We are just now beginning to put it all together, and I would argue it is out of necessity. We are under loads of stress that even our more recent ancestors did not experience. We are among the most adaptive species on the planet, and yet our bodies and minds have not evolved anywhere near the capacity we need to deal with innumerable stressors we experience in our modern existence.

To further this point a bit if it may seem obvious: Stress can be happening *within* and *to* your body without any observable changes in your behavior or appearance. We credit Hans Selye as the Hungarian born "father of stress research" who defined stress as "a wide-ranging set of events in the body, irrespective of cause or of subjective awareness. Stress consists of the internal alterations—visible or not—that occur when the organism perceives a threat to its existence or well-being."

So, you can feel stress and, yes, that tension can be stress, but it might not necessarily be stress. That is, it might not trigger physiological responses related to stress. And by contrast you may not feel the tension and actually be under stress.

With that said, let's take this one step further. Selye helped us define excessive stress as we know it today as occurring "when the demands made on an organism exceed that organism's reasonable capacities to fulfill them." For our purposes, what is also enlightening is that this stress can be triggered by emotional trauma, or even just *the threat* of emotional trauma.

We also talk about "good stress," the kind that motivates us, that gets us off our couches and into training and professionalization, learning or doing hard things. While we recognize there really are good stressors, we also want to point out that we are so blind to ourselves at times, and so biased, and so unconscious, that we often don't know the difference. And neither does our body.

If you're reading this book you probably already recognize there is reason for doing the work of understanding yourself as well as you can. You may also already recognize quite clearly for one reason or another that you are—and have been—living under the burden of stress for a long time. Too long.

We get stressed, and we don't always even know the source. If you don't even know what you're "so stressed about" how bad can it possibly be?

The short answer is, we don't know.

It's complicated. For one, there are "automatic" and completely normal and natural reasons for getting a little stressed. Stress is inevitable. Stress performs an inordinate number of responses within the body. The question isn't how good or bad these responses are to each person. They may vary wildly, and in large part due to the duration and intensity of the stress. Yes, stress is "normal" and sometimes even a way of spurring us on to get something done.

So, for the most part then, let's focus on what we can observe. The problem for our culture today is *chronic* stress.

The way the body and brain behave under stress has a massive amount of literature now. Some may find the way the body's systems interrelate abstract or boring, but this is also what so many often ask for: the *science* behind what is often called the "inner work."

First we should define our terms. Inner work is often defined as spiritual or soulful work. I value the Enneagram's contribution to the field of metaphysics. Not everything worth knowing, learning about, or experiencing is measurable, and to believe so is simply another distorted lens through which to filter your reality. One of the foremost resistances to this kind of worldview is that of the "subjectivity" or "lack of measurables" related to its study, application, and practice. And it's true, when it comes to spiritual development we are often left with anecdotes, personal histories, and self-reported transformations. One brilliant schema of the Enneagram is to help us to filter and interpret the psychological from the spiritual, to recognize and value their interrelatedness when it comes to the development of the human individual. I have experienced a personal reawakening in this area as a result of working with and understanding the Enneagram.

With all of that said, as promised, this book invites the religious or spiritual skeptic to the table too. Inner work is defined in a lot of ways, and in more measurable ways, it also means self-awareness work based on self-observation, journaling, gratitude, yogic, and meditation-related practices. I wouldn't know where to begin with pointing out the research done in these areas. Just consider the field of neuroscience alone. As briefly mentioned at the beginning, the contribution to studies involving neuroscience and brain research has seen a dramatic increase in such studies and promises to continue developing in the decades to come. It is an exciting time when it comes to validating where and how the brain operates under various conditions, and the ensuing efficacy of these inner work techniques.

While there are as many reasons as there are people for why people choose not to opt-in to the inner work, the first and simplest answer is often the most accurate: It is hard work. Not everyone works out and no one today is going to argue the short, medium, or long term benefits of physical exercise.

The world is not in need of another book on how stress works in the works in the body. We can summarize some of the empirical highlights here in order to better understand the current science.

We hear a lot these days about autonomous machines, and how automation is coming for many of our jobs. Strangely enough, our reactions to the environment have already long since been run by a system way ahead of its time: the incredibly complex *autonomic nervous system* (ANS).

ANS: It's easy to remember. Just think: "It's totally automatic." It's the part of your brain that's also called the "reptilian" part of the brain. What we call "higher" brain functions, the kind that leads to rational thought, scientists consider the "newer" part of the brain in that it separates our cognitive abilities from that of most other life forms on the planet.

These autonomic systems of ours adapted to environments for many thousands of years vastly different from today. Modern experiences can trigger stress reactions in the body many times throughout each and every day of even ordinary days. Our ancestors were wandering in the woods and tending crops. Our body's reaction to something relatively small or "normal" may nevertheless be a *big deal* to the automatic reactions of our nervous system.

There are a couple of branches of the ANS. There are the *sympathetic* and *parasympathetic* nervous systems. The sympathetic part (SNS) is the one we think of when we talk about "fight or flight." The *para*sympathetic part (PSNS) is responsible for these other "totally automatic" parts, such as rest and digestion, or "feed and breed" responses. In other words, according to Maslow's Hierarchy of Needs, these two parts of our nervous system are the first two levels of the foundation: the Basic Needs.

So, when the automatic part of the SNS kicks into gear, your senses become heightened and hyper-focused on the "threat," or source of stress. The heart rate rises and muscles become tense. The part of the brain that requires a higher quality of rational thinking is diminished, as the body leaps into protection mode. Survive and advance. Each and every day. Your own self-awareness also fades into the background as the SNS focuses more and more attention on the sources of the stress.

Autonomous systems that turn on without a user guide are great, right? The problem is the SNS doesn't just turn off, and in fact, you could say it does require something of a user guide to prevent it from "ruling over all." If it does stay in charge you'll find yourself anxious, hyper-vigilant, suffering from insomnia, you get the picture.

It should come as no surprise that the result of all this leads to mental and physical health problems. Chronic stress shuts down the SNS on its own, and depression symptoms set in low motivation, mood, sex drive, you name it. While this can occur from a single traumatic stress event, it probably even more often manifests from "a thousand little cuts" over time, or as mentioned above, from double-bind experiences.

It is essential for basic functioning (much less high-level functioning) for you to be able to switch from the SNS to the PSNS. The PSNS allows for reflection, which ultimately leads to health and an authentic sense of well-being. Literally, this is another dimension of self-awareness. Knowing how and why your body reacts to daily grinds.

But here's something that may surprise you. You're going to have stress in your life. Not only that, but stress activates you. The goal of this book, and the wisdom and applied research it holds, is not to eliminate stress from your life. Stress is necessary and vital for your life. Having stress in your life means you have things, people, and work you care about. You have a meaningful life and stress comes along with that. The challenge is to get good at stress so you can enjoy your meaningful life.

The Cross-Stressor Adaptation Hypothesis is the notion that when we purposefully stress the body through chosen activities, such as exercise, the body's physiological stress response is activated. This purposeful activation of the physiological stress response trains the body to adapt to stress more effectively. So, running and practicing Portuguese make you better not only at running and practicing Portuguese but also at dealing with stress at work, at home, and in life in general.

Learning is a deliberate engagement with challenge—with stress—to build new skills, abilities, and knowledge sets. True expertise takes a great deal of time and effort—of chosen stress—to achieve. Research from K. Anders Ericsson reveals that generally, expertise takes about 10,000 hours to develop (with all due props to Malcolm Gladwell for seizing on this idea and making it popular). Accomplishment as a highly qualified amateur may come after about 2,000 hours of practice, professional status may come after about 5,000 hours of practice, but true expertise takes an accumulation of 10,000 hours of what Ericsson calls *deliberate practice.*

Deliberate practice is different from just repetitive training. Deliberate practice means training activities specifically designed to enhance performance. It has the following features:

→ a well-defined task
→ an appropriate difficulty level
→ based on the individual's current ability
→ the individual putting in a high level of effort
→ opportunities for repetition and error correction

Good stressors are difficult *and* possible. Deliberate practice is difficult *and* possible. It's challenging. It pushes us beyond our current abilities just a little, so we can build our next range of abilities. It also is manageable, sustainable, and we have time to rest and recover. Even without the achievement of 10,000 hours and expertise status, the process of deliberate practice is valuable in and of itself. Deliberate practice as an ongoing process in life can become a vital strategy for addressing stressors head on. Hard work to learn something new is one of the best investments you can make to maintain your cognitive health as you age.

According to the research, stress—like so many operating principles in the world and what Gurdjieff called The Law of Three—comes in three components. First, there is the activating event. Something happens whether emotional or physical, which activates the stress stimulus, often called the *stressor*. The second component is the system which interprets the significance of the stressor. For humans, this happens in the nervous system and in particular, the brain. Finally, there is the response, involving physiological and behavioral responses constructed in reaction to the real or perceived threat. Another way to sum it up is: the significance of a stressor has everything to do with how your system assigns meaning to it.

I leave the deep research and discussion on stress in the capable hands of Dr. Mate who has done a lifetime of research on the significance of stress when it comes to disease. I begin with a simple, straightforward, and current definition of stress. It should be briefly said that there are Enneagram types who have functioned so well in the confines of their personality that they may be quite effective at pushing through stressors and ignoring signs of symptoms. We talk later about how some types are pretty notorious for having to "hit a wall" or burnout before they will pay any attention to their bodies and lifestyle choices.

I am also holding the word "shock point" loosely. Overall, I mean that you are at a point in your life where an activating event, some significant stressor whether as a bolt out of the blue or a long series of events, has happened. The other cumulative aspect is that you are at a time in your life where you are ready for this shock to be a defining point in your life. Your response to this shock is what counts. It is an opportunity to leap into a profound territory of personal growth. Your life can shift from resignation to regeneration.

Or you can suffer the experience and remain static, as many, if not most, do. In that case, it will turn out to be more of a "shock," but less of a turning point and therefore not a "shock point." Because this is a book featuring the Enneagram in praxis, and because Gurdjieff used the terminology of "shock points," let us briefly summarize our interpretation of what he was describing without getting into the weeds.

Gurdjieff called the Enneagram a living thing, a dynamic map always in motion, a symbol containing so much knowledge it could fill libraries. We sometimes joke that the sum total of human knowledge can be found on the internet. Gurdjieff essentially said it is contained in the symbol of the Enneagram. With that said, he fully recognized it would be no easy task to wake people from their ordinary, slumbering, mechanical, sleepwalking selves. And to that end, he developed techniques called "shocks." We all need shocks. They spring us into life and action, and if you are of a type that is so deep into your personality that you have survived and overcome all these years, then may we modestly suggest, this is all the more for you.

Gurdjieff spoke of the need for humans on a spiritual growth path to experience three shocks. The first he called the *mechanical or artificial shock,* the next was the *first conscious shock,* and the final was the *second conscious shock.* The mechanical shock means that you make an effort at the moment of receiving an impression. In other words, it is the willed choice to do more with your consciousness than what literally meets the eye. If you are shredding lettuce, you are not just taking the knife and watching that you don't cut your fingers and smelling the lettuce, you are observing yourself shredding the lettuce. You are aware of yourself at the moment you are perceiving.

The same is true with any given activity. As you read this book you are aware of the words and you are aware of yourself reading and interpreting the words. When you walk down the street, and so on. It is the idea of intentionally pulling in another apparatus of perception that is available to you that you don't typically use when you are in the habituated and mechanical patterns of your behavior.

Gurdjieff also discussed how humans have four centers: the head, the heart, the motor, and the reflexive/digestive. The latter are processes in our body that we don't think about are often unaware of: like digesting food, the heart pumping blood through the arteries, blinking our eyes, and so on.

The motor center bears a simple distinction. This is the center that has learned an activity and now it is virtually automatic. We think of the athlete who practices a throw or a strike, or any kind of repetitive coordinated movement. They are practicing muscle memory so that, especially under stress and in the heat of competition, their body will know what to do. Under more ordinary circumstances, we think of driving a car, typing on a keyboard, showering and getting dressed and ready for the day, or back to our kitchen comparison, dicing vegetables and preparing a meal. If you were to really document your day-to-day activities and experiences, you would find a great deal of your life is occupied in this center. And, to a large extent, this is what Gurdjieff was constantly referring to when admonished his students to wake up from their mechanical slumbering.

It may sound simple to observe yourself doing mundane activities, and I honestly hope it does because that way you will be open to practicing. And that is what it takes: practice. When you make the effort with anything you begin to build the muscle and at first it is hard and takes repetition and you can become easily discouraged or just not see the benefit. Over time, the rewards from the effort become more and more discernible. In *In Search of the Miraculous,* Gurdjieff says:

> Efforts to remember oneself, observation of oneself at the moment of receiving an impression, observation of one's impression at the moment of receiving them, registering, so to speak, the reception of impressions and the simultaneous defining of the impressions received, all this taken together doubles the intensity of the impressions. (188)

Gurdjieff called this remembering yourself. He referred to this idea frequently and to the layperson's perspective it at first sounds wild. Remember myself? Where did I go? But it is really not as mystical or complicated as it might at first sound. It comes down to observing yourself consciously and closely as often as you can. You remember yourself when you transcend the confines that your ego has constructed around your fundamental essence, or your truer, genuine, authentic self, your True Self, as we sometimes say. You constructed your false self for a lot of reasons. It has both served you well, and because of its distortions and over-corrections, it has also caused you a lot of unnecessary suffering. The root of the word passion comes from the Latin, *passio,* meaning "to suffer."

C.S. Lewis once wrote that "there are no real personalities anywhere else" other than in God. Everything is sameness until you find the originality of your real self. To my way of thinking, this giving up of the masks we wear actually brings us out of the labels of personality, and into the authenticity of who we are.

So, the idea of developing another level of awareness in your normal day-to-day life helps you begin to break you out of your personality's ingrained standard operating procedure, if you will. A great deal of Gurdjieff's teaching centers around the idea of self-remembering and the great struggle inherent within the process. This is the mechanical shock.

As for the second step, or the first conscious shock, lifelong student Jeanne de Salzmann describes it as follows in *The Reality of Being*:

> We are speaking of a very intense and active action. After the first shock of Presence, of awaking and coming back to myself, there is a struggle to stay in front of two movements, two levels in myself. With the need for this Presence to last, there is a second shock, the awakening of a new feeling, a new wish, a will...I will the Presence to last. (95)

Implied in this description is the need for a considerable amount of work, of concentrated focus and attention. But the definition of the first conscious shock is also straightforward enough. You continue the effort of observing yourself past an ordinary effort. The idea of shocks of consciousness such as explained and illustrated by Gurdjieff are important primarily to understand that there are levels of growth and effortful self-observation. If nothing else, in layman's terms, it will help you mature. By mature, we mean becoming more aware of your emotions so as to be in greater control of them. This leads you out. Taking control of your emotional reactivity, taking responsibility for your actions and reactions alone into and of themselves, not focusing your energy on another.

Gurdjieff used elaborate and detailed explanations of these patterns of growth in musical comparisons. The first conscious shock is like the third tone of a scale (*do-re-mi*), and the second moves in a similar fashion but at a higher frequency. He also uses the allegorical comparison of alchemy to show what you are doing when you make these conscious moves. You are essentially taking coarse or base metals and transforming them into finer or precious ones. Interestingly, he sees the first two steps as being in step with what nature has provided us already, but the third move we must create with great effort and it does not come from nature. We must generate that move on our own.

In fact, the "second conscious shock" is seldom discussed in any of the literature because to get there is rarefied air indeed. It involves the transformation of negative emotions. As A.G.E. Blake mentions in *The Intelligent Enneagram,* "It is salvation (356)."

This is incredibly difficult work to achieve and only very few do. Better for us to stay on our lower levels and put in the hard work here and now. We also leave the organic and universal applications of these ideas in the hands of the master himself (our bibliography should also provide a rich resource of related directions to move in).

We all have shock points in our lives that usually come in spite of our great efforts to avoid them. We burnout even in the midst of pursuing what we thought was our earnest pursuit of our calling. We burnout even in the midst of experiencing monetary or social success or both. We burnout even though we care deeply about the others in our lives and have done everything we can think of to change and challenge and love them. We burnout because we are hit by the unexpected in ways too numerous to name.

Carl Jung summarized those who needed therapy into

two essential camps, the "21-year-old and the 45-year-old." The younger person is looking backward and is in a struggle with how to move forward into the future and adulthood. The older person is looking forward and experiencing new thoughts and feelings often categorized now as "mid-life crisis."

On some level you are probably thinking how ridiculously easy breaking out of your current "mechanical" state sounds. All you have to do is muster up a little will, right? And you already observe yourself all the time, right? Let's just say it is not easy, or as easy as it sounds. Not to mention, on top of everything else, you aren't retreating into a hermitage where you're going to focus on stillness and breath and meditation all the days of your life, or even for a week in most cases. You have to actually participate with other human beings in this thing called living. And that means you are going to face this little thing called resistance (and we recommend Steven Pressfield on the subject of resistance). This is how Gurdjieff frames it:

> In humanity as a whole, as in the individual person, everything begins with the formation of a conscious nucleus. All the mechanical forces of life work to prevent this, just as our own mechanical habits and weaknesses work to prevent us from consciously remembering ourselves. (*In Search of Being*, 108)

Whether you are looking back and experiencing resistance with moving forward into your life's adventure, or your ego has taken you far into adulthood and you are preparing for a new level of growth, this book is here to help you move. What is moving you now? Is it internal or external? Either way, regardless of your center of intelligence, it is *emotional*. The emotions lead us to our truth. Let them be your guide.

Also, it will help enormously to become more cognizant

of your deeply buried instincts. As sure as you come from protoplasm, these cells are embedded in the organism that comprises you. Whatever the initial mover is that has brought you to these pages, now is the time to consider your way out. Perhaps this book can be your shock point.

And you can start by observing yourself throughout the day. One of the best ways to catch yourself in reactivity is when you are performing the most mundane of tasks. Or when you are naturally "triggered." Try self-observing when you are stuck in traffic, or waiting in line at the coffee shop when you have an important meeting to get to. Just as the Apostle Paul tells us to pray without ceasing, we similarly seek to be conscious all the time. Of course it is impossible. But the effort alone gets us a long way.

**THE INTROSPECTION ILLUSION**

So why not just do some self-observation? Why the Enneagram? And why not just hire a life coach for a few weeks?

Mentors and coaches are part of the communal response to growth and observation that we advocate. The truth is, you come out of the womb alone and you die alone, yes. You are confined to your body and your point of view. But you cannot do this on your own (sorry Fives!).

You don't know what you don't know.

But you knew that.

Believing you understand your motivations and desires, your likes and dislikes, has been dubbed the "Introspection Illusion" by psychologist Emily Pronin's 2009 research. More than half a century ago, Jung wrote: "In each of us there is another whom we do not know."

Jung was largely talking about the suppressed part of our personalities that we push into the "shadow," but the point is similar: *You don't always know your own thoughts and feelings as well as you think you do.*

You believe you know yourself, and why you are the way you are. You believe this knowledge tells you how you will act in all future situations. Time and again, research shows introspection is not the act of tapping into your innermost analytical capabilities but *is almost always a reconstruction.* You look at what you did or how you felt, and you make up an explanation. You make up explanations others can believe too.

There are so many ways we construct false narratives. We tell ourselves the potential is within us. We tell ourselves outside forces compel us. These truth distortions aren't necessarily wrong.

The question isn't how we lie to ourselves or distort our self's reality, but why?

The question "Why?" used to be what psychologists and researchers relied on when conducting their tests. Keep asking, *Why?* The problem, however, is that people don't always understand the why. You can be sincere *and* smart. It likely doesn't matter.

A 1977 *Psychological Review* study found that most subjects did not accurately introspect their way to objective self-reported reasons. However, when the connections were plausible cause-and-effect, they were a little more accurate.

Perhaps the most widely accepted view is that self-knowledge, even if not absolutely certain, is secure in the following sense: self-knowledge is immune from some types of error to which other kinds of empirical knowledge are vulnerable. "Looking within" is loosely applied. What does it mean to look within? Is it going to lead you to measurable change?

Most people believe they have an essential core, a true self. Who they are is demonstrated primarily in their *moral values,* and that seems to remain stable over time and experience. Books like Bruce Hood's *The Self Illusion* and Julian Baggini's *The Ego Trick* make a case that there is no centralized self operating either in the brain or as that special "inner voice."

Defining "true self" would be a book unto itself. The discussion ranges far back into antiquity and there are traditions and schools which discuss the concept from philosophy to theology to psychology. A recent excellent article which considers a range of arguments and synthesizes these ideas into a coherent form can be found in an article from *Frontiers in Psychology*, "The True Self: Critique, Nature, and Method," and can currently be accessed publicly. One assessment they make is the following:

> The basic function of the self is unity. It connects events in time and space into a single continuum of experience. To the extent that this unity is manifested, the true self is manifested. This can happen on different levels: (1) the core self—extending the continuity of the subjective sense of being—linking together orientation in space, time, and situation, and (2) the narrative self—creating unity throughout live events. Though we can say that there cannot be a narrative self without a core self, the converse is also true: The core self cannot actually exist—be aware of itself as a unity—without different moments in time being united within a time-structure.

We need both "selves" working in coordination. But put your "self" aside here for a minute.

I self-identified as an introspective person by my midteens. I began writing poetry as a freshman in high school, and ended up becoming an English Major in college. Turns out, I test better on analytical tests than verbal or mathematical, although I didn't become conscious of that until I was in my late-20s and had to take a series of standardized tests. The point is, over time, I evolved in my self-understanding, but I am fully capable of skewering myself inwardly.

I can make a decision slow and steady. I can go as far as a decision seems plausible and reasonable, but my over-reliance on my introspection can also lead to an inflated sense of "having it all together." Without the outward consultation of others (friends, family, mentors, colleagues), I can still be susceptible to gigantic mistakes, such as, for example, almost marrying the wrong person.

I had been engaged for about four months. I was going to graduate school at Baylor in Waco, Texas, and my fiance and I had made the long Thanksgiving journey to meet my parents in Richmond, Virginia. I was 22 and in love, or earnestly believed I was. My fiance—let's call her Stephanie—had told me all about her bulimic eating disorder in high school. It was behind her now, she said.

It had done some damage, she told me one night. She might not be able to have kids. I recall the night she added this little detail, and I recall being sobered by the reality but also, somehow, completely fine with it. I was in love, and this is what love was about. Marriage was about much more than having kids, and anyway, she said "might not." There was always a chance, I told myself.

Joining us for our Thanksgiving dinner with my parents and younger brother, was one other person, Ralph Starling. Ralph was the Minister to Singles at First Baptist Church, where my parents were members. Ralph was also an old friend of my parents and an uncle figure to me. He was tall, athletic (had been a semi-pro baseball player), funny, creative, and cool. And for whatever reason, even at the age of around 40, single.

We were having a typical polite and gratitude-filled Thanksgiving meal when Ralph—in his somewhat direct and unconventional approach—started asking me why I wanted to get married. I didn't care that I was being put on the spot. I appreciated the authenticity, the attention, the directness. But I had to admit to myself right there in the very moment that I didn't have a solid, clear answer.

"We're in love," I said, looking over at Stephanie who laughed somewhat nervously.

"Right," he nodded. "But why does that mean you want to get married?"

I was a semester into Seminary. I had been dating Stephanie for a year. I was going to come up with something more sophisticated. I stumbled my way to something about kids.

"Okay," he nodded. "And why do you want to have kids?"

By this time, my mom intervened. She backed Ralph off of the unexpected interrogation, and we resumed our otherwise forgettable Thanksgiving dinner. For as flustered as I was in the moment, I have always been grateful for the risk that Ralph took. If my parents had asked the same questions it wouldn't have had the same effect.

Over the ensuing weeks, I began to ask myself what the hurry was. I began to investigate deeper into my relationship with Stephanie. I started to see how her issues were still ingrained. It took a few more months, but by early spring—mere months before our wedding—I broke it off. It was the second-best decision I've ever made in my life. (The first was marrying Shelley a few years later!)

We tend to analyze only within ourselves, which creates an echo chamber. We also analyze to the point of *analysis paralysis*.

Timothy D. Wilson wrote a 2004 book with a title that echoes the Introspection Illusion idea in *Strangers to Ourselves: Discovering the Adaptive Unconscious.* He argues that although it is indeed worthwhile to "know thyself," you'd do better to pay more attention to what you do than how you feel or what you think. After all, this is what your friends do, and others are often more accurate judges of your personality than you are. This is true even if you haven't done much inner work, and remain at a lower level of awareness. The emphasis here is on following your actions, not your thoughts. Our actions, as every habit formation coach will tell you, are micro-votes for the person you want to be (or already are).

In the workplace, I've had friends blow off all things "psychology" because it's all self-evaluative. If you're only evaluating yourself on all these personality tests, let's say, then who's to say what's really real? How do you prove you're an INFP?

Fair enough.

One friend who even *minored* in Psychology says one of his professors "admitted" that it was "all bullshit anyway." Whatever the context of my friend's professor's statement, it clearly left an impression. Twenty years later, he still uses this statement as reinforcement to his concept that psychology was more or less useless because there are no external, measurable evaluations of one's own behavior. He was a Finance *major*, so that explains a little.

Unfortunately, we have stripped other important criteria from our understanding of psychology, and our very selves. In our "enlightened" society, emphasizing the intellect as the way to progress, we strip away many knowable parts of the human experience. Among them, the very idea of the aesthetic quality of life. Life is beautiful. How do you measure the quality of beauty? The Romantics tried to connect us back to feeling, but the march toward the rational above all has won the day for now. Now we can barely mention the concept of a soul without being taken for being gullible, "New-Agey," or superstitious. This has not always been so, even among the greatest thinkers. Plotinus, for example, wrote of the soul:

> Being born, coming into this particular body, these

particular parents, and in such a place, and what we call external circumstances…form a unity and are as it were spun together.

Further, it has been suggested from a variety of cultures throughout antiquity that we have a "daimon" or an angel or protector or paradigm or soul. In current times, it can be interpreted many ways. Heraclitus' famous statement (from a fragment), *Ethos anthropoi daimon,* has led translators to try a wide variety of what he may have meant. I most prefer, "Character is fate." The inner genius, our individual soul, is neither us nor is it our own. Ethos meant less moralizing as in ethics, and more related to the word habit. It is your way of being. Thus, your soul shows up in how you are, how you behave. It also reminds us of Paul telling his laity that you will know each other from the "fruits of the spirit" in Galatians 5:22-23. That is, those with a habituated commitment to doing the work will, in essence, "be" kindness and charity and joy.

Whether you are listening to your own inner voice, or really listening to others, we need some help along the way. That's where the Enneagram of Personality comes in. When it comes to a real source of aid on the adventure of self-discovery why not tap into a point on the map that can actually provide real guidance? This is not the stale pablum of self-help, tinged with the sponginess of hope. These are real signposts. The work still has to be done, but isn't it nice to know you'll have some verifiable directions to know in which direction to move?

If you've only just begun the self-knowledge journey, you may be surprised to learn that it is incredibly difficult to know yourself. Don't take my word for it. Lao Tzu, the ancient Chinese philosopher, who lived in the 6th century BCE, wrote: "He who knows others is wise; he who knows himself is enlightened." Similarly, Jung said: "Who looks outside, dreams; who looks inside, awakes." The sum total of philosophic inquiry is said to have been summarized by Socrates who said, "Know thyself." Plato similarly phrased it, "The unexamined life is not worth living."

Why would these revolutionary thinkers give so much status to achieving something that most of us believe we've already achieved? Numerous rigorous studies of thousands of people in the workplace show that people's coworkers are better than they are at recognizing how their personality will affect their job performance. As organizational psychologist and author, Adam Grant writes:

> People know themselves best on the traits that are tough to observe and easy to admit. Emotional stability is an internal state, so your friends don't see it as vividly as you do. And although people might not want to call themselves unstable, the socially acceptable range is fairly wide, so we don't tend to feel terribly anxious about being outed as having some anxiety. With more observable traits, we don't have unique knowledge.

Thus, people overestimate their intelligence, a pattern found more among men than women. People also overestimate their generosity. Why? Because in both cases, it's a desirable trait. People tend to believe they have fewer biases than others. Just because you believe something to be true about yourself does not make it so.

You are a mirror to yourself, but there is more than one way to view your behavior. The best method is probably to have more than one mirror held up by more than one friend or colleague.

And it is hard to receive feedback that we possess undesirable traits, or traits that are difficult to admit to. The good news is you can, and through the effort build yourself into the more desirable human you believe yourself to be.

Contemporary psychology has fundamentally questioned the notion that we can know ourselves objectively and with finality. It has been argued that the self is not so much a "thing" as it is a process of continual adaptation to changing circumstances.

And the fact that we so often see ourselves as more competent, moral, and stable than we actually are serves our ability to adapt. Some even point out that a fair amount of self-delusion and self-ignorance is actually helpful to this extent.

While psychology over the past two centuries has contributed the most in the realm of self-knowledge, we would do well to begin with philosophy's contribution. In philosophy, self-knowledge generally refers to knowledge of one's own sensations, thoughts, beliefs, and other mental states.

At least since Descartes, most philosophers have believed that our knowledge of our own mental states differs markedly from our knowledge of the external world, which includes our knowledge of others' thoughts. Ichazo has pointed out that Descartes actually got his "I think therefore I am" argument from reading Augustine, which would put the line of this thinking to a much earlier date. Regardless, Descartes is considered a marker for the Enlightenment and validating the reality of the world through our own thoughts.

But there is little agreement about what distinguishes self-knowledge from knowledge of anything else. Partly for this reason, philosophers endorse competing accounts of how we acquire self-knowledge. The most famous argument on self-knowledge is the certainty of a particular instance of belief. This is Descartes' "cogito argument," which demonstrates that so long as you carefully attend to your own thoughts, nothing can prove that you are not thinking and, therefore, you exist.

Perhaps the most widely accepted view along these lines is that self-knowledge, even if not absolutely certain, is especially secure, in the following sense: self-knowledge is immune from some types of error to which other kinds of empirical knowledge—most obviously, perceptual knowledge—are vulnerable. That is where inferential ways of knowing become the primary way for us to suggest that we can know the self. That is where the term "looking within" uses a spatial comparison to express a divide between the "inner" world of thought and the "external" world.

Self-knowledge is a skill, not a trait, talent, or divine insight.

Your self does not lie before you like an open book. You can't just open up the hatch in the back of your skull and root around until you locate your "self."

Think of all the self-portraits of artists over the centuries. A "portrait of the artist as a young self" has become almost a rite of passage for writers and artists. The attempt to look at yourself is fraught with much more difficulty than looking outward. It can be frightening to look within. We may not like what we see.

We are often blind to ourselves and the effect we have on others because we literally do not see our own facial expressions, gestures, and body language. You may be barely aware that your blinking eyes indicate stress. You may not hear how your tone communicates much more than the actual words you say. The same is true of all kinds of body language. The slump in your posture betrays something that weighs on you.

Emily Pronin's Introspection Illusion research gives us empirical validity to the distorted view we have of ourselves. Our self-image has little to do with our actions. We don't realize it. We may see ourselves in a way that stands in complete contradiction to the way we live. We may say we love the outdoors but never do anything outside. We may say we value time with family, but give all our enthusiasm to our job or personal pursuits. We may believe we're a talented artist even though we don't produce any art.

There are many ways we construct false narratives about ourselves. We tell ourselves the potential is within us, but we just never have the time. We tell ourselves forces outside us compel us to behave in ways that aren't truly "who we are." These truth distortions aren't necessarily wrong.

The question is not how we lie to ourselves or distort our self's reality, but why?

Let us begin with the simple premise that the pursuit of self-knowledge is practical. You will be happier and more effective in your life if you know yourself. And, to that end, the Enneagram more than any other system of knowledge, guides us to the motivations behind our behaviors.

Strangely enough, in order to succeed at things that are going to be fraught with challenge and possibly hardship, you might need to possess a little delusion. Elizabeth Dunn and Timothy Wilson report that mild self-illusions can be beneficial.

It's not always to your benefit to know just how stacked the odds are against success in your field. Is it always good to know how many more talented baseball players have tried to make it to the major leagues if that is something you aspire to? If you want to succeed in the music industry do you really need to know how much more talented thousands of people are than you before you start putting in your daily practice? Sometimes, as with running up a long hill, it's better to see just enough in front of you to take the next step and keep on moving.

Extreme self-illusions, on the other hand, can undermine well-being. If you're small and slow, it's probably not the healthiest to dream you can play for the NBA. If you value great wealth and having lots of things, but you just like watering your ferns, petting your cat, and making grilled cheese sandwiches, you may not possess the drive it takes—or find pleasure in what you're doing that could bring you greater financial agency.

Overall, self-knowledge is better for you than self-ignorance. It's probably impossible to go through life without any self-beliefs, so this is a fair enough starting point. When it comes to knowing yourself, ignorance is not bliss.

Without splitting philosophic hairs, let's start with this premise: You are no more or less than the sum of your thoughts, actions, attitudes, emotions, abilities, values, and physical characteristics.

With this in mind, you can begin to paint a portrait of yourself that lines up with your inner and outer reality. What you seek is a self that integrates these pieces of you. You seek unity.

Albert Einstein once said, "No problem can be solved from the same level of consciousness that created it," and that is exactly why we access our depths through other forms of consciousness.

When you continue to ask the same questions and make the same choices, you get the same results. To move in a different direction requires insight into where you have been and where you are, clarity on what no longer serves, and direction on how to move into where you would like to be.

Tasha Eurich has made a career demonstrating the strong links with scientific evidence that people are happier when they know themselves and how others see them. They are better decision-makers. They have better personal and professional relationships. They raise more mature children. They become smarter, more adept students who choose better careers. They also tend to be more creative, confident, and overall better communicators. And because knowing yourself does require a sophisticated level of learning and understanding, you also learn about the fundamentals of morality.

Daniel Goleman, one of the pioneers of Emotional Intelligence Theory, says that recent advancements in positive psychology have made self-awareness more accessible than ever. Goleman suggests that self-awareness is one of the four main pillars of emotional intelligence, and is imperative for success in any field. Most people think emotional intelligence is about managing other people's emotions. Identifying and managing your *own* emotions is paramount first and foremost.

It's not so much that you live up to a perceived ideal of "authenticity." Knowing yourself means recognizing when disparities occur between who you aspire to be and how you live out your life. People who know themselves well also tend to be less aggressive and less likely to lie, cheat, and steal.

When your values line up in integration with your work situations you tend to be a better performer, one more likely to get a promotion. People who know themselves well are more effective leaders with more enthusiastic employees. Research even shows that self-awareness is the single greatest predictor of leadership success.

**THE PARADOX OF OTHERS**

We've established that it is better to be more self-aware than to be less self-aware. Our well-being grows as our conscious goals and unconscious motives become more integrated. But we're also working through the issue of how your self-awareness cannot be complete in isolation. But if you can't fully trust yourself to tell you who you are, then who can you trust?

The answer is: Others. But what do others know anyway? Aren't "others" the very ones we like to criticize and judge? On the one hand, with people's responses, it's really *not* about you. But almost as soon as that idea begins to absorb, we have to paradoxically remind ourselves that, truth be told, it *is* sometimes about us. Sometimes we do create the conditions for the reality we experience. The wisdom is in learning to know the difference. And that is, presumably, why you are here, to gain access to that perennial wisdom.

As an editor for a magazine, and later of an independent publishing house, I frequently found myself on panels discussing how and why a work is accepted for publishing. As a writer myself, I would frequently find myself as surprised by the content that was taken as by what wasn't. One thing I did know was that a writer's work isn't observed in a vacuum. There is always context.

Your work may be read in the morning or afternoon, which has an impact on the freshness of the editor's reading. It could have been the first in the stack or 41st. It could have been among 41 other entries or 4,001. It could have been on a topic that was thematically in line with the values of the editor—or just the opposite. One editor may like tightly-constructed sentences, and another may like a discursive, associative style. Does an editor believe this work will contribute to the marketplace (be sellable), or is it art for art's sake? There are nearly limitless reasons for acceptance or rejection that may have little to nothing to do with the perceived quality of the work.

Similarly with teaching. While good teaching is about patience and clarity, and the art and science of challenging and encouraging students, you may be meeting a student at a time when they are eager and ready to learn, or at a time when the field is fallow. I've also had back-to-back classes in which I would teach the exact same thing with the exact same level of enthusiasm, and with the exact same punchlines, and the reactions of the class were *entirely* different.

The class that laughs at your every joke and eagerly asks questions and raises their hands to contribute to the discussion energizes you. They make you feel like you can do no wrong and what a joy teaching is. The reserved, non-responsive ones make you aware of the sweat that's breaking out on your forehead as you try to persevere.

Good work is good work, but what we can't control are the responses from others to the work. The same is true of the processes we put in ourselves. That is why a Stoic-influenced perspective suggests that maintaining your own values and priorities is all the reward you need. In those cases, adjust your expectations. Realize it is not about you. It's about them.

Until that is, you run into the occasions where it really *is* about you.

One of the earliest leading indicators that an issue lies within ourselves is when we repeatedly experience the same type of conflict with others. Most people have a vague sense of their behaviors but remain more or less exactly the same year after year. In general, this is because it takes real courage to look at long unexamined (or perhaps never examined) shadow sides of ourselves. We don't like these parts of ourselves, much less admitting to them. It doesn't feel good, and it's hard to go to the source and bring up unconscious things over and over again to reflect on them and analyze them in order to create any real change.

The freedom you gain from breaking a pattern often brings great relief, like a burden has been lifted. I have seen those who put in the work find enormous releases of stress. When the breakthrough happens, and when you're able to step back and recognize it, few things bring on as much calm and clarity and, yes, even transformation.

Through the calm comes confidence. From the calm and confidence comes resilience and adaptability. You realize it's okay to be wrong—about others and yourself. Integrating your conscious values with your unconscious ones makes you a more whole person. In turn, you are more desirable for others to be around. And that is the beauty and perennial wisdom of the Enneagram.

Thanks to the early pioneers and legions of current practitioners and researchers, it has never been easier to do the difficult work. There is more information and evidence out there on how to grow in this area than ever before.

The evidence proves that you will be not only a better human, but a better friend, parent, student, and/or colleague specifically. You can become a more creative, confident communicator. This impacts your relationships, your ability to learn, and how well you function at virtually any long-term project.

No one likes to receive negative feedback. It's okay to feel uncomfortable. You have to let yourself feel the reaction, and that takes time to process. It takes courage. But it is worth the effort and the dividends payout for the rest of your life.

You aren't here to hear about how terrible things are. You are here because you've hit a shock point, you are struggling with chronic stress, which may or may not be burnout, depending on how you define it, depending on how much stress you can handle. Some types can absorb a lot of punishment while in personality.

But you can indeed make an impact. You can take a stand. As Parker Palmer says in many different ways, "Doing the inner work is subversive." In this culture it is.

He also says, in an interview:

> When we bring our inner lives into our work, what-

ever we're working with ceases to be an object to be manipulated and becomes instead a partner to co-create with. That's what good teachers do with students, good doctors do with patients, good writers do with words, good potters do with clay.

To that end, we are going to provide both descriptions and prescriptions. We recognize that while the mechanism of recognizing yourself as a "type" is supposed to be liberating, and not labeling, that you are a complex organism with a complex array of experiences and responses. You can't control the greater forces outside yourself, but that is why you should start with yourself. That was a great reminder from the Stoics. It is the result of doing what we call the inner work on and within your personality.

And you begin that work by recognizing yourself and your behaviors and the motivations behind them first and foremost. You *can* grow yourself up. You *can* trust in the perennial wisdom of the Enneagram as a typing system, as well as the latest psychological research to support the theories as they are in process—just as you are in process.

Here's to freeing ourselves from burnout and sustaining the practices that prevent it from recurring.

# PART THREE.
# THE ENNEAGRAM IN GROWTH

# 3

# HOW OUR INSTINCTS BECOME SUBTYPES

*"The fault, dear Brutus, is not in our stars, / But in ourselves."*
—Shakespeare, *Julius Caesar*, I, ii

To this point I've used mostly empirical language when it comes to stress, with a few nods to the idea of soul and spirituality. I want to begin now with a premise that may sound obvious or simplistic, but is met with various levels of resistance by many. We are organisms. More specifically, we are animals. I am not trying to step on the toes of a theologian's need to emphasize the *imago dei*, or how humans are also made in the image of God. Like so many things, paradoxical or otherwise, both can be true at the same time. I want to emphasize the importance of recognizing that we are animals because by looking away at the idea, by ignoring a real and distinct part of our biology, we overlook, from the start, who we are. And if we are to dig into our psychology, motivations, and even spirituality, we must recognize this basic fact.

Denying our animal nature is nothing new. Charles Darwin's theory of evolution was controversial enough when *On the Origin of Species* came out in 1859. For all of Darwin's brilliant pioneering work into the origins and development of birds and bats and ants and turtles and armadillos and butterflies, he left his own species out of the equation. Well, on the third to last page, he did say that "light will be thrown on the origin of man and his history." Twelve years later in *The Descent of Man* he tells us that had he written about humans in his first book it would have prejudiced his readers against his ideas even more. He wasn't wrong, although he still didn't examine our collective origins much in that book, either.

This isn't the place to dive into our complex and rich history as a species. One of the issues for 19th century archaeologists, however, was simply that there was scant evidence of where we came from and how we may have evolved. You mix this in with other competing and related groups like Neaderthals, and it gets even more complicated. But researchers now are making significant discoveries almost by the decade now. Most recently, the earliest ancient-human presence outside of Africa had been a Homo erectus fossil found in a cave in Dmanisi, Georgia. It was dated to 1.85 million years ago. Now there is a new discovery of a community of early humans that lived roughly 250,000 years earlier than that group, and did so 3,500 miles to the east in what is now China. That means about 2.1 million years.

The long and short: We go way back.

Our egocentricity wants to keep us locked in to the anxieties and stresses right in front of our face. The ego doesn't care about how far our ancestors go back, or how many of us there are now. The ego behaves as if our one single perspective is the beginning of all consciousness.

This book wants to open up new pathways for you to understand how your personality behaves when it is under the authority of the ego. Don't let your ego be too troubled. You need your ego. But you need your ego to have a little perspective. You need it to recognize with a little perspective that it doesn't have to keep puppeting you in order for you to survive.

So, if you think about how we've only had workable electricity for a little over a century even in the most "developed" countries (not to mention indoor plumbing and running water), you might say things have changed. Now, living off the grid is the choice of a conscientious objector. Now, we watch the 14th season of *Naked and Afraid* and stare in amazement at two people's ability to make a fire and survive in "harsh terrain" for 21 days.

This is what we did. For thousands—millions—of years. Generation after generation.

The point here is that we have instincts based on surviving for a reason. We are animals. Animals with varying levels of consciousness.

Among the many contributions of psychologists and Enneagram pioneers and researchers over the decades is the application of the instincts. Humans are not *tabula rasa,* or a blank slate. We come through epochs of time that our ancestors evolved from and through, though we know nothing about it.

As John Bargh, author of *Before You Know it: The Unconscious Reasons We Do What We Do,* writes: "We have two fundamental, primitive drives that subtly and unconsciously affect what we think and do: the need to survive and the need to mate." He also notes that there is a third innate drive, of cooperating with each other, which also is essentially related to survival and reproduction. Bargh calls these unconscious behaviors "ancient, unremembered drives," or "effects" of the mind that operate without our knowledge.

Another contributor to our more recent understanding of our collective instinctive behaviors, Edwin H. Friedman wrote about emotional dynamics within his system's theory after working in organizations and systems for over four decades. Friedman worked in about every sector you can think of from the military to the nonprofit to the hospital to the church to the corporate setting. He found universal applications of dysfunction within groups and across cultures based on these timeless recurring issues.

"Emotional is not equated with feelings, which are a later evolutionary development," he wrote in a *Failure of Nerve*, published in 1999 (written a few years earlier). "While it includes feelings, the word refers primarily to the instinctual side of our species that we share in common with all other forms of life." It is important to develop awareness that can identify and separate our instinctual behavior from the personality. We will discuss this ahead.

In particular, Friedman saw leadership as a fundamentally *emotionally charged* process, of which few were prepared for. Our culture seems to prefer compliant non-selves instead of differentiated selves. No doubt, it is not easy to aspire to grow into our truer (or truest) selves. It can be a lifelong journey. At the same time, there is plenty of room for levels of growth that lead to less autopilot reactivity, that break us from our own ingrained and often unconscious behavior patterns, and free us, therefore, from how we engage and participate in social patterns.

In that light, this book is a paradox. It is both meant to show you your patterns—patterns all the more likely to emerge and show themselves under the shock points of stress—so that you will take responsibility for freeing yourself from them. You may or may not be the leader of an organization or a family. Either way, you can be the leader of your own self.

About a century before Bargh's 2009 book, a critically important figure (who has fallen out of favor in many schools) on the subject of instinctual drives was Sigmund

Freud. As dogmatic as he could be, Freud's thinking did evolve, but one thing that was central from the beginning was his idea that we are subject to drives, and these drives activate our psychological organization. In 1915, he first suggested that there are self-preservative and sexual instincts. He saw conflict between the two drives. Eventually, he would describe a sexual drive (*libido*), an aggressive drive (*thanatos*), and later he would state that the drives lead toward life and toward death. All of life was effectively dealing with our drives, whether acting them out or defending ourselves against them.

There are many ways we might categorize or conceptualize our instincts. As Enneagram practitioners, we have more or less "agreed" to break them down into three instinctual drives, which we call the Self-Preservation, Social, and Sexual (which can be called One-to-One for contexts like the business world where to use the term "Sexual" might be misunderstood and misapplied). On their own, without the distorting influence of the meat grinder that our personalities run them through, these basic drives work for a reason. They are free and necessary and we see them function in the behavior of animals all over the world. For many of us, who are extremely disconnected from nature (and not just our own nature), we might have to look these examples up on YouTube. When you observe a pair of birds bringing mouthfuls of worms to their nesting young, you see an aspect of the Social instinct at work. When you see the elaborate display of a male puffer fish working tirelessly for days on end to create what looks like a sundial on the ocean floor you see an aspect of the Sexual instinct. When you see Emperor penguins protecting their egg, you witness the Self-Preserving.

Of course there are endless variations, but the point is these instincts aren't bad or good. They just are. If you want to call them "good" because they are created from the God source, that is fine too. The point is they are in us. They are deeply embedded, even deeper than some of our unconscious emotional passions, or our mental blind spots.

We humans are a bit strange. We walk upright on two legs, which is strange enough. Most distinctive, we also have these highly developed brains that help us make a tool for just about anything. Another result of these brains is the development of an ego structure. That is where the purity of the instinct collides with the frailty and flawedness of being human. That is also why we don't emphasize or teach the instincts separate from or before teaching your type, as a few practitioners like to do. Only through understanding your type will you then begin to recognize the manifestation of your instinct's presence, which we call your subtype.

In terms of where the subtypes fit into Enneagram theory, they weren't clearly understood, researched, or documented throughout the 1990s and even into the early 2000s. Naranjo was working on them, researching, and discussing them in various parts of the world during much of this time, but it wasn't until he was invited to speak at an event in North America in 2004 that Beatrice Chestnut first heard the descriptions he had been working on for years. She began to recognize the critical importance of this understanding especially through the lens of the Enneagram's structure. It had been vague, especially in North America where so many other variations of Enneagram teaching had originated.

Now, she felt we had an even more finely-tuned instrument into discerning behaviors and the apparent contradictions even between types, than ever before. She made it her mission to bring this understanding to the world, and first did so with a major contribution to the field with, *The*

*Complete Enneagram: 27 Paths to Greater Self-Knowledge.* While I go to the source of Naranjo as directly and often as possible for my own interpretation and examination, you will be hard pressed to find other original sources beyond Chestnut's adaptations. We are strong adherents of the vibrant Chestnut-Paes Enneagram community, and want to make sure that credit goes where credit is due, even as we aim to bring new applications and points of study and reflection to the world.

So, to repeat an important point before we push ahead: When you connect any one of the three different instincts to our types, you then call them subtypes. On their own they are called instincts. When filtered through our personality's construction, they become what we call a subtype. Instincts are pure and free-flowing and perform a necessary function in us when they are not restricted by the fears, motivations, blind spots, and shadow sides of our egoic behaviors. Subtypes are subjected to all the above, and, spoiler alert, you will never be completely free, no matter how mature and spiritual and transcendent you become. But you can grow in your levels of self-awareness and this will show in the fruits of your spirit as you become more fully awake to yourself, and subtle shifts occur in your motivations and behaviors.

Breaking them down from the 9 types into 27 subtypes, our aim is to further illuminate them, to help make them more known to how you function the way you do and why. Although different practitioners call them by different names, we tend to follow the language of the original sources, based on Naranjo's work. Oscar Ichazo taught them, too. He called them Conservation, Social, and Syntony. We are more familiar with Naranjo, who (as stated in our opening section on the pioneers) first brought these early teachings to North America where they took shape among many of those early students and beyond. Although, we must say that the idea of "conservation" may be helpful in further defining and understanding what we mean by the "self-preserving" instinct.

When the Self-Preservation instinct is most pronounced, you tend to be most occupied with survival, especially through material security. You may have sensitivity to your own state through signals in the body, such as through sensations and physical impressions. Your biological drives direct your energy toward safety and security. This focus tends toward having enough resources, maintaining a sense of structure, often through processes and routines and resourcefulness.

When the Social instinct dominates, you are oriented toward achieving a sense of belonging, a place and status in the community. You may think in terms of navigating the layers, boundaries, and subtleties of social situations and dynamics. Your biological drives direct your energy toward whether you are included or well-positioned in groups. It also relates to your power or standing relative to others in a group, as well as to the world at large.

When the Sexual or One-to-One instinct is most deeply instilled, you tend to focus most on the quality and status of relationships with individuals. You may broadcast yourself, or put yourself on display with the intention of attracting some and repelling others. Your biological drives direct your energy toward pursuing and maintaining relationships, which does include sexual connections, but is also about bonding with others more broadly.

Understanding the instincts on their own can lead to misunderstandings about their application. Where the power for self-awareness and growth really hits is at the ignition level of understanding your instinct *in combination with* your Enneagram type's passion.

Most source books on the Enneagram do not discuss

the subtypes. I recognize it can be a lot to absorb. But I also strongly believe that these descriptions offer the most clear and accurate measure of the personality types than our single type number indicates. These subtypes also highlight why two people of the same type can look strikingly different when we more deeply understand the impact of these biographical factors on our behavior and the motivations (unconscious or not) behind those behaviors.

What gives our subtypes that distinct human flavor is the combination of our instinct with the passion of our type. Our passion is that emotional part of our personality that influences (usually highly unconsciously) our behavior, and ultimately, causes us so many of our issues related to bad stress, and suffering.

The passions of the nine types starting at point 8 and concluding at point 7 are lust, sloth, anger, pride, vanity, envy, avarice, fear, and gluttony. These passions do take their original form from esoteric traditions and ancient sources that were co-opted in various forms and with different meanings. Their meanings have broad application and have been seen in the behavior of humans for as long as we have recorded history. I give precise definitions in each section under discussion.

When the special sauce of your passion and your dominant instinctual drive come together, they reflect an even more specific focus of motivation, attention, and behavior. Just as we have all nine Types within us, we also have all three instincts operating within us. As the current theory goes, we tend to have a dominant instinct, a secondary more neutral one, and a repressed one. There is no test to take that will spit out your instinct. Only through self-observation and over time will you come to understand and discern your dominant and repressed type.

Naranjo observes that in a healthy person instinctual

drives are free-flowing and unrestricted. They become distorted through the influence of our personality, specifically through the lens of the passion, or the key emotional driver of our Type. Generally speaking, however, one of these instinctual drives emerges in us due to a feeling of lack. Sandra Maitri describes it in *The Spiritual Dimension of the Enneagram,* as, "[O]ne particular instinct becomes the most 'passionate' in the sense that our personality is geared around its insecurity and vulnerability." Our instincts don't flow as freely when they are tied up with the concerns arising from our particular type.

For me, I always readily identified with the broad brushstrokes of the characteristics of the Enneagram Four type. But there were some other behaviors I often exhibited that made me question whether or not I might be an Eight. Some Eight characteristics I exhibited, which cannot be explained only by the broader characteristics of my Four type, are: I cared about the underdog and the misfit; I could be intense and challenge perceived injustices; and I could be competitive. Also, Eights value authenticity, much the way Fours do.

I recognized that the competition often arose out of my Four sense of "lack," and battling to be superior because I didn't want to feel inferior. That is nearly the opposite of the way Eights are extremely armored and go boldly wherever they need to go. But still, there was something that wasn't adding up with the typing descriptions. For a period of time, I began to think the Enneagram was "pretty good" at explaining some pretty universal human characteristics, but it wasn't necessarily any better than a number of other typologies.

My competitiveness led me to be intense, especially when the competition aligned with my values or something I knew I cared about. And then I read Chestnut's descriptions of the subtypes in *The Complete Enneagram,* and everything changed. When I was introduced to the subtypes, it became abundantly, painfully clear: I was a Sexual/One-to-One Four. As you will see as you read further on, this subtype is named Competition. These Fours express their feelings openly and outwardly. Much to my dismay, this subtype was also called by Naranjo as the "angriest" of all the subtypes. I chafed at that. I resisted. Then, slowly by degrees, I began to self-observe and see the latent irritation and anger buried not so deeply underneath.

After a period of some acceptance, I then wanted to disown that part of me. I felt shame. I didn't like my type and subtype. I felt like apologizing for it when I introduced myself to Enneagram communities. Then I learned that many of us go through that part of the process as well. Confrontation with the reality of our type and subtype can be strong medicine. At the very beginning there is a sense of excitement, curiosity, and wonder. To be identified is a way of being known and understood (some of us want to be understood more than others). It can be exhilarating to see how and why we function the way we do, even if it might slightly threaten the ego who wants us to believe that life begins and ends with our fixed experience and responses to that experience. Sometimes, almost at the exact same time you feel the excitement, you feel vulnerable. Suddenly, you realize that you are known, not only for your superpowers, but your blindspots too.

But that is right where the genius of the Enneagram resides, and why it is not like any other personality typology that we (at Big Self School) have ever come across. The subtype work digs into the complexity of human behavior and motivations with a finely tuned instrument—and without making things too complicated. This analysis and this perennial wisdom is packed together in a powerful map.

For many typologies that is where the process ends.

Congratulations! You are _____, which means you like _____ and _____, and do not like _____ and _____. For the Enneagram, it is where the process begins. Now you have a growth path. You can specifically target and identify healthy behaviors and consciously work to integrate them into your reference point. Perhaps better than a map is the idea of a compass. All the wings and arrows can help you break out of the patterns you didn't even know existed.

Many people don't like typing systems because they don't want to be labeled. Well, here you go. A system that wants to support you in your unlabeling.

The guidelines for our growth out of our personality's fixations are expressed in the virtues, starting with point 8 and ending with point 7: innocence, action, serenity, humility, veracity, equanimity, nonattachment, courage, and sobriety.

Now that I have offered up this overview of the subtypes, I will give brief descriptions of the subtypes in each succeeding chapter on the types. For these sources, I rely primarily on the work of Claudio Naranjo, Oscar Ichazo, Beatrice Chestnut and her collaboration with Uranio Paes.

Almost every diagnosis in the DSM is the result of a dysregulated nervous system. What creates a dysregulated nervous system is not one size fits all. It is highly personalized and built around your core personality structure. And of course even the DSM has its cultural biases. Naranjo has pointed out, for instance, that the Type 3 doesn't have a condition listed for it in the DSM while the Type 4 may be over-represented. North America is a Type 3 culture, and we are suspicious of "negative" displays of emotions, such as sadness. Ironically, one of the conditions we have created in our Type 3 culture is the widespread malaise of loneliness and isolation, which leads inevitably to depression.

This book will use your Enneagram type and subtype to give a starting point for understanding the highly specific psychological stressors in your life. We'll give you questions to ask and practices to begin for unearthing and managing your stress, for good.

Think of it as your personalized syllabus for identifying and managing the stress in your life, while also creating a long-term plan for staying mentally and emotionally healthy.

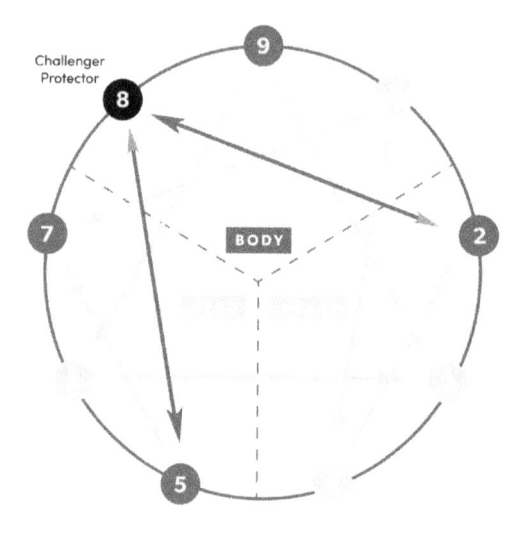

Challenger
Protector

8

9

2

7

BODY

5

PATH OF ENERGIZING    PATH OF RESOLUTION

# EIGHTS:
# TOO MUCH AND NOT ENOUGH

*"When we were children, we used to think that when we were grown-up we would no longer be vulnerable. But to grow up is to accept vulnerability...*
*To be alive is to be vulnerable."*
—Madeleine L'Engle

**In a single syllable:** Yawp
**Persona:** Battle Mask
**Mantra:** "I am powerful. I can do."
**Reactivity defense mechanism:** Denial

**Passion:** Lust

**In a Nutshell**

Ichazo's Ego-Venge, or what we most commonly call the Challenger, is a great starting point. (We will keep each of the Centers of Intelligence together, so we begin with Eight in the body center and Nine and One follow.) In *Keys to the Enneagram*, A.H. Almaas (Hamaad Ali) suggests beginning with point Eight because "its ego ideal is easiest to understand, and its idealized aspect is the most accessible to the average person." The primary motivation of an Eight isn't just about challenging, however. They want to be protected. They want to live in a world that needs protection, all of which threatens their vulnerability. Eights often have a strong—even large—physical presence. Even when they are not physically big, their expressions and gestures are often so. They can be fearless, even shameless in expressing themselves and making their needs known. Underneath the strong outer shell is the vulnerable "little child," but this child rarely comes out to anyone other than their closest relationships. Naranjo remarks that it is probably this "over-development of action in the service of struggling in a dangerous world that can't be trusted" that is perhaps the most essential way in which Eights keep themselves trapped.

**Defining Characteristics of the Eight Type**

Eights are known as fast processors. Western culture has prized the head type for centuries, the analytical thinker. In the past decade, we've also put a great deal of emphasis on the importance of emotional intelligence (EQ). What we seem to still overlook and undervalue is the way that body types come to their own sense of knowing. Every type has an intuitive process, and body types are no different. One Eight panelist on our podcast said, "I go into action without any cognitive thought process coming through my body, my body is telling me what to do."

We have heard from Gurdjieff and other practitioners that if the speed of a thought is 1x, the speed of an emotion is 10x, and the speed of a gut instinct is 100x. "That puts the body-gut types at odds with the others because we are already 100 times down the road, when the same thing is filtering through," says Enneagram practitioner Stacey Ruff. "When you're talking to me I am not just hearing your words. I'm hearing everything that's coming in through my body and gut. And I tend to respond to all of that. And so that gut may sometimes hear, you know, someone's saying something really polite and respectful and the gut is like, 'Danger, danger, be careful.'"

Eights most exemplify the willfulness and vitality of the Body Center. Naranjo described them relating to the character of dominance, with such traits as arrogance, power-seeking, competitiveness, and the need for triumph. No doubt, not all Eights demonstrate these raw or coarse characteristics. Many are simply assertive and strong and with easy access to the emotion of anger.

Some women report finding so many of the descriptions of the type Eight to be "hyper toxic," or highly masculinized. While culture and cultural expectations play a role in our identity formation, there are not more Eight men than women by any means. There is a beautiful way that we can talk about power, one that is both masculine and feminine.

Eights move through the world with an innate sense of confidence that usually produces an impact. They have big energy. They tend to be direct, and are known to be confrontational, even though many Eights say they don't enjoy confrontation, they just don't fear it. They are "larger than life," impulsive, aggressive in groups, and less inhibited than most of the other types. Culturally, in much the same way that Twos have been overly feminized, Eights have been overly masculinized.

Also of note in cross-comparing types and their relative proximity on the Enneagram symbol, Eights neighbor their Nine wing, which indicates a paradoxical relationship with indolence and falling asleep to the self. The response of not feeling completely alive, in the case of Eights, is to become aggressive and intense. No other type is considered quite so intense, except perhaps in Fours. Fours bear an interesting place on the Enneagram from Eights, almost at the opposite end. Eights' intensity comes out in an embodied, active presence. For Fours, it is more emotional. Also, as Naranjo observes, Eights tend to reach out toward the satisfaction of their need without guilt. By contrast, Fours tend to yearn for the source of their satisfaction and then feel guilty about their neediness (128).

In light of these defining characteristics, you can probably see how Eights have a tendency toward power (and empowering others in some cases), and are intuitively aware of (and resistant to) when they are being controlled. The central emotion for each of the body types is anger, but where and how it is directed varies. For Eights their anger is directed at their own sense of vulnerability. To maintain their own authority and autonomy, Eights get tough. They embody the notion that "the best defense is a good offense." Displays of assertion or even aggression or attempts at efficiency are ultimately (however consciously or not) attempts to protect themselves. They are among the most likely to express anger of any type, and they are equally among the least intimidated by anger.

They can project toughness toward others, but they also close themselves off to their emotional reserves. When they become preoccupied with self-protection they can also at the same time force others to meet their needs by increasing their aggressiveness and command. They tend to have a self-image of being strong, and when lacking in self-awareness, they can become increasingly intolerant to what they perceive as weakness in others. They can interpret anything that gets in their way as an insult, confrontation, or a test of will.

### The Passion of Lust

The Eight passion of lust is not meant in the narrow sense of only the sexual kind. The meaning of lust's exuberance is similar to the id, the idea of filling a need or an emptiness through physical gratification. One meaning of the word lust is an unquenchable craving and yearning. Naranjo says lust a "passion for excess or an excessive passionateness to which sexual gratification is only one possible source of gratification."

To a large extent, this powerful way of moving through the world, and this need for intensity and efficiency, means that the functional part of the Eight trapped in an unaware personality is highly resilient. As Naranjo also observes, "Even though the lusty type is passionately in favor of his lust and of lust in general as a way of life, the very passionateness with which he embraces this outlook betrays a defensiveness—as if he needed to prove himself and the rest of the world that what everyone else calls bad is not such (140)."

Lust conveys a sensory-motor disposition. Unlike the Sevens' gluttony, which wants a sampling of a little bit of everything available, lust is an intense craving for a particular thing. There is a pleasure in the attaining of one's lust, but there is also pleasure in the anticipation of the object, as well as in the very pursuit. Finally, embedded within this passion sits the fixation of vengeance. It might be said that when the fulfillment of lust combines with the extra excitement of attaining vengeance, it is all the more delectable.

### Functional Versus Authentic Personality

For Eights, their functional personality has a lot going for it. They can be inherently bold and confident. They aren't afraid of those who intimidate others, although sometimes without knowing it they are one of those very people. But in functional personality they probably have to admit they don't mind that people are sometimes a little afraid. It keeps them at bay, and often it keeps them in service to Eights so as not to upset them. Sometimes, too, ignorance is bliss, as the saying goes.

If you are an Eight, perhaps you really are insensitive to others' suffering or needs or the way you might barrel over others and tend to dominate. Better to dominate than be dominated in this "dog eat dog" world, right?

But when you do make contact with tapping into your resources and become ready to grow beyond the narrow confines of your mechanical reactivity, you will recognize that you are covering over an innocence that was probably taken away from you very early. That innocence, that vulnerable kid within you, is still there and available to more than the one or two closest people to you.

Eights value authenticity in others. In fact, they can sniff it out immediately. In many respects your personality arises out of your essence, your true and authentic self. Ultimately, the path toward authentic growth and the cultivation of a higher self that doesn't need to deny stress as a way of dealing with it, is through the virtue of innocence.

This requires breaking free from deeply entrenched fixations with the external world. You will need to find the "little you" that likes to play, that is safe. Finding that deep sense of authentic joy comes from tapping into your innocence. You find that innocence in the self-image of a small child. You will need to be able to feel the loneliness, the helplessness, the memories of your social environment that wasn't always fun. Sometimes it was frightening and a stress-filled struggle.

The process of exploring our most vulnerable feelings of loneliness and longing is incredibly difficult and at the same time incredibly important part of the development of our inner work. For Eights it is all the more important and transformative.

**Psychological Roots and Key Patterns that Create Stress for Eights**

Generally speaking, we see the psychological roots and key patterns that create stress for Eights emerging from early experiences of feeling powerless. Eights who have done a good bit of inner work report issues revolving around not getting their needs met in childhood. Sometimes these experiences were traumatic enough that they internalized the need to be strong as a coping mechanism. Often we see Eights with histories of having to take on big early responsibilities, including, by not limited to, taking care of themselves and sometimes others as well. Sometimes they found themselves in a combative environment related not only to parents, but also siblings and peers.

Thus, we see from an early, formative stage in their personality development and ego construction that Eights have founded their identity on being strong no matter what. If you aren't strong enough, then you are weak. This in part explains why Eights handle pressure and heavy amounts of work with what appears to be relative ease to most other types.

At the same time, this denial of vulnerability can act as addictive-like forms of behavior. The end result is that you are kept trapped and looping in repetitive behavior, which by its very nature keeps you stuck. Sometimes in coaching, we will see Eights who begin a session feeling overwhelmed, but then after the relief of a session, they gear up and feel ready to jump back into the very stress they've been in all along.

In a way, when you truly feel stuck and don't have control over your environment, this denial of vulnerability or emotions can help you function. But deep down, Eights feel deeply tired. When Eights begin to do the inner work and stop denying their stress, they recognize how tired they really are. They often take great pride in their ability to be super tough and possessing of a great deal of energy. Eights should shift their mindset. No one needs to be too strong. You shouldn't need a physical problem to slow down.

### Self-Preservation Eight: Satisfaction

These Eights have a strong desire for the timely satisfaction of their material needs. Naranjo calls this subtype, "the most armed of all." SP Eights go after their needs. They don't need to talk much. They are the most practical and potentially ruthless. They know how to survive even the most difficult situations and people. They will seek vengeance without even knowing why (while the other two subtypes usually have a specific reason).

Their drive for satisfaction leaves little room for reflection or self-understanding of what they may really need. The passion of lust shows up in the intensity of their drive.

SP Eight, Mindy Klein says that for her the passion of lust is expressed in how she does everything to an extreme. She decided to start running and was immediately training for a marathon (and then did several). She decided to "clean eat" and overnight became a strict vegan. She tried a "dry January" and then ended up in sobriety for two years just to prove that she could, not because she had an issue with drinking. She says, for her, the passion of lust plays the role of creating unwanted stress on her to take everything to the furthest extreme.

Sometimes Eights barely recognize that they're having feelings, but toward the virtue of innocence, they can learn how to allow for vulnerable feelings, especially in relationships. They often can do this through consciously learning to trust and how to depend on others as reliable sources for getting their own needs met.

### Social Eight: (countertype) Solidarity

Naranjo called this type, the "social anti-social," like the child who became violent protecting his mother from his father. This type especially represses the inner child, and is "red in tooth and claw." They are also the more intellectual of the three types. For these Eights, being a loyal friend is what they perceive as critical to resolving their social insecurity. The reason for the countertype of this subtype is that Eights generally represent a rebellious person, one who goes against social norm, but this type is also oriented toward protection of others. Their lust and aggression manifests in service of others.

Social Eight, Stacey Ruff, says:

> "My entire life I've talked about 'my people.' I know social Eights are really known for protecting their people almost to the detriment of themselves. And so when we started talking about that, and how much you're into the justice and fairness in response to other people who might be being abused or taken advantage of…and that's one of my growth things right now is trying to figure out, okay, perhaps you're important as well, not just taking care of all of your people. And once you're one of my people, I can feel, I mean, you're just there, you're almost stuck there."

We've heard especially from Social Eights that they do have big feelings that aren't recognized. They say that they do have an inner vulnerability, and they do have a sensitivity "under there." The issue is generally they've built these strong exterior layers on top.

In fact, these Eights do appear easier going than the other Eights. They tend to be less quick to anger. Their growth path toward the virtue of innocence is to be open to the love given by others, to learn to receive and trust these expressions from others.

## Sexual/One-to-One Eight: Possession

This subtype is the most emotional of the Eights, as well as most clearly the "Eight-ish Eight." They have the most anti-social, rebellious tendency, and are the most likely to go against convention and norms. More than the other Eights, also, this type strives to feel powerful. They are seen as "get it done" people. They are often fascinating and charismatic people who can win others over, even if they are surprised to learn that they don't listen as well as they realize.

Sandra Maitri notes the paradoxical nature between possession *and* surrender in this subtype, but that in either case, whether surrendering control to a worthy partner, or taking possession, they are very much in control. Their lust shows up as the desire to possess the body and soul of their beloved. While they are passionate and quick to fight, they are also quick to make up and move on. But their possession is not necessarily just about the "other," it is also seen as a more encompassing behavior directed toward their environment at large.

For these Eights, their move toward the virtue of innocence will show up in the vulnerable expression of their emotions. Through this conscious work, they will become more aware of their motivations for rebellion, as well as to manage their emotions to give more space for others. They can also grow from working in their mental center and not just through the body and emotions.

### Working with Arrows in Growth and Stress

Much of the theory about basic stances have Eights *moving against* people due to the core emotion of anger and how they process it. Eights challenge and confront situations rather than back down. They speak their mind and make their desires known. If they don't like what's happening, they tend to do something about it. When Eights are under stress they often move beyond assertion to aggression, and become intimidating or bullying. They get their way at others' expense and can become vengeful and vindictive. At their best, they are virtually tireless in their pursuits, and can be incredibly effective at making decisions where others would need far more time. They move in the world with confidence and purpose. Their self-reliant determination keeps them moving forward undaunted by challenges. They also have a capacity for energizing and inspiring others.

We can observe differing levels of nuance in these behavior patterns, however, depending on the subtype. The Self-Preservation Eights, for example, may have a stance as much inclined to move away from the world as against it in their defensive posture. The countertype of Social Eights is not nearly as easily defined by stance. They certainly have the capacity to move against, but they may well move toward others, especially those considered a part of their tribe, or the ones they view as the underdog whom they want to champion. The basic stance of moving against, however, is helpful in identifying the "challenging" spirit of lust and invulnerability that characterizes the core of the Eights' motivations.

Wings are not—as commonly misunderstood—subtypes. Wings are a personality's neighboring styles, and you may be conscious of your tendency to "fly with one wing" more than another. Wings are what we call the first steps in conscious personality development work, and require gentler stretches. The wing looking back is the Seven wing of the Eight, and the wing looking forward is the Nine. We may find ourselves unconsciously manifesting characteristics of either or both styles, but when it comes to conscious, and deliberate work in order to grow ourselves out of our mechanical patterns, we encourage first a conscious attention for Eights on their Seven wing. The high side of the Seven wing takes them out of their body center and into their head center. Their Seven wing, when done consciously, will see them willing to act more spontaneously, to tap into their own sense of humor, try things out with curiosity and a sense of adventure. When it manifests under stress or unconsciously, the low side of their Seven wing might see them unwilling to look at anything but the positive data at work, home, or in their relationships. They may find themselves leaping from task to task, simply looking for what is fun and avoiding boredom at all costs.

The next growth move for Eights would be to focus on their Nine wing. When done consciously this move—also in keeping with their body center—can produce surprising results from the typical stance of the Eight. When done with consciousness and intention, Eights focusing on their Nine wing will show up with an easygoing nature, ready to get along and go along with the flow. They embody a democratic spirit valuing everyone's opinion and contribution rather than having an us against them attitude. Rather than coming at things ready to wrangle, they are willing to listen more empathically, and engage. By contrast, when they go into their Nine wing under stress or unconsciously, they may find themselves tuning out, procrastinating, or narcotizing themselves in a variety of ways like binge-watching TV or scrolling through endless social media channels.

When Eights are ready to do the bigger work on the conscious development of their personalities with arrow work, they move first to the point Two, which is a *move towards* others and into the heart center. When done consciously and patiently, they will find themselves operating with compassion, understanding, and empathy. They build others up instead of beat them down. They approach others with tenderness, grace, and even charm. Their desire for protection of others can be fierce but also heartfelt and not merely reactive from the body. It compels their loyalty and the protection of those close to them. When Eights overdo their moving towards tendency and go to the point Two under stress or unconsciously, they may make others dependent on them so they will be beholden to them. They manipulate the weakness they perceive in others, and use their strength to attach people to themselves.

When Eights have grounded themselves in thoroughly practicing their move consciously to the Two position, they are ready to move to a different head center, that of the point Five, in which they *move away from* others. On the conscious side of Five, they reflect before they act. They aim before they fire. They are open to first learning all they can from experiences instead of approaching situations with biases and preconceptions. They might even find themselves in the sweet pocket of leadership, both in recognizing how to boldly go where everyone needs to go, but doing so with discernment and a focus of their intensity. When Eights find themselves unconsciously or under stress moving toward their Five arrow, they become too detached from their feelings and from others. They can become cruel and unsympathetic and impatient. Or they can turn their strength against themselves, punishing themselves and withdrawing if they think they've been unjust or that others have done them wrong.

### Reactive Impulse Under Stress

We often hear from Eights and their body way of knowing and interpreting situations that they process things fast. This can be a great strength, especially when it comes to crisis situations. They also balk at only using the term "reactivity" in a negative way. Sometimes, we've heard Eights say that reactivity can be a *good* thing. You're responsive. You're quick. You don't need to filter things through your heart or your head. By contrast, we've also heard many Eights say they have frequently acted too fast, sometimes without having gathered enough information, or sometimes just cutting themselves off from feeling or thinking and just acting.

Eights also really like to be in control. Sometimes, similar to Ones, it's connected to their independence and their lack of trust that anyone else can do it as well as they can. Sometimes the control is a form of perfectionism leaking in. What often gets left out in the process is self-care. They deny their need for assistance. Eights typically don't feel that they can stop until they're finished. Often that means they have to hit a wall before they finish.

When Eights are under stress they may at first want to attack it. They want to touch base with it, do something about it. But all too often they come back to *denial.* Many times this defense mechanism may help them. That's the role of defense mechanisms, they actually do help. You can see how they might at times keep us from burnout. At the same time, of course, you can see how they lead us right into the center of burnout.

Eights are famous for pushing through stressful situations. But because of this, they are known for driving through until their body "hits a wall" or just shuts down. For example, one Self-Preservation Eight tells us that she just kept on pushing through her stress until she had a heart attack at age 39, and even in the moment wasn't sure what was going on, and *drove herself to the hospital.* While this may sound extreme, we hear many such stories from Eights, who work through the pain until the pain often has to catch up to them and force a stop.

## Defining Characteristics in Personality

- → Tendency to go "all in"
- → Resists vulnerability—sees it as weakness
- → Core need for protection (even if it's a blindspot)
- → Mobilized easily by anger and indignation
- → Tendency to move against: natural inner rebel
- → Attuned to issues of control and domination
- → Tends to protect the underdog
- → Insensitive to subtleties

**Superpowers**

Eights are able to handle a lot. They can meet any challenge, expending a great deal of energy. As a result of their self-confidence they are also expert at being able to see the macro view. That is, they can assess the bigger picture intuitively in order to know where the next specific action needs to take place. While they don't necessarily like conflict more than anyone else, as a result of not being in touch with their vulnerability, they also are less likely to avoid it. Besides all the ways in which they move through the universe boldly going where they need to go, their eye for the underdog also places them in a unique position of empowering people (especially people they like). Many Eights are generous with their time in this capacity, and often can make excellent mentors.

**Common Stressors for Eights**

- → Working with others that slow them down, or that they feel are not as competent as they are.
- → Collaborating with others they don't fully trust or that they deem as weak.

→ When others take a long time to make a decision.

→ When people don't keep them updated about what is going on.

→ When others bog them down with details.

→ When people beat around the bush and aren't direct.

→ When people call them controlling or intimidating when they are just trying to get a job done.

→ When authority's misuse or abuse their power.

→ When others try to control them.

### Type Eight Patterns to Observe to Make More Conscious

→ Depending on your subtype, you may need to learn to verbalize your needs, to trust and rely on others. Also, allow yourself to need and be supported by others.

→ Allow the purity of your virtue of innocence to emerge. You don't always have to provoke, challenge, and move against in order to mobilize your energy and be at the center of everything.

→ Remind yourself that you're human just like everyone else. You don't need to see a physical problem before you slow down or at least practice a little self care.

→ Slow down. Be gentle to yourself. Listen to the signals your body is sending. Notice when you're getting tired. Don't just push the feelings away and try to power through.

→ When you feel an emotion, don't stuff it or ignore it. Often, bringing your feelings to the surface can be a huge release of stress and tension.

→ Similarly, stay in contact with your mental center. Slowing down to think things through is often exactly the right move, especially if efficiency is what you really want.

→ When getting in touch with your vulnerability, remind yourself that it's a sign of self-respect.

→ Vulnerability can mean being vulnerable with yourself, as well as others. How are things impacting you? Being tough and strong is not always the best thing for you.

→ It's not always helpful to step into conflict. Because you can process quickly, you should practice patience, as well as specific methods to help them slow down.

→ Learn the empowering energy of saying no to things. Many Eights ride that line between not enough and then way too much.

## Activities To Lower Stress And Practice Self-Development

**Reflect and respond to past times of growth:** Allow yourself to be open to other points of view, some that may even run contrary to your values or beliefs. Consider a time or times in your life where you allowed yourself to be open to other perspectives. What did you learn? Who were you able to trust?

**Self-inquiry:** Ask yourself: Do you value power over your relationships with others?

**Act against your *against-ness:*** There is a desert Christian tradition (Ignation) that practices a concept called *Agere Contra,* which means "to act against." This practice involves intentionally acting against your ingrained patterns of behavior, for Eights this means acting against your impulses to leap into action, and to rebel against the expectations of social or conventional norms. For Eights, this can involve meditation or journaling practice that lowers the temperature on intensity and allows you to rest, reflect, and simply be.

**Develop your three advisors with decision-making:** Before making a decision start with your head. Ask yourself: What do I need to know about this decision? Then, move to your heart. Ask yourself: What should I pay attention to regarding feelings and value with this decision? Finally, go to your body. Ask yourself: What action should I be taking or not about this decision? Write each of these answers down. Why write them down? It helps to clarify your positions. If your advisors are in alignment with each other, this is usually a good sign that you are integrating all your centers into a sound decision. If they are not, this is a good sign that you are in conflict. You may need to reflect on the differences and consider which advisor is speaking with the most clarity and truth.

**Be present and attuned in your body for deep healing:** Many Eights report having afflictions, or pain in their body. The pain is often overlooked or ignored as weakness. You can come to recognize pain as the very source of inner healing. If the pain is not too great that it completely dominates then it may be available to you. We resist pain by ignoring it, but this only intensifies the pain. Your body needs you to recognize your pain. Use the effectiveness of your body center of intelligence and apply it to yourself in a centered, slow, and patient way.

Develop a daily ritual and give yourself several weeks to come to this practice as often as possible. Create a space to be aware of your pain. In tiny moments your awareness will grow. Accept the pain. Welcome the pain as a source through which you can enter a new reality of growth and healing. As Thomas Merton said, "True love and prayer are learned in the moment when prayer has become impossible and the heart has turned to stone."

Your pain can stimulate a long-frozen grief within you. With diligence and over time your mind will call out for relief from the pain, and it is in your heart that you will find the source for healing. Just like with "Chinese handcuffs," the more we pull away, the more the bonds tighten. Eights need to access their child heart center to connect with their virtue of innocence. The paradox of this great truth is that you can find healing through your emotions by connecting to the wounded part of you in your body.

Mediator
Peacemaker

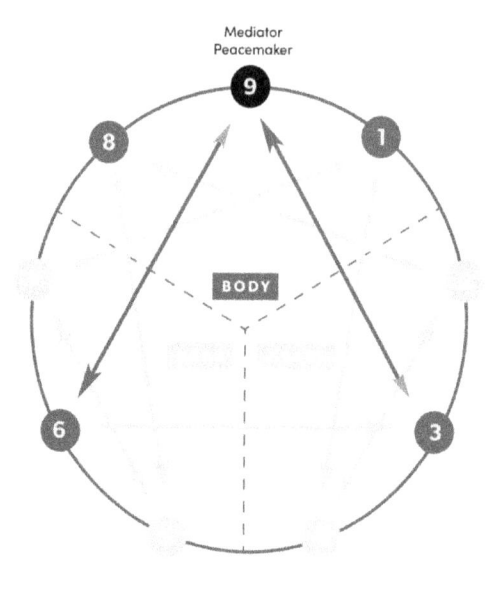

**9**

**8**

**1**

**BODY**

**6**

**3**

PATH OF ENERGIZING   PATH OF RESOLUTION

# NINES:
# WAKING UP TO WHAT YOU WANT

> *"But there are a thousand things which prevent a man from awakening, which keep him in the power of his dreams. In order to act consciously with the intention of awakening, it is necessary to know the nature of the forces which keep man in a state of sleep."*
> —G.I. Gurdjieff (from P.D. Ouspensky's *In Search of the Miraculous*)

**In a single syllable:** Ahhh
**Persona:** Sleepwalker
**Mantra:** "I am comfortable."
**Reactivity defense mechanism:** Narcotization
**Passion:** Sloth

## In a Nutshell

Ichazo's Ego-Indolence, or what we most commonly call the Peacemaker, contrasts significantly with the bold and invulnerable Challenger. The idea behind the study and application of the Enneagram is to learn how to wake up to ourselves. That means, in part, when we learn about ourselves, we don't do so merely as typology. We learn about the patterns and habits of our limited consciousness in order to awaken to them. They may be entrenched behaviors, but they are not fossilized forever in amber. We begin with this concept as we introduce the Nine type because Nines have fallen asleep to themselves. In this respect, the Nine type "embodies the primary element inherent in all fixations," as Almaas writes. What we mean by this sleep is that, more than most other types, Nines are unconscious of who they truly are, especially what is going on inside. This loss of interiority makes for a person who is open to the ideas and needs of others "outside" of themselves, while having great difficulty in first listening to, and second expressing, their own selves (and their corresponding ideas and needs). Nines live in a world that is anything but peaceful. They do their best to maintain the peace through merging and tamping down on their own relationship to anger, and they will sometimes settle for calm where no peace is to be found. The issue is, as Virginia Woolf observed, "You cannot find peace by avoiding life."

**Defining Characteristics of the Nine Type**

Similar to Eights, Nines have a strong sense of gut knowing. It can literally feel like it's in the stomach. It can also feel like an anxiety, a physical sensation, like an embodied understanding that comes quickly, but it may be hard to bring up for Nines. They may not always trust it, though. As those who want harmony they often ask for feedback from others before they fully trust their gut or body knowing. They're great at seeing all sides of a situation, but because of this—and their desire for harmony—it may be hard to make a decision, especially in a timely manner.

Nines are often called modest mediators, and that can definitely make for great leadership. In fact, it may come as a surprise that Nines make great leaders and can navigate corporate environments with grace and effectiveness. Conflict may feel terrible for a Nine. Dealing with the internal chaos is something they avoid.

For all their harmony and merging, Nines—being in the body center of intelligence such as they are—are also connected naturally to an internal anger. Of the three body types (Eights, Nines, and Ones), Nines tend to repress their anger the most. Some who are slightly more self-aware may recognize they are becoming resentful, or begin functioning in a passive-aggressive manner. It often bubbles up under the surface, and while on the surface it may not at first appear to others that anything is wrong, it certainly is.

When it comes to the idea of how Nines may "fall asleep to themselves," we hear from Nines that they find themselves taking on the agendas of others. Even strong Nine leaders can find themselves putting their own priorities last. Some we know who have done work in this area make it a priority to document in writing each and every day at least one thing they are going to do on behalf of themselves.

The type Nine ego structure needs to maintain its idealized self of being the peaceful person, where everything is tranquil and copasetic, no one gets upset, differences are resolved in a respectful way, no one gets ignored, and everyone is included. Any of the prior examples generate tension and Nines, who are highly sensitive to tension more than most people, experience tensions in their bodies—whether the tension has an internal or external source.

When they are in health and less in stress, this type is a paragon of groundedness and connection more than any other type of the Enneagram. They are natural mediators with a multifaceted and holistic perspective. All of this amounts to people who are intuitively accepting, curious, and empathetic.

But without self-awareness and inner growth, they tend to be so uncomfortable with their inner world that their fixation of indolence (mental diffusion) in combination with their passion of sloth, allows them to maintain their calm. Nines simply diffuse their attention and are inattentive to their internal feelings and experiences, all to keep their idealized position as the peaceful person.

Narcotization is a defense mechanism in which Nines numb themselves to avoid feelings that seem too large, complex, difficult, or uncomfortable to handle. Nines may narcotize and distract themselves by engaging in familiar activities that tend to require little attention and provide comfort like washing the dishes, mowing the lawn, playing the same simple video game they've played for years, channel surfing, or shopping. Anything will suffice from food to drink to sex to exercise so long as there is a reassuring habit or routine or mindless busywork to help them numb out and forget themselves. Nines do this most often when they feel stressed, often about their capabilities to execute. Sometimes it is because they feel overlooked or forgotten.

It can be difficult to determine if something or what is upsetting Nines when they engage in narcotizing behavior, because even *they* may not know for certain. However, when they engage in narcotizing behavior—especially when there is something else they should be doing or something they need to say—it is a clear indication that they have deadened themselves with something distracting and soothing.

Whatever the case, Nines are usually adept at getting along with others and find it easy to merge with others' agendas. They naturally support people, and are generally found to be easygoing and affable. While they don't necessarily speak up or offer their own opinions, they are sensitive to when they are being overlooked or excluded.

## The Passion of Nine

The Nine passion of sloth means a laziness toward the self. Nines can, in fact, be diligent, persistent, hard-working people. It can mean that the end result is a general laziness, but that is not the key indicator of the passion of sloth for the Nine. It is a drive away from attending to the self. As Maitri writes, it is "a muffling and damping-down" of the inner life, which seems perhaps dull or uninteresting. Some Enneagram practitioners like to begin with Point Nine when introducing the Enneagram for the very reason that Nines broadly represent the universal human condition of being so cut off from who they truly are that the difference between their current reality and the potential within themselves is the difference between waking and sleeping. What they fall asleep to most is their anger. Interestingly, they are smack in the middle of the body center with their Eight neighbors who externalize theirs, and their One neighbors who internalize theirs. Nines do everything they can to fall asleep to theirs. This leads to a peace and calm, which tends to produce a dreamy numbness to self.

We also see this tendency to merge with others as yet another way of distracting themselves from acting on their own behalf. We will see in the subtypes that each has a different pattern of focusing on this fusion.

The way out is through the virtue of right action. Nines need to wake up to their anger consciously, and to more clearly and proactively act in their own self-interest. Channeling anger into a deeper channel of positive self-regard and showing up in the world on their own behalf can help grow out of the spiritual laziness of sloth. We will examine areas for concerted focus and growth through the work with wing stretches and arrow movements.

## Functional Versus Authentic Personality

Every personality type has functional aspects, which make it easy for them to remain stuck in place. Many don't want to grow out of the confines of their ego structure because for them it works, and it is uncomfortable to venture out of the prison yard. But even when people do say they want to grow, they don't often know what they're getting themselves into. In the early stages of putting your toe in the pond of self-development and awareness, it's good to self-inquire: "What does my personality actually do for me?"

For Nines, their functional personality of being good at mediating conflict, giving off easygoing vibes, and not rocking the boat, can go a long way. Not only can it work well in relationships, especially with a strong-willed or vocal partner, a Nine "strategy" can be as effective as ever in today's workplace. While in the past, the style of Eight might have been a classic leader in the workplace, now you might say, it is the Nine. Among other things, the Nine approach to negotiating the often complicated and political dynamics in organizations, is ideal. Not to mention, their desire for consensus-building, and general affability.

### Psychological Roots and Key Patterns that Create Stress for Nines

Nines often report that they grew up in environments where they felt overlooked, and their own opinions and preferences and feelings weren't as important as others. We believe our middle son, Lucas, is a Self-Preservation Nine, and it sometimes saddens us that Lucas must have felt like the typical "lost middle child" (especially in that Shelley is a middle child herself). He found himself wedged between two intense siblings who, as we sometimes say, took up a lot of oxygen.

At least we are now aware of some of the sources where his personality emerged, and we can make sure to let him know we value his opinions and want to know his feelings. He is growing into being more comfortable with asserting himself with us and his peers (from what we can tell from afar). Sometimes he may make his preferences known by saying he's coming to the dinner table and then not doing so until dinner is almost over. Like many Nines, his "Yes" may be a disguised "No," and we're learning to roll with his style. Another thing about Nines that we see a lot, as well as in Lucas, is that they are easy to be with. There is just something about Lucas's personality that makes you want to be near him, even if he isn't saying or doing anything.

As children, Nines had a sensitivity in the early "differentiation" stage, which involves negotiating the tension between connection and belonging to others and separating. Differentiation is the experience of children who continually reconcile their innate desire for independent, autonomous existence with an equally powerful impulse to re-immerse themselves in the enveloping world from which they have come. For Nines especially, this separation was painful in a particular way that makes them want to remain merged, or recreate the conditions of merging to experience union. This is also why they may tend to forget themselves or dissociate from the experience of not being held when they still needed it. It could also mean that they were not recognized as a separate and independent entity that belongs to the group at the same time.

Sometimes Nines, especially when they zone out and just sit around passively on the couch, can actually get more stressed. Partly this is because they are ignoring their needs. They aren't tuning in to the ways their emotions are wanting to be processed in anger or sadness. The very inactivity can snowball into creating more stress from the stress they're already feeling.

## Self-Preservation Nine: Appetite

Naranjo describes the fictional character of Don Quixote's sidekick, Sancho Panza, as illustrating this subtype. This subtype can be very loving and amiable, although of the three subtypes, this one is the more practical, stubborn, and potentially irritable, the most Eight-ish of the bunch. They are sometimes called the "sensualists" of the Enneagram because of their focus on physical comfort. We can think of "appetite" as "I eat therefore I am" (as a framework of being in the world as compared to Descartes famous "I think therefore I am" *cogito ergo sum* dictum).

At the same time, we shouldn't take the appetite concept too literally. It's about the merging of any physical need in service to comfort, and in place of engagement with the self, or a more active and involved (and potentially stressful) life. For this type there is such a degree of abnegation that they are even willing to give up the need for love when it comes to meeting their comfort in simple, practical activities almost as compensation for the lack of what they really need.

They may remain stubbornly entrenched in their habits, putting a great deal of energy into making sure not too much is expected of them. They are generally low-key and easygoing, but can surprise others with intensity and aggressiveness if their boundaries are infringed or significant demands are made on them.

This subtype can also be a late bloomer, taking a long time to figure out what they really want to do, as well as acquiring the skills or completing the necessary studies. They often never fully follow through developing their interests or talents. When they finally do, and are able to channel their energy into distraction-free focus, they often discover talents and dreams that are surprising to those around them.

## Social Nine: (countertype) Participation

Social Nines are arguably the most workaholic types of the entire Enneagram. There is this constant motion in service to the group and service to the community, and they forget themselves in those decisions. This is how they are the countertype to sloth behaviorally. They do express sloth, however, through merging with the group, and the priorities of the group over their own. Naranjo calls this type "the jolly good fellow." They give a lot. They care deeply about participation from everyone, and when they are working hard, the last thing they want to do is burden others with their own pain or stress.

The internal conflict that may emerge can take the form of tension between how much they give themselves over to relationships versus how much they keep for themselves. Social Nine, Lesley Scearce has said on our podcast:

> "I keep a list that literally every morning are like the three most critical things. And then one personal thing, for me, that is top of mind. And I'm going to have to keep the discipline of one day a month with nothing on the agenda, to just be alone in silence with my own thoughts, silence to just breathe, envision, and reset on leadership, reflect and just reconnect to myself. Because that is always the thing that is easiest for me to let go."

The congenial, light-hearted Social Nine is often a fun person who may feel like an outcast or misfit, and so overcompensates to fit in with the group or community. The paradox is that they don't feel completely comfortable in social situations, so they put forth tremendous energy to make it seem effortless. They tend to do this by employing socially acceptable forms of behavior and communication. At stake, however, is a loss of who they really are and an ongoing sense that they really don't fit in spite of the energy they put into fitting in. This type can suffer from the conflict between wanting attention and recognition while also feeling that being singled out is elitist or arrogant or could threaten their connections with others.

This type can be mistaken for Twos because they are seen as being selfless in constantly putting others first. They can often look like Threes when they work very hard without letting their stress show.

### Sexual/One-to-One Nine: Union/Fusion

Sexual or One-to-One Nines are looking for total union with another. It is a need to be in fusion, to use relationships to "be." This type, Narajano says, is like a "wallflower." She erases herself from pictures. It is a betrayal of their own needs in meeting the needs of others. Sloth is acted out through a total focus on the other. The problem with this is like the allegory of Shel Silverstein's *The Missing Piece Meets the Big O,* in which the missing piece is looking to "fit perfectly" with another. The Big O teaches the missing piece to realize that the two need to roll together on their own and independently.

Sexual Nines may seek their fusing with a peer, parent, sexual partner, or any important person. This connection gives them purpose, especially as they will take on the feelings, attitudes, or beliefs of the other. When this happens, they are lacking in their essential identity and their focused intensity (not typical of Nine behavior generally speaking) and flair for the dramatic can lead to them being mistaken for a Four.

The good-natured part of their "Nine-ness" makes others feel supported, understood, relaxed, and comfortable. In order for growth to happen, however, this subtype needs to find their own being without the "other." They need aloneness, conscious boundaries, and to find their own interests. This will lead them to a deeper connection with themselves and in turn make them happier and healthier partners for others.

### Working with Arrows in Growth and Stress

Nines tend to *move away from* others and situations. In personality, they allow things to happen and events to unfold at their own pace. Nines have a hands-off stance towards the world. This works great in a lot of situations in life whether at home or in the workplace. Not only does it imply a degree of intuitive wisdom, because for a fact not everything does need to be stressed over, it is also a key way to navigate organizational vicissitudes.

Of course, when stress occurs, they may double down on these patterns and avoid conflict and confrontation and hope that putting things off or not dealing with them directly will lead to some kind of resolution. While benign neglect may have worked for us kids raised in the '70s, it generally isn't the best approach to relationships. Thus, when they become too removed from the situation, they put off what needs to be done, and conceal their real intentions often even from themselves.

We can observe differing levels of nuance in these behavior patterns, however, depending on the subtype. We do see definitive shifts in the stances toward, against, or away from others and situations especially when it comes to the growth work in wings and arrows.

The wing looking back is the Eight wing of the Nine, and the wing looking forward is the One, both in keeping with the body center (and as we will see, a similar pattern for Threes in the heart center and Sixes in the head center). We may find ourselves unconsciously manifesting characteristics of either or both styles, but when it comes to conscious work in order to grow ourselves out of our mechanical patterns, we encourage first attention for Nines on their Eight wing. The high side of the Eight wing takes them into the challenger part of their personality, the one who addresses perceived right and wrong without worrying about what others think or how they might respond. They move in the world with confidence and purpose. Their self-reliant determination keeps them moving forward undaunted by challenges. When Nines go to their Eight wing under stress they often move beyond assertion to aggression, and become intimidating or bullying. They get their way at others' expense and can become vindictive.

The next growth move for Nines would be to focus on their One wing. When moving consciously into their One wing, Nines will show up with an idealistic vision of how people and situations could be and a growing desire to move reality from where it is to where it has the potential to be. They are more willing to move against the *status quo*, the present state, to raise it to a *status meliore*, a better state. Under stress and less consciously, Nines in their One wing can be predisposed to react resentfully when reality falls short of perfection. They may be quick to spot flaws, criticize, and fix things.

When Nines shift consciously to their first arrow Three, they *move against* others and their situational context in a problem-focused, energetic, get-it-done approach. They attack their problems rather than ignore or fall asleep to them. They assertively express and work for what they want. When Nines move to their Three arrow unconsciously or in stress, they become busy for its own sake, even compulsive about their To Do lists. Their anger falls asleep in endless distraction, busy-bee behavior, and repetitive routines.

When Nines move consciously to their Six arrow, they *move towards* others. Their loyalty and commitment to others may get them moving, doing for others what they might never do for themselves. They find the courage to support themselves and their agenda. When Nines move to their Six arrow in stress or unconsciously, they become overly concerned about what others think. They want to get others on their side at all costs. They side with external authority which may move them farther away from their inner authority and guide.

When in leadership positions, they may lose their efficacy by seeking consensus in relationships and teams rather than asserting their authority and own ideas. Interestingly for Nines, just like for Threes and Sixes, they find themselves remaining in their primary center of intelligence while they work only on their wings. The arrow work takes them completely out of their primary centers and enters them into each of the other intelligences.

### Reactive Impulse Under Stress

The Nines defense mechanism of narcotization also supports their being distracted from their own inner thoughts, feelings and sensations. They simply start doing non-essential or routine things, narcotizing by cleaning the house, falling down the rabbit hole doing endless internet searches, washing the dishes, losing themselves for hours in their collections of books, purses, albums, shoes, you name it.

When in stress, Nines turn their body's energy against themselves in the form of repressing or diffusing any expression that would be disruptive or upset the apple cart. They can also become stubborn. They will usually express their anger passively, and sometimes defensively aggressive in the form of just wanting to be isolated and left alone. If they get their way in their self-abnegation and narcotizing they become angry, even if they barely recognize it. Their fixations will often lead to neglect of themselves and the others in their lives.

**Defining Characteristics in Personality**

→ Diffuse attention by forgetting what they were discussing or not remembering something clearly stated

→ Asleep to their own needs, opinions, values

→ Display forms of procrastination

→ Bring the same work home without ever completing it

→ Follow entrenched routines

→ Engage in comforting activities for extended periods of time

→ Work hard for the team or organization and not for self interest

→ Collaborate well with others

→ Can be the ultimate conflict avoiders

**Superpowers**

Nines have many skills to consensus build, and to do so with such grace and aplomb as to avoid many of the conflicts that often arise from making decisions and moving groups in a single direction. They are attentive to the needs of others. They are supportive and conscientious of others. Generally speaking they are also receptive to others' opinions and perspectives. They may have a tendency toward inertia, but the flip side of this is that they are grounded. Typically, Nines don't like to be rushed, and when it comes to diplomacy and discernment, this can be a great strength. In today's corporate world, their mediating skills are a major asset. Not to mention, Nines are likable. They are almost always easy to work with because they are friendly and considerate and they don't have a need to get credit for their hard work the way some types do.

### Common Stressors for Nines

→ When others race to make a decision without considering everyone's input and building consensus.

→ When they continually avoid taking action and the results of their procrastination builds up as stress or anxiety.

→ When people take advantage of their easygoing personality and use them for their own agendas, not asking them what they actually want and need.

→ When people give them commands and tell them what to do, rather than asking.

→ When they aren't given an easy "out" or way to say "no" (in which case they may say "yes" and mean "no").

→ When they are not included in decision making and projects that they are involved in, especially when the decisions impact them.

→ When expectations aren't clear, which leads to conflict that could have been avoided.

→ When people get into conflicts, especially those that seem silly or unnecessary.

### Type Nine Patterns to Observe to Make More Conscious

→ Act on your own behalf.

→ You can do body work. You can literally ask yourself, "How am I doing?" Acknowledge your importance, and similarly to what we would say to an Eight, remember that these actions are just basic self-respect.

→ Vigorous exercise can help Nines feel more confidently in their body.

→ Speak back what you're hearing, but remember who you

are and what you stand for and your own opinion and way of knowing.

→ Say things that need to be said with clarity. Clarity is kindness.

→ Right action. Bring your energy back into your body and re-discover your power.

→ It could even be an emotion like anger. Putting off emotions for Nines is common. You heal through recognizing them.

## Activities To Lower Stress And Practice Self-Development

**Engage with presence:** Nines can overwork just like Eights and Ones. But there's also very little self-monitoring. Whether working too much or sitting on the couch a little too much, Nines can easily overlook their feelings. It's important to have a routine or some method of developing a practice of tuning in to yourself. Ask yourself how you are doing? This simple check in is a simple but powerful method for the first step of self-inquiry. At first it might sound counterintuitive, since Nines struggle with inertia and just getting going. However, the kind of stillness it takes to tune in means you have to stick with it. Practice engaging each of your center's: your heart, your head, and not only your body when you practice this form of meditation.

**Right action:** Break out your weekly planner at the same time each week, and ask yourself, "What is the hardest thing I have to do this week?" And do that first. No dithering. Follow through and kill that inner procrastinator. Watch your stress level actually go down.

**Self-inquiry:** Ask yourself: Do you value harmony with others over having your own identity? Why or why not?

**Trigger your body's need for sensation through nature:** Study after study shows the replenishing effects of nature. All types need the experiential benefits of engagement with nature, and it can be especially true for body types and their relationship with anger. For Nines, falling asleep to their anger often means more generally falling asleep to themselves and, therefore, their own needs. Never underestimate the potential powerful effects of nature and how it reduces stress. Try one of these simple techniques:

→ Go outside: If you have few options for getting outside access what you can. Maybe a few trees and a bench outside your apartment building? Sit there rather than inside.

→ Walk outside: Walking is considered the overall best exercise. It is low impact, helps with posture, develops your cardio, and allows for a mental refresh and reset. Any kind of walking routine will yield wonderful physical and mental rewards.

→ Fake it till you make it: Some research suggests that even just imaging yourself outside can help. Google a guided meditation in nature and give yourself a few minutes to escape. Chart how you feel afterwards. Check out material from UCLA , which offers guided meditations as short as three minutes at: http://marc.ucla.edu/mindful-meditations).

**Mental Shifts That Connect You to Your Body With Controlled Breathing:** As we well know by now, there is an intimate connection between our minds and bodies (no matter where your center of intelligence resides). Clear space in your mind and alleviate stress that may be building in your body. And if you really just don't believe you have the time, then this controlled breathing exercise can be done in under a minute:

> Take a deep breath, expand your belly. Pause. Exhale slowly as you count to five. Repeat four times.

That's it! This brief exercise has been shown to tamp down stress hormones, sharpen your thinking, and possibly even give your immune system a small bump. This small action further shows your body the self-respect it deserves. It also helps you to deliberately recognize when you are unconsciously doing when you tune out and narcotize.

9  •  1 Perfectionist Reformer

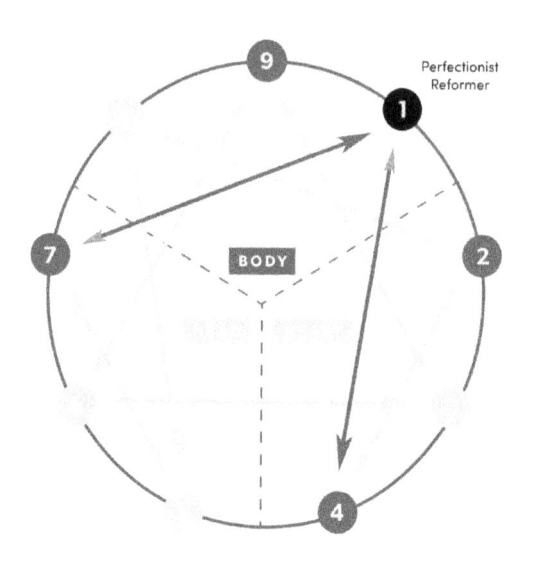

7  •  BODY  •  2

4

PATH OF ENERGIZING    PATH OF RESOLUTION

# ONES:
# GOOD ENOUGH PERFECTION

*"And why should we feel anger at the world? / As if the world would notice!"*
—Euripedes

**In a single syllable:** Firm
**Persona:** Critic
**Mantra:** "I am right. I am good."
**Reactivity defense mechanism:** Reaction formation
**Passion:** Anger

**In a Nutshell**

Ichazo's Ego-Resent, or what we most commonly call the Reformer or Perfectionist, creates an ideal out of rightness or goodness or improvement and related traits. Ones often feel a lot of responsibility—with a wide variety of levels of awareness—to fix themselves and others, not necessarily in that order. As a body type, they also tend to know things quickly, but they also tend to expect others to know things as quickly as they do and as well. When other close relationships fail to do this, they can also be quick to anger. Anger for Ones, however, is not usually expressed directly and overtly, as it may be in Eights, or emotionally as in Fours. In Ones we often hear the anger being housed literally in the body. The anger can be so readily absorbed, and so intense, that it is hard to hold inside for Ones. They may think they are holding it in, but it usually leaks out even in ways in which they are unaware. Freud taught about the superego as being the ideal part of the ego structure, and there is no clearer example of the superego at work than in the One type.

**Defining Characteristics of the One Type**

If you've ever felt a little like there is no pleasing a One because you are bound to be (or at least feel) criticized and judged regardless of what you do, it may help to understand that Ones are notoriously harder on themselves than everyone else. Ones do want to see greater perfection in the world, but the problem is that the perfection is always their own assumptions and beliefs about how things should be and how people should behave. When these emotions and expectations of the self and others are continually unmet, and therefore suppressed, the characteristics of usually low-level anger inevitably leak out.

If Milan Kundera's theme of *The Unbearable Lightness of Being* means that we are lightest when we are freed from meaning or expectations, then Ones represent the polar opposite. They are burdened by expectations. Their expectations of themselves, others, and the world at large. Nothing lives up to their sense of what is best, and as a result, they themselves suffer. Kundera's theme of meaningless, however, is not the healthiest response. While there may be wisdom in avoiding affiliation with ideologies and human institutions with their agendas and flawed and fatal policies, it is not "right" per se. Kundera, of course, may be dramatizing or showing a kind of reaction formation of life in these lonely, isolated, disconnected times we live in.

Ones live under the oppression of an inner voice constantly admonishing them to do better, to be better, from the biggest idea to the smallest detail. If that sounds tough, try walking in their shoes for a day.

And as body types, they tend to go to the immediacy of their "felt" sense of knowing. Kristi Rider, a panelist on our podcast has said: "For me being a body type means that I know things quickly, might take action quickly. I have a gut knowing that I've interpreted as an intuition, when I need to discern what's the right thing to do. And, I'm really good at it. And I don't often doubt when I know something, and probably one of the trickier things about that is I assume that everyone else should know also like I know." This very superpower of Ones can make it hard to "lighten up" because they immediately and directly see imperfections wherever they may reside.

"Type One is like being in judgment, and critical of yourself really more than others," says panelist Randa Hinton on our podcast. "It makes so much more sense that I have all of my emotions, literally physically, and it takes like a lot for me to let them kind of come out. So I think for me, I've had to do a lot of work and find ways one to relax, to let things go. And to not carry the weight of the world on my shoulders."

So it probably comes as no surprise that when stress hits for Ones, it comes with a lot of intensity, and also often a lot of emotionality. Ones hold a lot of tension in their bodies and tend to keep them in. Reaction formation is a defense mechanism that all types are capable of. It is the tendency of a repressed wish or feeling expressed in direct contrast to the way you really feel. For Ones, this hits the bullseye as a conditioned response. As they are in conflict with their anger, they often repress it and one of the ways of doing so is to get extra friendly or upbeat at the precise moment they feel the curdle of irritation.

Ones tend to repress a lot, anything they see as in conflict with an ideal of what is right. They might suppress sexuality, their relationship to food, their relationship to working out, their relationship to politics or religion, you name it. Sometimes Ones look for authority in what they need permission for and in this way almost need to be re-parented. They can be hypersensitive to judgment or criticism, especially because they try so hard to be above it.

Another identifying characteristic of Ones is that they often speak in the language of "shoulds" and "oughts." Thus, when Ones seek to break out of their ingrained personality patterns, and out of stress, they need to lighten up. Easier said than done, but relaxing the passion of anger holds the key to the kingdom. They also need to be on guard for reigniting the whole program of goodness when they start to work on themselves. If any type needs to do less and do things messy or "worse," it is the One type.

**The Passion of One**

Anger is the passion of the One. Ones have over-identified with denying the instinctual part of themselves by identifying with only the parts they deem as "good." On the one hand this can look like fighting global warming or advocating for abortion. It almost doesn't matter the cause, it's more about the response to what is viewed as virtuous and just. Ones identify with what they have deemed "good" and seek to control themselves to adhere to those principles or ideals. The instinctual part they feel in themselves when the world around them (i.e.—reality) doesn't correspond is anger. They constantly seek to force the world or others to conform to their sense of right and wrong, and when it inevitably doesn't live up to their projections they are frustrated, resentful, or outright angry.

Of the three body centers, Ones are the most ambivalent toward anger. Eights express it in their outer projection of confidence and invulnerability. Nines fall asleep to it. Ones are in conflict. They often turn it inward, and often come to their coaches and therapists in depression (because what is depression but self-directed "inert" anger?). Sometimes it leaks out in irritation, frustration, resentment, and irritability, which is thinly disguised and often a blind spot that they don't realize is so obvious to others. Sometimes, too, it boils over in intense outbursts of rage.

The way out is through the virtue of serenity. One approach to the process of engaging with serenity is to look for the positive in others, as well as in the self. Also, getting in deep touch with the gut knowing, pushing through reaction formation and into personal affirmation. Affirmation can lead to a deeper degree of acceptance. This is the pathway to the Ones' virtue and can break them from the tyranny of their rigidity and inner-and-outer-focused judgment. We will examine areas for concerted focus and growth through the work with wing stretches and arrow movements.

**Functional Versus Authentic Personality**

Goodness for fixated Ones depends on a borrowed morality, not a genuine one, such as Plato's idea of "the Good." In personality, of course, they may get a lot done, and they may get a lot done exceedingly well (even if it may sometimes take a little longer than other types). A mantra of a One might well be, "If it's worth doing, it's worth doing well." There is something to be said for this ideal. You should see their lawn. It practically glows and is trimmed and hedged symmetrically. They follow the user guidelines as laid out in the company handbook, and, yes, by the way, they have read the handbook (you mean you haven't?). And what's wrong with wanting to do right? Don't we all need a little more right in this world?

The problem is that for as "correct" as they may be they are forever proving their worth in order to be loved or accepted. The mantra "Would you rather be right or happy?" applies particularly to Ones. In their authentic personality they can come to know, first of all, that they are good enough just being who they are. They don't need to constantly oppose or manage or improve anything. This can open them up to a freedom they never knew existed. In this new freedom they can dictate their own terms and conditions for how they want to live. They can relax their unnecessary hold on being "right" and perhaps get more in touch with their sense of humor (which a lot of Ones have). However they approach it, relaxing their grip on rule-following and fill-in-the-blanks self-righteousness can lead to a lightness of being and make themselves more joyful within, and more pleasant to be around.

### Psychological Roots and Key Patterns that Create Stress for Ones

No one wants to be called "anal" but in terms of how the term has come into the parlance of our times, no other type defines One better. Like all body types, Ones had an intrinsic need for holding. The core issue around the need for structure and adherence to rules and standards is seen as a reflection of unmet needs that supported a stable holding environment at an early age. Ones often report having felt a need to control and conform their behavior to the structures or expectations of others.

Unlike Nines who seek to merge in order to maintain a sense of inner cohesion and comfort, Ones adhere to correct behavior, authority, and standards. Most Ones tend to report that they took on responsibility too early. Whatever the roles or responsibilities, they had an early unmet need of wanting to be recognized or acknowledged for how hard they worked, especially to be good. The composition is that of excessive demands and little acknowledgement so that there is a sense of constant frustration at not getting what they need or strive so hard for. In stress, as with all types, you can see the doubling down of what they unconsciously tend to do. So Ones can become especially self-critical of themselves and of others.

Ones may be one of the most discussed in the psychological literature of the past century and a half as the "obsessive" type, and perhaps the most over-represented in films and literature. (We can think of the character of Melvin Udall played by Jack Nicholson in *As Good As It Gets* and his obsession with handwashing.) Importantly, though, it is not just a case of repressing passive oral needs that creates the self-reliant angry attitude, such as Freud generally proposed. Neither is it due to a premature self-control and increased tolerance for frustration, such as Fromm built upon with the toilet training theories. It is this combination of meeting the excessive demands that are at the same time deemed as legitimate or what is to be expected. Thus, as the theory currently goes, the reaction formation drives both the anger and its defense in the form of reaction formation.

**Self-Preservation One: Worry**

Of the three types, this is the one that most embodies perfectionism. They are so attuned to "being good" they repress even their natural emotional stance of anger into a reaction formation. They camouflage anger's heat into warmth, and rather than show even irritation, resentment, or frustration, they show the colors of tolerance and friendliness. Naranjo's name of "worry" for this subtype focuses on the survival fear of having everything under control as much as possible. They tend to constantly anticipate what might happen in order to get ahead and make sure things remain "correct."

They tend to turn their gaze inwardly, and their perfectionism creates a powerful and difficult inner critic to overcome. Sometimes their excessive sense of responsibility comes from having to grow up early. Because of the intensity of their inner critic, this subtype can actually be very angry. When in stress their anger will leak out sometimes as frustration, irritation, or a thinly disguised self-righteousness. If it builds up enough it may explode in the form of angrily doing what hasn't been done right in their estimation.

Even here, however, perfectionism might be cloaked in an anxiety focus around lifestyle. They may make a fuss over keeping their home in an ordered way that seems virtuous and ordered. It could be emphasized through any manner of habits or processes, usually though, for this type, the object of focus centers on boundaries. The boundaries could be how to properly eat, take care of one's finances, trim and maintain the lawn, parent, or lead a team. Usually the focus is on the mundane, the way to perform ordinary tasks in a certain order or method.

Because of the inclination toward anxiety, this subtype is most often confused for a Six. The differentiating factor is that the Self-Preservation One has a solid grasp on what they know "to be right" while the Six's first inclination is to continually second-guess themselves and their actions. Less frequently we see mistyping as a Three, especially of the same instinctual variant as Self-Preservation.

### Social One: Rigidity

Naranjo calls this subtype the most rigid of the three. Their core issue is needing to be superior. They have a particular way of going about this superiority, however, which differs from other expressions of it as might manifest in, say, Fours or Sixes. This type is looking to experience their sense of integrity in relationships, they seek to belong. They seek to do this through imposing their idea of what is right or wrong, appropriate or inappropriate. Their social standards are a reaction formation to their fundamental sense of needing to be good enough to belong. Another name for this subtype could be "rectitude" since by definition it implies setting a moral example of how to be and behave, as well as what the "right" cause is to get behind in the first place.

These are often our reformers. They have a sense of responsibility and obligation to identifying the correct mission or purpose and then setting an example of how to pursue it with integrity. So long as others in their purview live in accordance with the appropriate standards, this type can be seen as warm and outgoing. They may generously offer their time in service as mentors, teachers, coaches, and as leaders concerned with an ideal associated with the good or just cause. Their hearts may well be in the right place, but they tend to remain on the outside of the causes or organizations they serve for the very reason that no one and nothing can quite live up to the principles and ideals they project.

They are known as the most intellectual of the three One types because they tend to channel the passion of Anger into the truth they seek to embody. When done skillfully, even in personality they may appear less reactive than the other subtypes because of their apparently distanced or aloof perspective. As a result, this subtype is most akin to mistyping as a Five. Similarly, a Social Seven might at first look like this type. The Social Seven (countertype) inverts the passion of gluttony into anti-gluttony, and turns gluttony into a focus on helping others through their pain.

## Sexual/One-to-One One: (countertype) Zeal

Sexual Ones have the most outwardly manifested anger. Naranjo says this subtype feels entitled to what they want. "Why not me?" they might ask, and find reasons to justify their demandingness. Interestingly, that very question—consumed with the fundamental question of perfection—can be turned on its head, especially in insecurity. As Ichazo has said, "Union with another is always threatened by someone more perfect." Similar to the other Ones is the sense of the motivation behind what is right and wrong. If the Sexual One tells you what to do it is from a sense of what is honorable, superior, or morally right.

The focus on rightness here is proving and demonstrating traits that make them desirable. They don't necessarily seek a partner who is like them, but they do care that as a couple they model the best way to be in a relationship. This type is less focused on criticizing themselves, however, and tend to direct their focus on the "other." In this respect they may infatuate the ideal. This very infatuation may make them aspire to be attractive in a wide variety of ways whether it be adventurous, athletic, humorous, or simply physically attractive. The high ideals of this type may keep their partners at a distance. No one can quite live up their ideals or high standards.

Because this type is the least self-critical of the three subtypes, and because they are the most comfortable expressing their anger, they are viewed as the countertype. Just as a reminder, the countertype is a behavior that runs "counter" to the passion. The outward expression of anger in this case isn't directly counter to the One's basic emotional reactivity, but does stand out in that it isn't as intensely self-directed. The characterization of "zeal" comes from Naranjo's adaptation of Ichazo's interpretation, which is a "special intensity of desire." But the "zeal" here is a double-entendre. It means both an intensity and excitement in seeking the object of its desire, as well as a passion for doing things with intensity and care.

Angey Liskey, a Sexual One, says on our podcast, "I can make myself have a fever, because I make myself so hot and upset, my cheeks get so red, I feel tingling through every part of my whole body. And what most of the time happens is it becomes energy that I use to fuel and get things done. And so like rage cleaning, or organizing or whatever."

This subtype is sometimes difficult to tell from Eights who also have no problem in expressing their anger. One not-so-subtle difference is the under-social functioning of Eights, and the over-social functioning of the One. Eights are sometimes tone deaf to others, while Ones are very much tuned in and constantly seeking to improve what they view as not up to standard.

### Working with Arrows in Growth and Stress

Ones are generally inclined to *move against* people. On their high side, Ones have an idealistic vision of how people and situations could be and they desire to move reality from where it is to where it has the potential to be. Ones move against the *status quo,* the present state, to raise it to a *status meliore,* a better state. On their less conscious side or under stress, Ones can react angrily and resentfully when reality falls short of perfection. They are quick to spot flaws, criticize, and fix things. Their defense mechanism of reaction formation is the classic example of doing the opposite of what they want to do. When they feel irritation at someone in the workplace for not following the rules or paying attention to details, they may overdo how wonderful everything is and how pleased they are with the others' performance.

The wing looking back is the Nine wing of the One, and the wing looking forward is the Two, the latter remaining in the body center, and the former pushing the One a neighboring step into the heart center. Ones focusing on their Nine wing consciously will show up with an easygoing nature, ready to get along and go along with the flow, an approach they are usually in conflict with. They embody a democratic spirit valuing everyone's opinion and contribution rather than believing their way is the right way and everyone needs to get on board. By contrast, when they go into their Nine wing under stress or unconsciously, they may find themselves tuning out, procrastinating, or narcotizing themselves in a variety of behaviors and interests, some addictive and some merely distracting.

Once Ones have worked consciously on the easier-going nature of their Nine wing, they are ready for work in their Two wing. In conscious moves to the high side of their Two wing, Ones value relationships, connection, and support. Rather than criticize and judge, they will find themselves affirming and approving of others, putting others at ease, thinking of others first. When they go into their Two wing under stress, they may find themselves giving in order to get, or putting everyone else's needs before their own and forgetting they even have needs.

When Ones have consciously worked on the gentler shifts in their personality work through conscious wing work, they are ready for the arrow leaps. The first arrow point to target in their self-development journey is toward the Seven. When they make this move consciously, they *move towards* people in an accepting, affirming, optimistic way. They embrace reality with flexibility and possibly even spontaneity rather than rigidity. By contrast, if they are in their Seven arrow under stress, they move towards pleasure to avoid pain, sometimes getting caught up in addictive behaviors. Or they may appear overly friendly when reaction formation works to disguise their underlying anger.

After they have thoroughly engaged with the future-oriented and optimistic nature of their Seven arrow, they are ready for the second arrow to the Four point. When Ones shift to their Four, they *move away* from people in an adaptive style which allows them to reflect on their own feelings and desires instead of getting caught up in fixing others. In stepping back, they can attend to their own inner journey, and in the self-referencing style of the Four, they can let others "be" even when the others may be struggling or in apparent need of help or improvement. When Ones fixate inside their Four arrow, they can withdraw due to their sense of lack, being misunderstood, or not appreciated for all they have done.

### Reactive Impulse Under Stress

A lot of times Ones sincerely just want to show up and help. In unhealthy expressions, Ones may feel like they're just helping, but others find them critical and like a parent that can never be pleased. They may feel like they're "always apologizing," but when it comes to the big things, they really never are. They may feel like they're being encouraging, but others feel more like they never affirm. When Ones can uncover some of these blind spots and begin to function in greater degrees of self-awareness and observation, they can function more from a health perspective. Usually, for Ones, this means doing less. Like, rather than show up and help, Ones may find that they're actually being the most helpful by just showing up.

### Defining Characteristics in Personality

→ Dominant or "ever present" inner critic

→ In leadership positions, it can be especially tough to self-observe and not seek to control things and get angry that they aren't being done up to their standards or their perceived potential

→ Resist giving in to joy and excitement for fear of losing control

→ Obsessive adherence to rule-following

→ Rigidly contrarian and then wounded when others don't see the value of their contribution

**Superpowers**

When channeled appropriately, and in the right context, Ones' ability to see what needs improvement and action can be a powerful asset, especially in professional applications. Ones like both to do things the right way and "to be" the right way. If you want things done well and done the right way, the One is who you are looking for. They can be extraordinarily disciplined, and their high expectations of others is really because they want to live a life of integrity and through that, they don't expect anything of others that they don't also expect in and of themselves. Ones also tend to be good at creating processes and structures where none were previously to be found. When other types flounder in their mental or emotional centers, overthinking, dramatizing, or simply talking too much, Ones go directly for clarity. They are organized in their approaches, and tend to be clear in their communication and practical in their implementation. Even when Ones—like all humans—don't live up to their own standards or ideals, they are earnest in their attempts to work hard and do well. You can count on Ones.

### Common Stressors for Ones

- → Receiving feedback that contains right and wrong judgments.
- → When they are not told authentically and directly that they are doing a good job.
- → Breaking out of black and white, either-or thinking, rigidity even when they want to.
- → When others don't follow the rules or follow through with what they said they would do.
- → When they are not in control of a situation.
- → When others act unethically or irresponsibly.
- → People who make excuses for poor work and/or repeat the same patterns of behavior that lead to poor performance.
- → When people are not logical or rational in their thinking or approach to problem solving.

### Type One Patterns to Observe to Make More Conscious

- → The way they will seem mad to others and don't realize their body language or lack of engagement in verbal communication make it hard to engage with.
- → The way they may insist on doing it their way only because it's the only right way.
- → Becoming aware not only of suppressed anger, but also of the tendency to shift into reaction formation behavior.
- → The way they tense up and get stressed when things don't follow a prescribed pattern or expected set of agreed upon rules.
- → Their relentless need to constantly improve may make others in their orbit (whether at home or work) become frustrated or criticized.
- → The way their standards are not necessarily as objective as they may think or believe they are.

## Activities To Lower Stress And Practice Self-Development

**Start a program and don't track your progress:** You can't relive the past, and you can't prepare for everything that will happen in the future. It's important for Ones to be in the moment. Stay present to yourself in the here and now. Get out of flogging yourself over what has happened in the near or distant past. Stop the voices about what you're anticipating. One way Ones can do this is develop an exercise routine because of the way they hold so much in their bodies. But the big trap for Ones is to start a self-improvement program that they must follow "the right way."

We recommend for Ones to start running without tracking your mileage or pace. Or to lift weights with no plan other than to get your heart rate up for a few minutes to clear your mind and relax your body. Don't give yourself too much homework! Start with any of these suggestions and just do that.

**Do something completely out of character:** Wear a loud Hawaiian shirt. Put a silly bumper sticker on your car. Slurp a beer at your next get together (and don't call it a get together, call it a party!). Roll down the windows while you drive and let it mess up your hair. Maybe these examples work and maybe they don't, but you get the idea. Do something that is out of character, and that encourages you to lighten up. That's the first step. The second step is the next day when your Inner Critic starts talking, laugh at it. Make fun of your Inner Critic.

**Facing up to the inner critic:** If you don't want to completely "break character," but still want to do something about that nagging inner critic, practice self-observation: When is the Inner Critic loudest? Change up your practices and habits to break free from the tyranny of the inner critic by changing up your patterns and disrupting the voice. Some name their inner critic so they can make fun of it.

**Tap into the virtue of serenity:** Make time for yourself to tap into the virtue of your serenity. Serenity is feeling calm in your body, your mind, and your heart. Ones may have a hard time achieving this when there is always something they could be improving, achieving, or industriously checking off their list. Sometimes Ones can improve their chances of achieving serenity by going for walks in nature. Others by just doing nothing, laying in bed, or listening to relaxing music, or floating in a hot tub and staring up at the clouds. Some like an environment, perhaps their office or some personal space that only they control. For Ones, self-care for the body is even more important than for other types. Ones may need to schedule their serenity. Scheduling exercise routines, especially those related to stretching the muscles and improving mindfulness, like a massage or yoga or a long walk.

**Knowing what is theirs to do, and what is not:** Ones may think that others want their advice because they assume everyone is like them and wants to be and do better. When Ones realize that unsolicited advice often implies criticism and character flaws, they will realize that most people don't want this kind of advice. They should also feel better recognizing there is less for them to be responsible for.

HEART

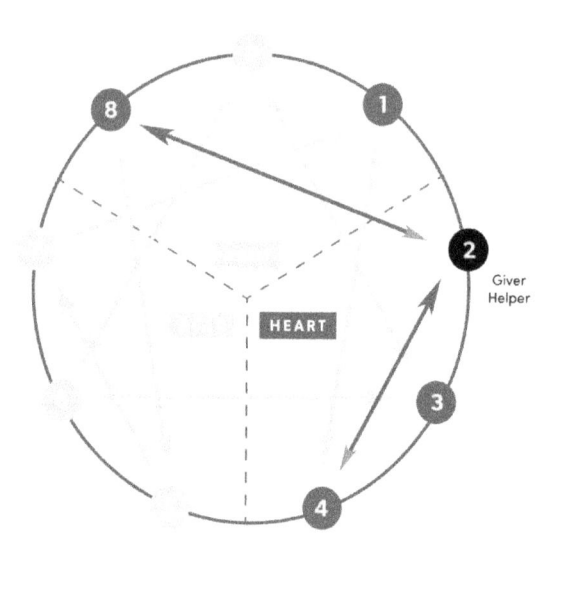

**2** Giver Helper

PATH OF ENERGIZING    PATH OF RESOLUTION

# TWOS: DEFLATING THE PRIDE BALLOON

> *"A proud person is always looking down on things and people; and, of course, as long as you are looking down, you cannot see something that is above you."*
> —C.S. Lewis

**In a single syllable:** Use
**Persona:** Flatterer
**Mantra:** "See all I do for you."
**Reactivity defense mechanism:** Repression
**Passion:** Pride

## In a Nutshell

Ichazo's Ego-Flat is most often called the Helper, which can be a misleading name and many misinterpret and go overboard on how Twos just love to *help, help, help*. Twos flatter to get what they want, and what they want is love and belonging. The belonging is to an idealized other from whom they can receive the recognition and worthiness and support they feel they lack. Generally speaking, the helping is strategic and not often even conscious. The first of our three Heart types, Twos feel deeply and have an intuitive sense of how others are feeling. Twos may be considered the most emotional of all the types (even over Fours) because they are not only a feeling type, but often also "anti-intellectual," as Naranjo says. For all that, many Twos report not feeling the freedom to openly express their emotions because of their consideration of others. Twos are so good at getting others to like them that they can even make a competition out of it. All subtypes will take on some of the hardest people to get along with. It can be a point of pride when they do win over that difficult person and prove to themselves that they really are that amazing.

**Defining Characteristics of the Two Type**

For Twos, information comes to them through their emotions first and foremost and fast. Twos we call "other-referencing," which means their first focus of attention is on others first. They scale on the side of other referencing more than self. Twos strategically help people in order to create *indispensability*. They're often called strategic helpers. And when they become indispensable to somebody, the love factor really gets met (their emotional need for being valued and understood). They tend to repress their own needs and feelings, and are highly attuned and emotionally sensitive to the others in their orbit. Their core motivation is gaining approval and love from important others.

Twos tend to be warm and friendly. Twos have that kind of affable demeanor, which can sometimes come across as seductive. My wife Shelley, is a Two, and says, "The word 'seductive' was one word that always kind of hung me up a little bit." And while it may be true more so for the Sexual/One-to-One subtype, seduction proves true across the board for all Twos just in different manifestations, or you could say the targets of seduction vary. Shelley also says that upon further review, when considering how she was called one of the "blonde bombshells" at her alma mater, Georgetown College, she has since realized that to her she "was just being friendly," but the unconscious mission was to win people over, "to get them to like me." And through some inner work and reflection, she has learned about the way Twos are "kind of strategic about who we let into our heart."

Twos also have big emotions. But as Narajano observes and many Twos attest, part of the strategy is to repress the emotions. They may be having firecracker emotions going on inside, but never stop to label them and understand them. For some Twos, the emotions are so big they overwhelm. For less conscious Twos, they don't really even see how the world doesn't filter and interpret reality through this same filter. For them, life is a felt experience. In order to be more effective in relationships of all kinds, and especially in stressful situations, an important first step is to become more conscious about how heart types show up in relationships.

Once that committed work on self-awareness has begun, the next step is work on healthy boundaries. Twos are compulsively driven to focus on the needs of others out of a buried fear that they will be alone and unloved with no one to help them if they stop. The process of recognizing these patterns, and of developing strategies and habits to focus on what a Two needs first is a growth point.

When Twos come to coaching or therapy their first instinct may be to ask, "How are you?" It is important for Twos to be in relation, but their task for forward movement and growth is to keep the focus on them, not on the person with whom they're in relationship. Twos need warmth and empathy as a way of developing trust and a psychological safety net, but if ever they need to keep the attention on themselves it is here. They need to be able to connect without having to be anyone, and they often need affirmation that who they are is already enough. Unlike the body types that need holding, these intensely emotional heart types need mirroring. They need to feel heard, and they need permission to feel, a safe place to grieve and let their emotions surface unfiltered.

### The Passion of Two

Pride is the passion of Twos. Pride is deceptive in Twos. They tend not to recognize it at first blush. But it is also deceptive to the others who participate in its courtship because, after all, isn't this person focusing their attention on you? Aren't they serving your needs and interested in your interests? Don't they defer to you before they take themselves into consideration? It may in fact be that because Twos are not aware of their love need that this unconsciousness supports the passion of pride. What creates pride in a child more than being worthy of the love of his or her parents? But if you don't know the motivation behind why you are pursuing this "worthiness" in the first place, it makes sense that you will feel a sense of pride when the other acknowledges your efforts and fulfills your need. It's almost as if Twos feel like, "Well, of course you are giving back to me. I've done so much for you. I know that I am worthy of this."

Naranjo makes the fascinating insight that just as we might understand anger as a reaction-formation to gluttony, "we may in this case understand pride as a transformation of envy through the joint action of repression and histrionic emotionalism (190)." In other words, through the combination of repression and emotionalism envy is transformed into pride. That is, rather than soliciting emotional support from others (such as Fours do in their passion of envy), Twos provide emotional benefits to others as the source of their passion of pride.

"It's like this pride in like, I can fix you, or I can fix your situation," as panelist Jonathan Bow reports. "Or if I just do this to help you, then your life will be better. Right? Like I'm not your hero, but I can try to be, and trying to be that person is exhausting. So I think that that is part of the issue. And it comes to pride for us too. But also, it's just not attainable, right? Like we often put ourselves on pedestals. It's interesting, because, you know, we are the type that is most known to be focused on others. But I think when our pride shows up, we turn very self focused in 'Look what I can do to help you and to fix you.'"

He goes on to say that is the same pride that shows up in him when he just says he pretends he doesn't have needs, or doesn't pay attention to any wants or desires. And that ends up hurting himself and the people around him, because he is "better" than those who have needs. And it's also a self-deception.

Humility is the antidote for pride. So, as a Two, Shelley thinks about it every morning (well, most mornings). She thinks, *What's the smallest thing I can do today, or the most anonymous thing I can do today to keep moving things forward in my life? It's challenging, like thinking about how do I integrate more and have more humility? To not have the answers, to ask for what I need, to be basic.* We will examine areas for concerted focus and growth through the work with wing stretches and arrow movements.

### Functional Versus Authentic Personality

Like all ego structures, there are aspects of the personality that function in the world with great efficacy even while it is at the expense of the true or authentic self. Here we see behavior that approximates a form a love that we may idealize. Twos fixate on intimate relationships and/or relationships with important people. In all cases they are affirmed for their self-worth—they are treated as "Enneagram royalty" as Ginger Lapid-Bogda describes them—through the special treatment that they get from these connections. And in personality we may find them warm and generous. When they cast their vision in your direction it feels like sunlight. You feel important, recognized, understood, affirmed, possibly even loved. And what is wrong with that?

For those who benefit from their charms you might say that nothing is wrong, and please don't change. Of course, the benefits are only temporary. This is a love or a giving that demands a return on investment, and one way or another the beneficiary will need to understand. Either that, or on the lower levels of functioning and interpersonal dynamics, we see codependency, manipulation, victimization, and Quid Pro Quo exchanges.

The deeper spiritual aim is to recognize that the expression of love through intimate connection is only an idealization (and therefore a distortion) of a fuller and more complete love. You could say that in personality, the Twos are really onto something when it comes to what love looks like, but it stops at the gates of true understanding and expression. You can merge in love while still maintaining your own individuated self, separateness in togetherness.

The key to growth through the virtue of humility is to bring into recognition and self-understanding (and self-acceptance) that the over-identification on relationships really originates from an emptiness. The Twos' ego is constantly fretting that it is not enough, that it must prove itself again and again. There will almost surely be pain of one kind of deficiency or another, a recognition of limitation—usually of something the person values highly—before they can grow into "a wider vision of who they are," as Chestnut and Paes write in *The Enneagram Guide to Waking Up.*

It is no easy task to convince pride that it needs to shuffle along. In Christianity, pride is sometimes regarded as the chief of all the sins due to its attribution of Lucifer as deeming himself greater than the Creator. While there may be a good moral foreground for characterizing pride in such serious terms, through the lens of our psychodynamic interpretations of personality we regard all passions with equal seriousness.

Carolyn Swora, a Sexual/One-to-One Two, says, about her struggle with pride:

> "A big aha for me was starting to realize the layers of pride. I realized that pride shows up for me in being a super person, like a super woman, and that there's not a challenge that I can take on that I can't win, or be in…and finally I've started to break that cycle…It's just insidious in how it shows up."

### Psychological Roots and Key Patterns that Create Stress for Twos

All heart types have the same unmet central need at a major early stage of development for mirroring. The display of mirroring often begins as early as infancy, as babies begin to mimic individuals around them and establish connections especially with particular body movements. The ability to mimic another person's actions allows the infant to establish a sense of empathy and thus begin to understand another's emotions. The infant establishes connections with others emotions and in turn mirrors their movements. Mirroring establishes rapport with the individual who is being mirrored, as the similarities in nonverbal gestures allow the individual to feel more connected with the person exhibiting the mirrored behavior. When this need is not adequately met the experience for all heart types is that they are not fully seen, recognized, affirmed by, or understood by their primary caretakers.

One of our podcast panelists, Jonathan Bow, says:

> I felt like my job was to hold everything together. And so I became a therapist for my family in a very unhealthy way. But when I'm sitting in that seat, trying to be the one who holds it all together, and then learning very quickly, Oh, but if I am this superior, moral, great loving child who's super polite, does all the right things, doesn't do any of the wrong things, that immediately gave me that sense of like, Oh, yeah, you're loved and you're appreciated and you're valued.

Naranjo documents the "association between hysterical personality and simple repression" as the earliest relationship reported between a defense mechanism and a neurotic disposition, and also "the most thoroughly documented and agreed upon," when it comes to the Two type. Repression stands for a defense mechanism where the ideational representative of impulses is impeded from becoming conscious. In other words, it may be unconscious but it also may be unconscious because there is a motivation "not to know." It manifests itself as a pretense to the world that it doesn't know, but also deceives the self. Naranjano theorizes that emotions facilitate this process much like intellectualization functions to distort reality. In this case, "emotionalism."

### Self-Preservation Two: (countertype) Me First/ Privilege

The apparently more childlike, the "cutest" of the Twos. In not building up self-importance there is a use to remaining childlike: kids are more likable than adults after all. They at least appear to be without guile. Of the three subtypes, this one feels the most burdened by giving or helping others, partly because they have a harder time trusting others than the other Twos. Also because they give compulsively out of more of a survival-based fear. They feel they *need* to give and help.

They tend to be selective about who they associate with and often have a tight-knit circle of friends and family that they can rely on, especially as this can be protection from the expectations of others outside that circle. They are supportive and giving of those in their smaller orbit, but at the same time can be demanding. While there may be a good deal of dependency connected with these Twos, it is also often a blindspot. They wouldn't want to admit that they need others or that they need help. In fact, what we often see is this type diligently striving to put others first for the benefit of all involved.

Their strong sense of obligation and responsibility can look like the warmer Six subtype (Self-Preservation), but Six nonetheless with more anxiety and fretting than one might expect from a Two. Their support style tends to be more practical like to help with others in skills related to caretaking or providing financial support. In men this is especially true. This subtype has a huge reserve for selflessly giving of their time and resources. In times of crisis they are sought out, especially when no one else is to be found.

This type can easily get caught up in a vortex of helping intensely followed by breakdowns into helplessness. The others who benefit from their giving may become dependent on the services, and also not realize the reciprocal expectation. Because these Twos are already so prone to overlooking their own needs, when they are also not met by others, they have a tendency to need time away in an effort of self-care. However, often the self-care is more in the form of self-indulgence or breaking away with a hard boundary that resembles a tantrum more than a healthy boundary. And the self-indulgence doesn't actually replace healthy self-care.

One of the traps these Twos are prone to falling into as the indispensable one is to lose their identity—including their own gifts and talents—in giving others support. This subtype begins the process of awakening to their self by giving to their own self with just as much focus and intensity as they do for others. This is not easy for Twos predisposed to always thinking of others first. When they do access their virtue of humility they can move into realizing that working on themselves in healthy ways provides them with the support and care they really need.

**Social Two: Ambition**

This subtype needs to be "someone." They still "seduce" but more in a leadership or standing above and set apart way. They don't fashion themselves as wildly as the Sexual/One-to-One subtype. They operate in a more "civilized" way. They are especially attuned to connection to the group. They are among the more social of any of the types and have an intuitive sense of how to "work a room." They are excellent networkers, sensing who is "in" and "out" of groups large and small. They are hard workers, ambitious, intentional about their place within the group or community at large. They take pride in their ability to bring people together and make connections of their own, and are especially skilled at flattery (consciously or unconsciously).

Pride is most evident in this subtype as they are often known for their leadership and accomplishments. In some cases, with this subtype, the reward of high-level connections and strategically helping others is its own reward. For many, however, they find themselves in positions of power and leadership. When they are, they can be tenacious and exceptionally hard-working, especially when they connect with the right organization that aligns with their values. They will champion their people and take pride in making sure that even the "lower level" subordinate, or misfit is included and helped to achieve their goals.

It may take time for Social Twos to climb the proverbial ladder of success, however, because they are so good at helping others, and often don't see their own ambition. For many of these Twos, they are not willing to acknowledge their pride or to allow for vulnerability, and this makes others suspicious of their motives, which is often a blindspot. Also, because of the very fact that they see themselves as special and set apart with skills at getting others to like them, they can be reluctant to ask for help which might lead to insight and growth.

Social Twos are powerful and effective leaders when they are functioning in their higher selves. They can be savvy at opening the right doors, and can be incredibly supportive as mentors and coaches, especially taking pride in seeing subordinates succeed. They are also not afraid to have "hard conversations" because of their people skills in delivering bad news in direct yet gentle ways. When they are functioning in their lower selves, this subtype can be demanding and prone to unexpected displays of intense emotions (usually in the form of anger).

They may be mistaken for Threes in their image-centered focus, as well as their discipline and hard-working nature. From a distance they may seem like Eights as well due to their sometimes denying vulnerability and their tendency to be "turfy." Growth work comes in the form of humility for this subtype by being open to the way they give-to-get, as well as in their motives behind why they help people of any status, and recognizing pride for what it is.

## Sexual/One-to-One Two: Aggressive/Seduction

This is the subtype known as a "seducer," or in gendered terms, a "femme fatale." Whether man or woman, charm is their strong suit. They have an intuitive gift for making others feel special, and can push toward the object of their attention with an approach that makes the connection feel inevitable. This subtype might be the most effective at forming close engagement with others of all the types. The flattery involves their alertness to the needs, interests, habits, and values of others. In other words, they tune in to what makes the other person tick. At the same time, they are also deeply emotional (as emphasized above from Naranjo), which at their best brings out their sensitivity and empathy for others, often the underdogs. And also, at lower functioning levels, creates the conditions for interpersonal chaos.

When it comes to connecting with others, they seem to somehow know that just being the object of someone's attraction is attractive in itself. Under some circumstances, they may seek to prove their desirability by seducing a particularly difficult or challenging partner. These Twos are unabashed when it comes to making themselves "aggressively" attractive. They are also less ashamed than the other Twos of stating their needs. Pride shows up here through the ability (and constant affirmation) to attract simply through physical desirability.

Naranjo observed that this Two is like a "double-Two," a Two that doubles down its Two-ness. The instinct of the Sexual/One-to-One for connection and merging is made all the more intense and powerful in combination with the Two's prideful need to seduce and shape-shift for others to get their own needs met. They are known as wild at heart, people who love hard and fall hard.

In leadership they have the potential for being passionate and inspirational. They have a strong confidence in their ability to leverage relationships and influence others. They will work relentlessly toward a goal they believe in. They thrive on connection and in higher level thinking and functioning, they can have a missional purpose with a vision of "others" in mind. They can be passionate and unpredictable in their displays of emotions in lower-level functioning (as leaders or followers).

Their work on the path of humility is especially to recognize the false self they present to others in order to please and make themselves likable or desirable. The maintenance of boundaries is also a critical first step of self-awareness, how to maintain them between others, and still find ways to meet their own energetic needs in healthful ways.

### Working with Arrows in Growth and Stress

Twos tend to *move towards* other people and situations. They value relationships, connection, and support. Their natural tendency is to affirm, embrace, and approve. Fixations in these tendencies can lead them to become cloying, and sometimes enabling, and even suffocating, which is ironically, the opposite of what their best self intends. They become overly solicitous and flattering. At their best, Twos are empathic warriors who know what others are feeling and how to meet their needs. They are deep feelers who make friends easily. People want to be in their orbit, and many come to them for help and assistance.

The first step in the growth journey for Twos is to take a step back into their neighboring One wing, which has them step into their body center. When done with intention and consciously, stepping into the One wing means not always putting others before your own needs, but first and foremost doing what needs to be done and executing correctly. They escape from impression-management and how others see them and embody structure, routine, and self-discipline for themselves. The less conscious side of the One wing reveals itself in having an eye for flaws in everything, especially as it reflects on the image they want to present to the world.

After this work is established, Twos do well to integrate the Three wing. Conscious work here involves a focus on tasks and goals and working toward them with diligence. This helps free them from the constant expectations of other relationships in their lives. They can begin to set their own agendas and priorities for themselves, and not in "giving to get." The stressed side of the Three wing may find them busy for its own sake, or accomplishing to be admired by others.

When Twos have thoroughly engaged in the conscious wing work of their neighboring personality points, they are ready for the arrow work. The first arrow directs them to the Four point, in which they *move away from* people. This means stepping back to allow others to stand on their own two feet. This also means moving inward to discovering their own unique style of creativity, and focusing on what they need first (and possibly letting others satisfy those needs before they even think about meeting anyone else's). Unconscious or stressed moves away from others to the point Four may mean they feel hurt, misunderstood or underappreciated. They may also feel special and privileged because of all they have done for others.

When Twos have recognized their own needs and priorities, they are ready to shift to their arrow target at point Eight, and *move against* others. This means setting boundaries and limits, expressing their own needs, and making requests of others. They become clear about who they are and what they are responsible for and challenge others to accept responsibility for themselves. The less conscious or stressed behavior for Twos at the point Eight, may mean they move against others in an aggressive rather than an assertive manner. They may impose their services on others, becoming critical and domineering. They may fantasize or seek revenge for feeling used and taken advantage of. Or they might push others away, claiming they don't need them. The key for continual growth here is to focus on making their needs known in assertive and respectful ways and recognizing the need for boundaries in firm but gentle and loving expressions.

**Reactive Impulse Under Stress**

Often Twos start to take on more and more under stress. They worry more and more about how people see them. Big emotions rumble around and without necessarily knowing what to do with them. They can get moody, and then mad at themselves for getting moody. For Twos, it can be how they are doing with other people, and as a result they put more pressure on themselves to do more, to be more, to help more.

Twos try to repress stress, much like Nines. Sometimes, due to the repression, their stress may be invisible until it explodes. What they really need is to feel supported. Just talking about it to someone who can empathize can be healing for a Two. They expect others to tune in to their needs, but asking for help can help. And also moderating their workload.

Twos need to remember they are not responsible for other people's happiness or comfort. Especially as leaders, Twos need to be able to let go of other's expectations, and be okay if others feel disappointed or frustrated. Twos have plenty of capability to be creative and strategic, but they have to give themselves the room for it by stepping out of their (unconscious) pride of meeting everyone else's needs, and making sure to make time for their own.

- → Seduction of groups or individuals
- → Poor boundaries and may come to resent the people who break them but tolerate them anyway
- → Immersed in emotions to the point where it can be hard to think or move into action, especially on behalf of oneself
- → Focus on winning over the most difficult people in their orbit
- → Enable bad behavior out of fear of breaking connection or not being liked
- → Begin to take on everything themselves because no one can do it as well as they believe they are capable of, and then resenting the others who let them go ahead and do this
- → May seem democratic in the way they can be friends with everyone, but the deeper motivation is due to pride and how all of these people will actually make them feel more special and affirmed

**Superpowers**

Twos are super generous caretakers. They make for powerful allies. They make for great friends and leaders and parents. They are deeply relational and seek connection and due their charm and emotional intuition, they are all-stars at making connections that stick. They are friendly, warm, hospitable, and generally fun to be around. As leaders, they can inspire through their passion as well as their work ethic, especially when they believe in what they do. They naturally listen to others and can be incredibly empathic. They are networking all-stars. Of all the types, Twos may make for the most compassionate bosses because they care about burnout and stress in their employees and actively seek to foster humane workplace dynamics.

## Common Stressors for Twos

- → Hard to focus on themselves long enough to feel like it's okay to rest and take care of their own needs.
- → Not getting reciprocation for their generous efforts to serve others.
- → Not getting recognition or affirmation for their generous efforts to serve others.
- → Overextending themselves to the extent that they don't even know who they are unless they are involved in the lives of others.
- → Saying no to requests of any kind, but especially when they begin to recognize they are being used or will receive nothing in return for their effort.
- → When people put themselves above others.
- → When people seem to have no social skills and say things that are rude, offensive, caustic, too direct, or abrupt.
- → Being left out of meetings or communities that they expect or want to be a part of.
- → Getting over a confrontation or argument or criticism quickly without it showing, and then being called "overly sensitive" or emotional.

## Type Two Patterns to Observe to Make More Conscious

- → Develop a sense of self unto your own self. It's not selfish to do self work.
- → Giving to get. Everything does not need to be *Quid Pro Quo*. Can you give with no expectation?
- → Maintaining healthy boundaries. Learn that doing things for others isn't always as helpful as it may seem. Whether a manager or a parent, letting others learn to function on their own develops their own autonomy. Also, there are limitless possibilities for serving the underdog, but what is the price you are paying either individually or for your family when you give compulsively, and what is the mo-

tivation behind your actions?

→ Recognizing and discerning the many layers of pride and self-inflation and deflation.

→ Oversharing. Relational connection is so important to Twos, but clarity may be needed for a team. A Two might want to arrange for a weekly meeting "just to spend time together, to check in with each other and listen to each other's lives." Some Two leaders feel like that is just the natural thing to do. But many types don't prioritize relationships and may resent or be suspicious of the motivation behind such meetings. Discern what is yours to do, and the difference between checking in with a focused meeting as opposed to a vague meeting which may be seen as a time waster.

## Activities To Lower Stress And Practice Self-Development

**Daily meditate with this single question "What is it that I need right now?":** This question involves activating presence on your own behalf (since no one else will do it for you), and places you firmly in your arrow pointing to Four. Fours are like Twos in many ways, but one fundamental difference is that Fours are self-referencing while Twos are other-referencing. When Shelley went through a particularly difficult time and was in extreme burnout, she practiced this for a year and a half without fail and it sprouted huge growth and renewal in her as a result. You can't remove struggle from life, but you can improve your ability to handle challenge.

**Emotional reactivity recognition:** Integrate practices into your life that allow you to slow down and stop trying to prove your worth. Start by hitting the pause button before you react or say anything regardless of the situation. Don't repress your emotions, but learn to process and feel them, name them and move through them. Similar to how people with acute anxiety can't stop anxiety by not acknowledging it, but instead look it straight in the eye and allow anxiety to come at them like a wave but not letting the wave overtake them. Ride the emotion waves as they come, and through deeper self-observation you will learn to separate yourself from them and not become them.

**Tap into the virtue of humility:** If the deepest core need of Twos is for unconditional love, then self-acceptance and affirmation is where you must begin to deflate the tires of pride and bring yourself into the humble moderation of being plainly human, and plainly good enough.

You don't have to be amazing or extraordinary to be good enough. That's a limiting belief and creates a false self. While perfect love probably doesn't exist, it can be ennobled by a commitment to growth, self-understanding and acceptance, and pursuit of a higher plane of existence. You will go through trials. You will go through times when you need to be vulnerable, when you need to ask for help, when you feel powerless. These are humbling experiences, and you should let them be your guides. If you keep your eye out for daily humiliations, the small slights, the daily disappointments, all the things you really have no control over, you can learn the virtuous path of growth and break the neverending cycle of your ego's fear-based passion.

**Get off social media (and maybe take a media hiatus):** Do you find yourself getting triggered by what's going on in your feed (and yet feel helpless to stop the mind-numbing scrolling in search of nothing)? That's a signal. Or when you tune into the latest headlines are you finding yourself a little more anxious, and yet powerless to do anything about what you're learning about? Another sign. Go into yourself. Get away from the noise. The world will spin without you.

HEART

**3** Achiever Performer

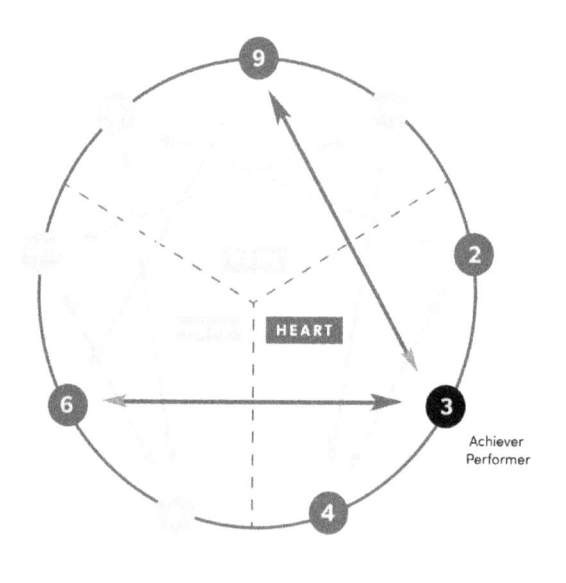

PATH OF ENERGIZING   PATH OF RESOLUTION

# THREES:
# WHO YOU ARE WHEN YOU'RE NOT SUCCEEDING

*"The worst of all deceptions is self-deception."*
—Plato

**In a single syllable:** Do
**Persona:** Ladder Climber
**Mantra:** "See how I succeed?"
**Reactivity defense mechanism:** Identification
**Passion:** Self-deceit

**In a Nutshell**

Ichazo's Ego-Go, often called the Achiever or Performer, is more concerned with image than any other type. All the heart types are image-focused, but the shape-shifting is so intense with Threes that they deceive themselves most of all. The real self is distorted through the patterns of what Threes perceive their culture values as the consummate person. The distortion may be two-fold in that it begins with the Threes' own impressions based upon their personal history, and also from the false qualities of what a collective society values. Generally speaking, this is associated with actions related to building efficacy, capability, and excellence. This constant grind for admiration is a search for the deeper essence they are missing in the authenticity of their True Self. Some may argue that healthy expressions of Threes are supreme examples of "having made it" as a human, and that they serve as role models for the rest of us. While their accomplishments may be truly remarkable, it still does not represent a person who as an individual self has realized their essence. If Threes make the world go round, they make your head spin impressing you with just how high they climb your culture's success ladder.

**Defining Characteristics of the Three Type**

Threes are in the heart of the heart triad center of intelligence, and yet, perhaps even more so than the other two center spots (Six for head types and Nine for body), they tend to not be seen as "heart centered" or leading from an emotional energy. Many are surprised to hear this because they "feel" like they are very emotional. Some may fear their emotions because emotions are messy, and Threes—image-focused as they are—like to be in control of how they are perceived. We have heard Threes say that they contain their emotions until there is an appropriate time to sit with them and let them surface.

They want to portray an image of control by way of seeking the approval of others. But in actual experience, you have probably noticed that Threes are generally impatient with emotions. They will tolerate them to a degree but you can almost sense them tapping their foot and restraining themselves from looking at their watch. For Threes, it's as if emotions are messy and inefficient, and if they are a necessary part of being human for some of those softer types, so be it, but let's get on with it as soon as possible.

Generally speaking, Threes' focus of attention is neither all self or other-referencing. They are more ambivalent than Twos (other-referencing) and Fours (self-referencing). To the extent that they focus on how to present themselves to others they are other-referencing (with differing levels of consciousness attached). But as you can imagine, vanity is at the same time a serious focus on self. Their orientation is a focus on achievement, on success, and how that plays out. They are driven to compete and win. They are not just adept at image management and shape-shifting, they are intuitively inclined to it. Task-oriented as they are, they suppress emotions in order to accomplish their tasks. They have them, and they may be conscious of them, but they really don't like to let them outside the house.

This can be a first obvious way to tell them apart from Eights, with whom they are sometimes mistyped. Eights, however, don't really care what you think. Eights do get a lot done like Threes, and they also find themselves in leadership roles and telling others what they need to do. Also, similarly, they can be demanding and controlling when functioning in personality and especially under stress.

With some experience and discernment, you can begin to tell them apart because of the different expressions and patterns of their passion. The passion of lust communicates much differently than the passion of vanity. Vanity cares about the ultimate focus shining a light on them for their achievements, while lust consumes everything in its path with the underlying motivation focused on being impervious to attack. Also, with understanding of the basic differences between body and heart types you can also see the difference between Threes and Eights. The difficulty here is the way Threes mask their heart-centeredness, as well as the possible (if only occasional) way that Eights may reveal vulnerability.

Longtime Enneagram practitioner and Self-Preservation Three, Jim Gum, describes his identity as this constant cycling between praise and blame. "You unwittingly ride this roller coaster of your emotional life based on praise and blame based on how you're coming across. And if what you do is being well received, I feel happy and joyful and confident. And when I'm not being well received, I am despondent and just want to give up and, at the worst case, you can kind of become despairing."

In this respect, Threes outsource their worth to this feedback machine. And to make matters more complicated, if you are a Three, you really aren't all that aware that you're doing it. But the Three has this energy to keep working for what's going to get that *thing*. Threes present themselves in public as very confident and together. But internally, they are actually quite fragile. It centers on a compulsive (often unconscious) need or desire for approval.

"I did an outstanding job? Well, thank you," Threes feign false humility because they want to be nice, but they also know they did work harder than everyone else they know. Threes live for that pat on the back and the exclamation, "Wow, couldn't have got that done without you." These kinds of affirmations can be intoxicating for the fixated Three.

We want to consider the most fascinating or distinctive aspects of each Type, and without a doubt, for Threes it is their seemingly indefatigable earnest drive to accomplish and be seen for doing well. I once worked under a university president who admonished the faculty: "Don't just do good work, be seen doing it. We want to see you." This is Three language (although they don't need to hear it because they already "get it").

Threes are distinct from other types in this respect too. Threes are the one type that still isn't listed in the DSM. That is, they are so in line with what Western culture deems as healthy and productive and efficacious that their type isn't associated with the kind of dysregulated functioning of aberrant behavior that gets diagnosed in the latest DSM or related literature. After all, what is wrong with getting a lot done? What is wrong with being the pace-setter, the trend-setter?

Naranjo cites Eric Fromm's observations about the this type's "marketing orientation." If we think of "market value" and the idea of value exchanges, the Three in personality is effectively "marketing" their personality. This reminds us of the past decade's emphasis on "branding yourself" in a wide variety of TedTalks and bestselling books. You aren't just a person anymore, the thinking goes, you are a brand and you should think of yourself that way. This is Three thinking—although Threes will adapt to variations on a theme—and we can see the interposition between personality and culture values in play.

The main issues that arise from some interpretations is that Threes lack depth because they are too self-assured. We also take into consideration Karen Horney's diagnosis of reluctant usage of the term "narcissism" here. She doesn't want to use it to mean quite the same thing as the self-inflation and empty arrogance generally associated with the word. Yet at the same time, she observes that there isn't a better single-word description when it comes to associating both the passion of vanity along with the myth of Narcissus. Why? Because in the traditional sense of Freud's interpretation of narcissism we see "indiscriminately every kind of self-inflation, egocentricity, anxious concern with one's welfare, and withdrawal from others (203)." Whereas for Threes, it is more accurate to describe them as in love with their own idealized image.

Also, a common misinterpretation of the Narcissus myth is that the moral is not to fall in love with yourself—or else you will pine away after your own image and possibly fall in and drown as well, depending on which version of the myth you've read. He displeases the god of retribution, Nemesis, by his indifference to the affections of others. Nemesis fools him into seeing his own image in the water, and only then does he "fall in love with himself." The *hamartia*—or tragic downfall—of Narcissus begins with his indifference to others, which is a different emphasis on narcissism than we typically take from this myth. Threes are anything but indifferent to the adulation and admiration of others. You could even say they live for it.

Besides the self-assurance, however, and in spite of the buoyant and outgoing behavior associated with Threes, they also get their energy from proving again and again how successful and impressive they are. This type is the stereotypical example of burning out hard and then Phoenix-like rising again to write a book about how hard they burned out and look at them now. (Not that there's anything wrong with that.)

### The Passion of Three

As Naranjo says, "Nothing could be more appropriately called 'vanity of vanities', of which the preacher in Ecclesiastes speaks, than living for an ephemeral and insubstantial image (rather than out of oneself) (199)." Ichazo first spoke of "deceit" as the passion of Threes, placing vanity in the fixations. Deceit became associated with dishonesty, however, and has been improved upon in our current understanding to self-deceit.

Self-deceit is an improvement on deceit because it's really not the "other" that the Three lies to, it is fundamentally to the Threes' self that they lie. The false front that Threes project is unconscious (unless they've done the work to bring it more into consciousness). They effectively "market" themselves to others, presenting themselves often in an upbeat and put together way. Also, there's nothing deceptive about how they get things done.

The problem is, in the end, they are perhaps the most lost of any type when it comes to knowing who they really are. They have deceived themselves at the expense of pleasing and impressing others. In a sense, too, they are impressed within themselves because of the mirror they put up to others. Others are impressed with me, I am impressed with myself.

The antidote for the passion of vanity is a move to the virtue of veracity. Veracity reveals a closer and more substantive understanding of the Three's True Self rather than approximating a mirror of approval from others based upon impression management. We will examine areas for concerted focus and growth through the work with wing stretches and arrow movements.

**Functional Versus Authentic Personality**

There are plenty of reasons why functioning in your lower-level, unconscious personality works for you. But if that could be said from all that we have learned, is it any empirically less true for any type more so than for Threes?

Only Sevens can be said to make such a strong case for remaining perfectly fine through the rose-colored glasses of their persistent optimism. Indeed, Threes "get her done" as they sometimes say in the American South.

Threes mirror the paragon of virtues we see on the silver screen. While normal men and women can't hope to actually be the amazing characters the leading actors play, or in most cases to be the actors themselves, they can emulate them in real life. They can mirror strength, vitality, empathy and lovingkindness, you name it. The problem is in personality it can be the ultimate deception because of the lack of veracity. You can play a role with verisimilitude, but you are still playing.

And that is why for those who are ready to do the difficult inner work, the antidote to vanity positions itself wisely through the virtue of hope. Depending on the subtype, different strategies for the relaxation of the image grip will come into play.

Recognize you were not put on this planet to be a projection of what you think others will admire. You have a real self in there. You have your own needs and desires. You are not so independent, you really do need others. You do have feelings—strong, intense feelings—that can also be a path toward aspiring to the virtue of veracity.

### Psychological Roots and Key Patterns that Create Stress for Threes

Similar to all heart types is a deficit related to not feeling fully seen or affirmed or connected to the primary caretaker at a critical moment in early development. Threes adapted by completing tasks as a way of being seen, as well as avoiding the emotions they felt, especially of sadness, the core emotion of all heart types.

Naranjo observed that this type is characteristically an ESTP on the Meyers-Briggs scale due to their typically extraverted sensing and their tendency to think over feel, but also interestingly their disposition of perception over judgment. While there are interesting correlations between types and Myers-Briggs profiles, they don't always line up so neatly. We find it interesting, however, that for Threes this profile does in fact seem frequent, but it is only a hypothesis. We need more information.

What we do see is that the psychological adaptation of being able to perform and/or achieve often does parallel with athletic types, as well as those endowed with high intelligence or physical beauty. The vanity has to come from somewhere, right? Their desire to attract attention in these effective ways was almost surely from feeling the deficit in early childhood of not being recognized enough for their capabilities and their response is to show others that they will not be ignored.

For all the above discussion of image management and self-deception, we would be remiss not to mention another common factor of early childhood experiences from reports by Threes. They often adapt their style due to high variations of expectations in combination with stern discipline.

Threes are among the most likely of all types to push on through stress. They are the least likely to show up for therapy or coaching until something outside of themselves and out of their control has stopped the show. They will feel stress when others on their team aren't working as hard as they are, which is almost inevitable and a very common pattern for Threes in the workplace. They feel stress when *anything* interferes with their tasks. They feel stress so long as a task is unfinished. At some levels, you could say they like to be involved in constant busyness.

Threes feel anxiety whenever they stop working. When they do hit a wall, they need their coach to be gentle, but in order for them to truly receive the message of slowing down they may need assertive truth-telling. Telling a Three to slow down almost never works. Show them the way through stress by following the clarion call of their emotions, and guide them through a deeper recognition.

### Self-Preservation Three: (countertype) Security

Self-Preservation Threes are so determined to be good and follow the perfect model that, on the surface, they run counter to the passion of vanity. This may make them hard to identify at first. They want "to be good," which on the one hand you could say everyone wants, or is perhaps most similar to the Sexual/One-to-One One, but this is different. They don't just want to be efficient and effective, they want to be *seen* for these things as well.

This counter-type has trouble with self-promotion. Their strategy to get attention is by doing, not telling people what they've done as much, and knowing (believing) that the hard work pays off. Their driven and competitive behavior generally works well in the workplace for the very reason of their productivity. They're also practical and all about efficiency. If a goal doesn't have to be perfect, they accept good enough in order to move forward. This can be a differentiating factor between the One type, which they are sometimes mistyped as.

They struggle with being good team players only because they rarely feel that others share the same work ethic. Their competition is actually inwardly-focused in terms of reaching a certain level of sales, or an amount of money, or a certain certification level of competency or excellence in order to keep the goals and tasks in perpetual motion. While this subtype still wants to look good for what they accomplish, they are more focused on the tasks at hand, and less flashy than the others. This more buttoned-up appearance can also be why they look like Ones.

Of all the subtypes this is the one most prone to burnout. The burnout comes not only from merely over-working, but also from a lack of personal alignment with what they are actually working on. In some cases, you might see a Self-Preservation Three earlier in life nail their profession. Whether through good fortune, earnest seeking, or alignment with family and cultural values, they effectively execute on their "mirrored" vision of what it means to succeed at their given vocation. Usually, early success indicates a connection to natural gifts or strengths. Much like kids labeled as "talented and gifted" at an early age who develop a fixed mindset and a fear of failure, the same can be true to this subtype of Three. Later in life, when they recognize a need for a shift in direction (for any wide variety of reasons), they may find it hard to change because they aren't able to see (or be willing to risk) how they could be good at other things.

When anxiety and stress run high enough that they cannot be bulldozed through work and outward success, this subtype is also prone to their own kind of inertia. "You have fight and flight," says Jim Gum. "And you also have freeze. And I was a freezer, I would just kind of like, 'Oh, I don't know how to handle this.' And typically, the effect would be I'd be quiet, wouldn't be very verbal about it. I would feel inadequate, young and incapable of handling emotional situations…And as part of my Self Preservation instinct dominance…so I have to get to a point where I have to unfreeze. And I've been able to do that, in tense situations where I show up now, and I say what I need to say, and I'm not just kind of collapsing."

This subtype is focused on doing what it takes to be a good person. Often they work on being the model parent, the model worker, or the model spouse. While the virtue of quality and doing good runs against the passion of vanity, they also want to be seen as doing the right thing, and that is where the vanity appears. Overall, they focus on goodness, ethics, and personal autonomy, which does contribute to their mistyping as a One. They can also look Six-ish at times when they aren't able to hide their anxiety in stress.

### Social Three: Prestige

For all the defining characteristics of Threes, we find in this subtype, the most Three-ishness. The passion of vanity stands out most clearly, as well as the shapeshifting. This subtype needs the admiration and adulation of the crowds, they need fans more than they need friends. While we aren't saying we know Gary Vaynerchuck's type, a Social Three would be our best guest. This subtype can be brilliant at marketing and promoting themselves. Their message can also adjust to the messaging of the broader cultural commentary of the moment. They are so good at the messaging, and coupled with the competitiveness and intensity, it may be hard to see any flaws.

We may often see this type in highly accomplished roles. They are talented and driven and can be sources of continual inspiration for others. Their charisma and enthusiasm also make them excellent at presenting themselves with personal warmth and connecting with people to amplify their own sense of self and possibility. As these Threes climb the corporate or social ladder, they may find their motives being questioned. Their agenda may appear self-serving. Their shapeshifting may come across as inauthentic. "You can't listen to the haters," is one Social Threes' personal motto. Social Threes tend to have an eye for trends and social movements. They can often become trendsetters for this very reason. Another motto for Social Threes could be: "I am seen, therefore I am."

The truth of the matter, however, is that Threes often aren't as political as they may appear to others, and aren't any more self-interested than any other given subtype per se. Messages may shift, for one thing, but it doesn't mean the first messaging was "not true" just because the market or tastes have shifted. For another, people grow and change all the time. Besides, company's (as well as people) shift their emphasis or strategy all the time. The Social Three should realize, however, that they are "putting themselves out there" as we say. They seek an audience and they want to "win friends and influence people" just as Dale Carnegie did. In other words, they should expect there are going to be "haters." Or, as Abraham Lincoln once wrote,

"You can please some of the people all of the time, you can please all of the people some of the time, but you can't please all of the people all of the time."

As leaders they can be remarkable. Their interpersonal skills in combination with their ambition is an area of great strength. They also possess the networking and marketing savvy to flourish in virtually any sector of the working world. They intuitively know what to say and when to say it, and also what not to say. Their interpersonal skills might be one of the more overlooked aspects of their strengths because they aren't generally seen as being a heart type. But make no mistake, they can read a room as well as any empath.

Panelist and Social Three, Steph Barron Hall, says, "I think I experienced myself as very emotional, you know, I just don't always show it on the outside. And I'm getting better at that, but the real hardest thing about emotions for me is that they're so messy... And so part of the growth path is showing up in authenticity, and in messiness, and all that kind of stuff. And that is incredibly difficult, you know, to not be polished, right?"

When these Threes are doing the work, recognizing they don't have to be among the elite or the rich, beautiful, and/or famous to be loved and valued (to be who they essentially are), they can break from the persona. Through the virtue of veracity they can come to a deeper understanding of who they are beyond their concept of what others value. They may even learn that there are reasons for them to be loved and admired that they hadn't even considered through the narrow filters of performance and production. They can open themselves up to what failure, burnout, stress, and other personal or professional setbacks might have to teach them (without having to rise up from the ashes and immediately teach everyone what they've learned).

## Sexual/One-to-One Three: Masculinity/Femininity

While this type is the most emotional of the Three subtypes, they are still likely to contain their emotions with a degree of vigilance. Another interesting point of comparison is that this subtype has the most ambivalence in relationship to their passion of vanity. While the Self-Preservation runs against (or counter) to the passion, and the Social runs with (or doubles down on), the Sexual/One-to-One is more in conflict. The way their vanity tends to show up is in their personal appeal. They want to be attractive to a significant other or others. They want to be seen as important and attractive or even charismatic to a special someone, and they can pull out all the stops to make this happen.

Narajano observes that in women it might mean being a pleaser with a passion for her family, that is, in this respect, more mental that sexual. The displays of attraction might be in knowing how to take care of yourself and extending that to others. For men, it might be his personal autonomy or being an excellent provider or how he will show his family the very best time, better than anyone else. So, we can see that rather than the appeal being as outwardly based on culture's standards, the projection is more on being the "fantasy" partner. The appeal, therefore, manifests itself as an "ideal" masculine or feminine archetype.

A way in which this subtype runs against the grain of vanity is the way in which they will support others. This is also an important distinguishing characteristic between the Social and Sexual/One-to-One Three. This subtype doesn't have to have the spotlight on them the way Social Threes do. You might see them smiling brightly on their Facebook feeds in what appears on the surface to be self-promotion. They may be on stage as a leader of their company, looking vibrant and polished and confident, but an immediate distinguishing characteristic is the spotlight of their attention. It will be clearly more self-referential with the Social, and far more other-referential with this subtype. Again, the vanity is how the spotlight on others is a reflection on them and what they have done for others. They are happy with an attractive image and in the promotion of others. Sometimes these are strategically or politically important others, and sometimes they are simply important members of their family, team, club, affiliation, or organization. This act of pleasing is all the approval they need, and so may not appear to be successful in the conventional sense.

Just as this subtype may show ambivalence toward their passion of vanity, so they are in their referencing behavior. They certainly do like to work on behalf of others, but like all Threes, they can fall into periods of strong self-referential behavior. This can occur when they are striking out in a new direction, determined to show significant others in their life how effective, valuable and inherently brilliant they can be. During these periods, they will become intensely competitive (even if it is mostly internally focused), and also impatient with the slow pace of others, all of which leads to varying degrees of self-focus and absorption. This can be a blindspot.

This subtype is seen as the most in touch with their feelings of the Threes, and this may be a powerful direction for inner work and growth. If they can access their emotions, recognize the emptiness or disconnection from themselves as well as from others, they can accept their inner sadness. They can then recognize the false self they put on when they are perpetually bubbly and optimistic (which can sometimes make them seem like a Seven). Focusing on their virtue of veracity can lead them to a deeper and more authentic place where they can develop a clearer sense of who they are, and not who they are because of what they do for others.

### Working with Arrows in Growth and Stress

Threes tend to have a stance of *moving against*. Threes are competitive, self-motivated, and live to check things off their To Do lists. They work towards their goals and thus often against others. They tackle problems and overcome obstacles with enthusiasm. Threes can get caught up in Type-A behavior where they overwork themselves and their team.

We can observe differing levels of nuance in these behavior patterns, however, depending on the subtype. For instance, with Self-Preservation Threes, it is most evident. They put their heads down and grind and don't necessarily come up for air unless it's thrust upon them for one reason or another. For Social and One-to-One/Sexual Threes, however, the movement against might not be as easy to identify mostly due to the "marketing style," impression management, and/or shapeshifting. Social Threes throw grass in the air to see which direction the wind is blowing and move with current, really in an effort to be ahead of the pack. In this way, they won't seem to be moving against at all, but in fact leading the way. Similarly, One-to-One/Sexual Threes are "other focused" inasmuch as they need to be to make sure they are remaining amazing and relevant to the important others in their lives. This may often create an ambivalence of moving toward or against others as the case may be.

When it comes to working with the small growth movements involving wings, we see that Threes are firmly ensconced on either side by their other heart-type neighbors. The first move would be toward their Two wing. This move can soften their edges, so to speak. They can connect more deeply with their feelings and not always set them aside. They can think more of how others relate to them, as well as what others are thinking and feeling themselves. On the other side, when getting in touch with their Four wing, they also will connect with their unobserved feelings and empathy, and they will care less about what others think, and more about how they process and handle their own thoughts and feelings within the privacy of their innermost soul. They may also connect with a little more of their own unique individuality, rather than always thinking of how others will respond to their need for presenting a successful image. When they do connect with others, they do so in more authentic ways.

When Threes are ready to do the bigger work of focusing on their arrows, the first move is to the Six. This move against their first arrow is a *move towards* others. It takes them out of their emotional purview and right in the middle of the head center. On the high side of Six, they grow into loyal and committed people. They commit to others as well as their own projects. They move past shapeshifting and recognize more clearly how their passion of self-deceit operates to keep them boxed in. They think through scenarios before jumping compulsively into behavior they believe they will be rewarded for. When they move less consciously to the Six arrow, whether in stress or anxiety, they lose their identity in their work. At home, this could mean having no identity other than doing things for everyone else, and at work they may "become" the organization they work for. Threes have the most likely tendency of all types to move from an organized person to becoming the organizational person. They can also find themselves spending far too much time in analysis paralysis, which feeds their doubts and insecurities, and compounds the fear they feel.

When Threes move consciously with their second arrow to the high side of the Nine, they *move away from* stress.

Interestingly, arrow work for Threes takes them decisively out of their feeling center and first into the head (Six) and then firmly into the body (Nine). By slowing down and stepping back, they create room for their feelings, something they rarely have time for in themselves or in others. When they make this move, they find themselves more at peace and less compulsively driven. They let themselves *be* and not just *do.* Threes moving in stress to the low side of Nine can make them prime candidates for hard burnout. They fall asleep to themselves and either become nothing but their To Do lists, or they procrastinate what needs to be done, which leads to even more acute anxiety and stress. Interestingly for Threes, just like for Sixes and Nines, they find themselves remaining in their primary center of intelligence while they work only on their wings. The arrow work takes them completely out of their primary centers and enters them into each of the other intelligences.

**Reactive Impulse Under Stress**

When it comes to the stress and our reactivity it is good to remember and recognize that this is especially the times when we are most likely to respond from what Gurdjieff called our mechanical behavior. Our automatic responses click into place and react and respond from what we broadly call our unconscious. As you can probably imagine, then, when Threes are under stress, especially chronic, they tend to double down on the things that drive from the ego. This includes first and foremost, an intensity in their already hard working style. They will become irritable and impatient with others who can't or won't keep up—whether or not they're in leadership positions. They delegate and collaborate less because they believe (whether true or not) that they will get the job done the best and most efficiently.

They are likely to do all this at the expense of their personal or professional relationships, and also importantly at the expense of their relationship with themselves. In other words, they cut themselves off from their emotions as well as any inter or intrapersonal dynamics, which would only be messy and inefficient anyway. So long as they experience the outer rewards for their accomplishments and maintain the capacity for enduring, they will continue in this behavior perpetually.

In some instances, their drive and ability to check off their To Do lists can decrease their stress and the intensity of their drive relaxes. In most cases, however, their defense mechanism of working harder creates more stress. This can be explained on both the level of interpersonal dynamics and ignoring the needs of important others in their life, or in the work setting where they don't always "play well" with others. Also, their interior life suffers, which, as illustrated by Gabor Mate's research in our early introduction on stress and stressors causes issues internally which may or may show up symptomatically in the nervous system for months, years, or even decades. Almost inevitably, however, the breakdowns occur, and opportunities for self-evaluation emerge.

### Defining Characteristics in Personality

→ Impatience in almost any form: they want the "executive summary" rather than having to attend the meeting; they don't have time for water-cooler talk and are never seen hanging out on Beer Friday; they are the first to push back when anything like a "process" is introduced; they complain to the principal that the car rider line wastes everyone's time and has a proposal for how to make it run better.

→ Impression management: you will see them in your

feeds on social media almost every day with an innovative or optimistic idea which either promotes themselves or others.

→ May seem manic or impulsive because they are always running around and checking their phones and watches, but lack spontaneity because anything they do they need to do well (and being seen doing it is icing on the cake).

→ Angry when people don't deliver on their commitments or do what they say they will do, especially when it reflects poorly on them.

→ Lose their identity in their job or "become" their job and become the ultimate organizational person.

→ Will attend social events because it reflects well on their image and they expect everyone to then attend their events because they want "fans" over "friends".

**Superpowers**

They make for great leaders. They have a high work ethic, and unlike other types, they sincerely love work. As a result, they stay engaged, are likely to be available to others night and day, and ready to step up and step in for whatever may be asked. They won't waste their time, much less yours. Their communication style is refreshingly clear and concise. They will not be the ones to slow you down, and in most cases they will be the ones to pick you up and do more than their share of the work to get things done. They possess an infectious energy and have a natural propensity to motivate others. They look good. They are optimistic and nice, and keep things on a surface level so nothing gets in the way of the work that needs to be done. They understand promotion like no other, they are the ultimate marketing superstars of self or others. They can read a room as swiftly and intuitively as any heart type. They often are actually beautiful, highly intelligent, physically gifted, or possessing qualities that set them apart from others.

### Common Stressors for Threes

- → People who do poor work or don't really care how well they do (or if a project fails).
- → People who get in the way of their goals.
- → People who consistently don't pull their own weight.
- → When emotional chaos at home interrupts their schedules or commitments, especially when the issues don't involve practical, tangible outcomes.
- → Distractions.
- → When others don't recognize them for their hard work or brilliance.

### Type Three Patterns to Observe to Make More Conscious

- → Threes need to learn to be comfortable in their own skin. They don't have to "be" anything else to anyone. They need to be themselves. But how? For a lot of Threes, their fear is a ruling denominator. It keeps them running on all cylinders to prove that they are the amazing person they want others to think they are. When Threes can work on recognizing and sitting with their emotions, they will find real growth, and a path through the debilitating realities of stress.
- → It can be a heavy burden to feel like you're working so hard just to be appreciated. Put that weight down. Recognize the power and authenticity of your own emotions. You don't have to constantly prove to yourself and others that you are enough.
- → Why is it so important for others to see you as something that you really aren't? What is behind that compulsive desire to make others perceive you as something you believe they want? Who are you really doing this for?
- → Why do emotions scare you so much? Why do you believe they are a waste of time? What could they possibly have to teach you about yourself? You don't have to fear your feelings. They aren't threatening. They don't get

in the way. Remember you're a heart type. Feelings are your path ahead. Threes are usually impatient, and usually with others. Take that impatience home. Listen to it. Talking about feelings helps you find the real wisdom in yourself that you need something.

## Activities To Lower Stress And Practice Self-Development

**Tap into the virtue of veracity:** Threes' defense mechanism of identification is key to understanding the virtue of veracity. Their identity merges into the successful role or image they play or portray. They shape-shift into any given identity that works. They have lost themselves in their false self, the ego with its defensive, survival-and-fear-based schemes. Only through pursuit of this higher level emotional self-understanding will they begin to recognize the features of what is true in them. Working with a good coach even if you think you've "got it all pretty well handled" can be an excellent step. If you've experienced trauma, you may want to consider enlisting the help of a licensed therapist.

**Make a job out of taking care of yourself:** Not everyone may agree with this, and of course it would be ideal to loosen up the grip that your personality has on you, but that may take a lot of time (that you don't have). Threes sometimes simply don't know how to stop. Because self-deceit is the passion of the Three, they can easily fool themselves that they're relaxing when they're not. They can even "make a job out" of relaxing. Sometimes the only thing that stops a Three is an accident, a collapse, situations in which they are literally incapcitated by life. And we are stating that you consider doing just that. Be as effective at giving yourself the self-care and gentleness it needs as you are at giving to the needs and impression management of everyone else. Mechanisms that you build into your life can be tremendously helpful. And then you will take ownership of them. Once they're established as habits or rituals in your life, you may find they're hard to stop.

**Learn the blunt truth from others who have come before you:** As we've covered, most Threes will not even sniff at coaching or self-development work until or unless they've become "burned out from exhaustion and buried in the hail" (as the lyrics from Bob Dylan's "Shelter from the Storm" goes). But just maybe with a little curiosity and just some small indicators, and good information and research like this book, they may bring themselves some preventive measures and medicine. But just reading some lines in a book, or even having a coach tell you "slow down" will not get it done. Sometimes these practical and effective doers want something a little more persuasive, a bit more substantive. We've already recommended a deeper dive into the insidious effects of stressors through the research and writing of Gabor Mate. Consider this longitudinal study called The Harvard Study of Longitudinal Development, conducted by Harvard Researchers that began in the 1930s with some 268 participants. The bottom line is that those who chose personal satisfaction over success lived longer.

> "When we gathered together everything we knew about them about at age 50, it wasn't their middle-age cholesterol levels that predicted how they were going to grow old," said Robert Waldinger in a popular TED Talk. "It was how satisfied they were in their relationships. The people who were the most satisfied in their relationships at age 50 were the healthiest at age 80."

Since that first generation, they're also deep into the research of a whole new generation. It's easy to find the study and they have reams and reams of data points on both sets of participants. Ask yourself from a values perspective, what really makes you happy? What really tends to grind you down? What is the biggest critique those closest to you would probably (or do) say?

**4**
Romantic
Artist

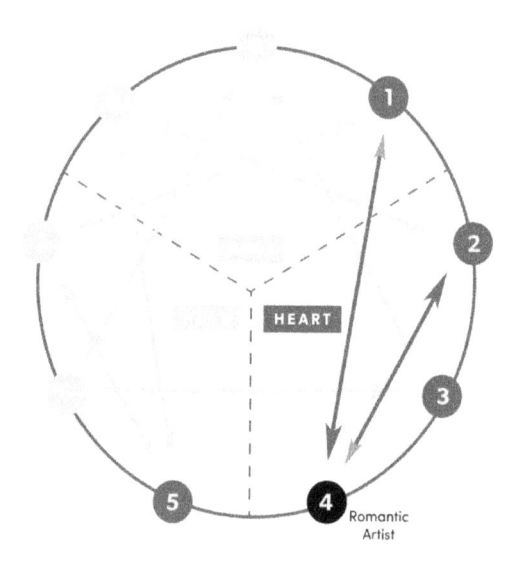

**HEART**

PATH OF ENERGIZING    PATH OF RESOLUTION

# FOURS: ENDLESS COMPARING AND INTROJECTING

*"But in the mud and scum of things, / There alway, alway something sings."*
—Ralph Waldo Emerson

**In a single syllable:** Match
**Persona:** Thalia and Melpomene
**Mantra:** "I am uncommon and so misunderstood."
**Reactivity defense mechanism:** Introjection
**Passion:** Envy

**In a Nutshell**

Ichazo's Ego-Melan, Fours are broadly known as the type most comfortable with the deep or difficult emotions that most types would soon avoid. Most Fours will tell you they not only don't mind sadness, they find something bittersweet in being able to hold the sadness or melancholy (think Shakespeare's "parting is such sweet sadness"). The Four is often labeled the Individualist, the Romantic, or the Creative, though none of these descriptions is quite adequate (but this could just be the Four in myself coming out here). For one, they are not necessarily any more or less creative than any other type. For another, there are loaded associations with the terms "romantic" and "individualist." C.S. Lewis, for instance, documented in his first book (*The Pilgrim's Regress*) twelve different meanings of the word "romantic." And "individualist" implies they may not be good team players, which is no more or less true for many other types and subtypes. Their passion of envy is key to understanding their attraction to the arts and artful expression. It is also why you can often tell them apart from all other types because they really want to be understood so they often express themselves in highly verbal, open-ended, sincere ways. If Fours are anything, they are sincere (the term "authentic" implies a truer form of realness, which not all Fours have conscious access to).

### Defining Characteristics of the Four Type

You could say the Fours' passion puts them naturally at odds with others in the form of whether they have more or less than what others possess. Other than Twos, they are the most directly connected to their emotions. The gigantic difference between these two heart types, however, is that Twos will think about others first (as a way of getting their needs met), and Fours will think about themselves first (also as a way of getting their needs met).

With that said, Fours are incredibly relational. This is why it seems important to discern the typical labels associated with Fours. You will find them in all walks of life. They may not tend toward accounting, finance, or computer science, but you will find Fours who are coaches, counselors, teachers, ministers, outdoor enthusiasts, human resource personnel, or even doctors and lawyers, to name a few. To some extent, you could say these jobs or vocations could fit any type, and you would be right. But let's be clear that the "aesthetic sensitivity" and "inclination to the arts" is overdone and inadequate when it comes to defining and describing Fours.

Let's focus on an aspect that seems underdone in the literature: their relational skills. Fours are highly empathic and attuned to the emotional space between themselves and others. In fact, Fours also have an innate ability to pick up on the feelings of others, very often without even knowing it. Many Fours report shifts in their own moods based on the emotions of others they pick up on, a concept known as introjection. A Four wants to "connect" with you. They are automatically considering whether they are experiencing connection with you and you with them.

Podcast panelist, and Self-Preservation Four, Shay Bocks says this about introjection and its connection to envy and longing:

> "We're all pretty familiar with the idea of projection where we take our internal experience and project that out on others and assume others are having that same experience. But what Fours do is we actually pick up and sense emotions, thoughts, feelings, outside of ourselves, and bring them in as if they are ours, or that they mean something about us. And so when people talk about Fours being self-referencing, and some people think of Fours as being very self involved, that's not my experience of Fours, really. I think what they're really describing is this sense that Fours pick up stuff, especially emotional content, and kind of swallow it as our own. And so not only are we being down on ourselves, because maybe you're having a bad day, and I just took that as like, I'm unworthy of being in your presence, but also, this is where envy comes in. We envy so much that we actually take on other people's negative emotions, and pretend like they're our own. And, so that's how we end up being so melancholic and seeing what's missing, seeing the negative, because this is the information we're picking up from the world around us."

When Fours aren't as conscious of their inherent relational abilities they may very well expend unnecessary energy seeking to connect with virtually everyone they come into contact with, from the receptionist at the doctor's office to the doctor herself to the UPS delivery driver to the online support representative. Why do they do this? Because, in effect, they want to be that one special person that has something different to say than the usual mundane exchanges that must take place in another's life. They will be the person to be "real" where no one else is. And while the inclination may be admirable, it is not necessary or called for in many situations. Also, it tends to leave a less conscious Four with the restless feeling that nothing was really accomplished and that they are still in "lack" of the connection they were seeking or expressing—and is therefore a waste of energy. Our energy is limited, and as a part of our conscious work, we do well to galvanize our resources and direct them in more powerful and productive ways.

What is not a waste of energy is to recognize the power of their relational intuition and to do something with it that brings them into the world and in contact with others. Because of their focus on "being real," Fours focus on their personal identity much more than most types. They love talking about their "passions" and "callings" and how they personally interpret their life in meaning-filled ways. Naturally, at less conscious levels, this self-referencing behavior can disintegrate into self-absorption. But when consolidated in healthy, mature, and more conscious directions, and they are able to turn the reference toward others, they can find themselves equipped for all manner of vocations that have to do with helping others discern what to do with their lives.

What is more commonly known about Fours, and which should not be overlooked, is their value on originality, often in the form of aesthetic and creative sensibilities. The depth of their feelings in combination with their value to be real or "truth-tell" translates into simple expressions not being enough to adequately express the insight or revelation.

Fours are also commonly associated with "longing," sometimes getting lost in themselves in nostalgia and confabulation. Also, perhaps because of the intensity and sensitivity to their emotions, they are prone to "making a big deal" out of something ordinary to everyone else. That is, they may get lost in the transcendence of a sunset, or take on the feeling of a windy autumn day with the leaves scattering along the empty road, or rain dripping from the gutters on a rainy spring day. You could almost say their natural predisposition to feeling tunes them into their surroundings, whether in nature in general or between other people, and they internalize them and "become" them. Thus, their inherent "specialness" is that they pick up on what others miss.

They want to interpret their finely-tuned sensibilities and communicate their profundity in ways that cannot always be expressed in words or other mundane or ordinary ways. So, they are either themselves often artists, poets, dancers, actors, musicians, novelists, memoirists, and other related artistic forms, or deeply appreciative of these human expressions which seek to communicate the extraordinary or layered nature of reality. Across the board of the three distinct subtypes, you can also identify Fours by their passion of envy (feeling deficiency or lack).

For all of that, there is another common perception of Fours that needs elucidation. Many Fours aren't necessarily "melancholic" either in their interior life or the outer expression of it. What they often are is emotional in general. That is, of the four basic emotions Glad, Mad, Sad, and Fear, they may experience any and all of these with intensity, or if not intensity, at least with ready access. Don't mistype a Four as a Seven just because she shows up to work in an upbeat or positive mood most of the time, or for an Eight just because he is often seen as irritable, intense, outspoken, or angry. These ranges of emotions are completely possible and common for Fours. A discerning evaluation of their overall behavior, however, might reveal some inconsistencies. For instance, Sexual/One-to-One and Self-Preservation Sevens are almost compulsively positive. Fours will reflect a wider range of emotions, and if they are not in a great mood one day, they rarely disguise it. And they are far more sensitive than Eights.

Furthermore, Fours can look like Twos when they "become" their emotions, which effectively means they are so connected with their feelings that they aren't even aware that there is consciousness separate from them. Unlike Twos, however, Fours are more known for getting into their heads, often in the form of analyzing their behavior and the behavior of others. Many Fours are actually highly analytical and intellectually curious, which seems a far cry from the stereotypes commonly portrayed and discussed.

Other than arguably Sixes, however, the difference between the Fours with their subtypes is the most distinctive. This underlies one of the principles we emphasize in the importance of discerning subtypes beyond mere general types. Some have theorized that the strong "variations on a theme" between the Fours is due to the intensity of their emotions.

### The Passion of Four

Fours manifest a painful sense of lack, and a craving for what is felt as lacking in their (often unconscious) envy. There's a perception that something good is outside the Four's experience, and somehow this indicates a deficiency on their part. It's the habit of comparing themselves to others and the feeling that derives from an ongoing comparison that puts them below or above another person. The inferiority/superiority complex is keen in other types as well (like Threes and Sixes) for different underlying reasons.

The passion of envy isn't as obvious or perhaps as well known as others which we hear about in literature and religion like vanity, gluttony, pride and so forth. Importantly, envy is not jealousy. Jealousy is of an insidious nature, meaning not only do you see something someone else possesses but importantly, you believe you deserve it too and if at all possible you will take it. It is a more overt form of competition still related to scarcity. It is almost as if to say, "You have something that I don't have, but I am equal to you in deserving it and it is inherently unfair that I don't (and something should be done)." By contrast, envy is *invidious* in nature, meaning you see something someone else possesses and feel that you are lacking because you don't also possess it. It may end up transforming into something that a Four may feel he or she deserves, and thus creating a form of competition to get it too, but this is not typically the case.

In general, Fours believe (internalize) they are inadequate. Deep down they believe they are amazing and talented, but that they have been overlooked for some reason. Some compare it to a "thwarted vanity." Naranjo says as much when he writes, "While an ennea-type Three person identifies with that part of the self that coincides with the idealized image, the ennea-type Four individual identifies with that part of the psyche that fails to fit the idealized image, and is always striving to achieve the unattainable (97)."

There are many ways envy manifests itself. We have noted envy within as an essential feeling of self-disregard or minimization. Interpersonal envy is another: someone who possesses gifts or abilities that the Four internalizes as meaning he or she lacks something. It shows up in craving and depending on love. Interestingly, it emerges from an idealization of self, or love, or other, of this grand possibility of what could be "if only." And it comes also in the form of social striving. The early 20th century French novelist Marcel Proust portrayed this very idealization of upper classes in the first several volumes of *Remembrance of Things Past*. Also, envy gets Fours stuck in an ever-perpetuating cycle of seeking the extraordinary and intense, along with feeling disappointment and disillusionment with the mundane.

It is important to remember that as heart types Fours' essential core emotion is sadness, which seems emphasized in this personality structure, and that they too are image focused. Thus, while there are many ways in which Fours may feel inadequate, the focus is on how they are perceived or recognized or understood for who and what they are.

For Fours, the path forward is through the virtue of equanimity. Finding balance and wholeness within themselves and outside themselves in how they perceive others. It's a new way to feel like "who I am is equal to who you are." Equanimity also emphasizes simplicity (as in humility and plainness in style) and emotional neutrality. We will examine areas for concerted focus and growth through the work with wing stretches and arrow movements.

**Functional Versus Authentic Personality**

What, you may ask, is "authentic" personality to the personality that values authenticity? In part, that's why in the opening introduction we didn't necessarily subscribe to the idea that Fours are "authentic" per se. They may be earnest at times, or sincere, as well as blunt or even caustic to others in their form of "telling it like it is." Authenticity contains the seeds of a little more self-awareness, as well as discernment for what is theirs to share, and some diplomacy in how to deliver their evaluation. Further, Fours have a tendency to overshare or hold someone hostage with having to track paragraphs worth of words with something that could be said much more precisely, directly, and clearly. Is all of that "authentic"?

Overall, we can see the functional aspect of Fours working well in their drive for originality and thinking outside the box. When the work they do aligns with their identity, all three subtypes can be highly effective and driven. Their moods tend to fluctuate, however, and they can turn from outgoing and vivacious to quiet, reflective, and withdrawn. Whether they know it or not, they are empaths. They have an intuitive ability to listen and absorb what others have to say and reflect back to them what they feel.

At the same time, their natural inclination is to consider what these feelings and feedback mean to them. Because of their tendency to go inward they may lose connections with friends or even loved ones without even meaning to. Often they won't know what they've done when they do reach out or try to reconnect. This is a pattern reflected in all the varied differences between the subtypes.

In essence, freed from many of the unconscious strictures and distortions of unconscious personality patterns, Fours can do two important things. Through the virtue of equanimity, they can find more interior calm and emotional balance. They don't ride the wave of the highs and lows that their intense emotions issue forth. Also, they can become more aware of when through their defense mechanism of introjection they are absorbing the emotional atmosphere outside of themselves. Through this awareness they can build clearer boundaries with others' emotions, which also will help them remain more balanced.

Second, they can grow in greater awareness of how they tend to think of themselves first before considering the impact on others. Whereas Twos need to work on putting themselves before others, the reverse is true for Fours. This level of awareness can aid in their social lives, and also make them more effective leaders and employees in the workplace.

**Psychological Roots and Key Patterns that Create Stress for Fours**

Like all heart types, Fours have a primary need for mirroring. When the need is not met adequately for one of a variety of reasons, the adaptive strategy to be seen and understood, and to maintain connection manifests in the form of introjection. Commonly this type has a predisposition to both idealize the love of the parents, as well as to fundamentally reject them for their inadequacies and failings.

For much of the 20th century, psychiatrists and psychologists have written a great deal on the ideas behind projection, introjection, and transference. The basic theory here is that you could say Fours have internalized aspects of the unloving parent, or put another way, of parental rejection. This is where the constellation of traits emerges of poor self-image and basic negative self-concept. It also explains the pursuit of distinction and proving of self-worth especially through means which they (as feelers) process their suffering through aesthetic expression.

They can be stressed by anything that relates to their passion of envy and of lack, or lack of their ideals. In the workplace they will let you know if you aren't working up to expectations. They will get upset if they don't feel supported or understood, and it may not always be clear how they need support or understanding. They will typically have a hard time genuinely being happy for another's success that they themselves haven't also had. And they may reject people they don't deem as possessing something that they value. This may mean people who aren't refined, or seem shallow, or who they generally regard as inferior to them. By contrast, they will overdo their suffering and victimization if they are rejected by someone who they admire or want to be in good graces with.

### Self-Preservation Four: (countertype) Tenacity

The Self-Preservation Four can look like a One in their strong need for self-determination and self-discipline. They have a high pain tolerance, and in this way they may be the hardest to identify without a lot of experience or information. Part of that is simply due to their countertype qualities. They express envy less than the other two subtypes. They tend to internalize their emotions rather than express them as the other two do. They are "tenacious" (some call them "dauntless") in that they will suffer their own pain without bothering others with what they may be feeling or going through. Sometimes they compare the experience to a person bearing a gigantic pack. They feel burdened by the weight of their feelings, but don't know what to do with them. In early characterizations of the three subtypes of Fours, Naranjo termed them "the angry hateful, the shameful guilty, and the depressed." The first two act out the feelings, and in the SP case, they double down on internalizing the feelings, which leads to depression when not addressed in healthy ways.

Perhaps another reason this subtype may be hard to discern is that SP Fours are more in contradiction than most. They tend to pay a lot of attention to the clothes they wear, but usually choose attire that doesn't stand out. Similarly, they may want their surroundings to reflect who they are, but that expression is often understated, such as intentional minimalism or small but unique artifacts. They tend to have strong opinions but don't often argue for them. They are usually industrious and detail-oriented, as well as outgoing, but will retreat into frequent self-examination. They crave stability and security, yet they want creative freedom and often desire to innovate.

They can even be mistyped as Sevens because in some cases they express a bright and optimistic, even light disposition. The general theory here is that these "sunny SP Fours" are likely to have the Sexual/One-to-One instinct in the second position, and Social in the third. We might go so far as to say this sunnier disposition is a reaction formation against how they really feel inside.

For the most part, however, the stoical disposition of the otherwise melancholic SP Four is a way of getting love by not being a burden on others. It is as they are saying, "See how much I suffer and don't complain?"

In the end, however, this subtype bears similar characteristics as the other Fours in both strength and self-awareness, as well as in stress. At their very best they lead with a focus on connecting to a higher mission. In an organization you see them connect with others through support and concern for others' well-being. When thriving in the right conditions they can harness their energy into ambitious endeavors, usually focused on making the world a better place and missional-related causes. When in stress they tend to withdraw and can fixate on self-criticism and devaluation. This can damage their self-confidence and keep them from realizing their dreams, as well as the meaningful connections with others they crave.

**Social Four: Shame**

Social Fours are almost the opposite of the Self-Preservation Fours. They can focus too much on feelings and making sure that everyone else knows about them as well. Social Fours central focus of attention is on expressing sadness (in contrast to Sexual Fours expressing anger). The sadness is packaged around feelings of inferiority related to envy. It's a self-recrimination which feels that there is something inherently wrong with them. They are often shy, especially of expressing their needs and desires. If they do feel anger it is usually transformed into shame in the outward expression of tears and sometimes a sense of victimization. As a result, they are often dramatic and can be extremely sensitive.

This subtype is the one most often associated with—or stereotyped as—Fours in general. Think Aunt Pepa of *Encanto* who has the rain cloud always over her head. Oddly enough, Social Fours are sometimes mistyped as Sevens because unlike their other two subtypes, their social focus of attention can demonstrate an openness and approachability, and through their shapeshifting, creativity, and sometimes eclectic tastes. In fact, some argue that Aunt Pepa is a Seven because she leads the song "We Don't Talk about Bruno," which is supposedly about avoiding difficult emotions, which Fours of course do.

Because they don't feel that they measure up to others, they can attribute this to a basic lack of understanding for how special and deep they are. They may come to believe that it is their place in life to suffer more than others. They see that others are happier than they are, but they scoff at how silly, hypocritical, or shallow these philistines are. In unhealthier expressions, they can believe that they are set apart from others. Like the poet T.S. Eliot said, to paraphrase: "The poet is not bound by the conventions and rules of ordinary people." They can look down upon holding down a mundane job or long-term relationship commitment because they get in the way of their finely-tuned sensibility of who they are, or what they stand for, or their search for exactly who they truly are.

Sometimes they may shape-shift to fit and be exceptionally fine-tuned and polished. It is possible that T.S. Eliot was, in fact, a Social Four. He aggressively pursued success as a compensation for nagging interior feelings of inadequacy, and by making certain achievements, they "get the world off their backs" in effect. They prove that they can play the game and succeed. By contrast, they may express themselves in compensation in exotic ways with very particular tastes and style. Think Robert Smith of The Cure and the ensuing Gothic subculture that followed the look and style in 1980s and '90s.

For all their self-comparing, Social Fours are not generally competitive with others the way the other Four subtypes are. They tend to connect with others in the workplace when they feel they are with other independent types who get them. Like all Fours, when their identity can discover alignment with the values they are working toward, they can be dedicated and creative. In growth and maturity these Fours can realize that they are no more or less than anyone else. They learn to chill out about their internal self-criticism, and the way they in turn criticize and blame others. They figure out how to take action in practical ways instead of getting lost in the intricacies of their finely-wrought sensitivities and the emotions they tend to wear on their sleeves.

### Sexual/One-to-One Four: Competition

For Sexual Fours it can be about getting angry and complaining a lot. This type often doesn't realize how intense and aggressive they can come across. They have a tendency to express anger, which is a way they process the envy they feel. The pain of envy and inferiority gets expressed as anger. Quite often the anger is turned into competitiveness. Like anything, this can turn in healthy or unhealthy directions.

When it turns into negativity, the competitiveness can be rage-fueled and destructive. They will seek to tear down those they deem as their competition and feel perfectly justified in the actions they take. It's as if they are saying, "If I'm going to suffer, then so are you." For a famous example, some point to the highly fictionalized character of Salieri in the 1984 film, *Amadeus*. In the film, Salieri is consumed with competitive hatred by the genius of Mozart, that really only he (Salieri) fully appreciates.

The intensity of this subtype comes across as demanding, especially in personal relationships. Their behavior is often consumed by endeavors that will prove them better than everyone else. They seek status, prestige, or to break through as a star or important person in their field of expertise. The ideal they seek is to be so set apart from the chaff that they will be seen as the ultimately attractive or special person they always believed they were. And by contrast so long as this doesn't take shape for them the more they will continually be frustrated and openly angry and irritable.

These Fours like intensity in everything. They tend to like intense and serious film, especially in the form of dramas or psychological thrillers. They like intense music, intense sports, intense relationships. When they work, whether out of pure competition, or in alignment with their values and clear purpose, they work with an intensity-fueled focus. Without intensity, things seem bland and dull, it may be hard to focus or find purpose or value in whatever it is they're involved in. For all these reasons, these Fours may be mistyped for Eights. The primary differentiating pattern, however, is the emotional filter they see through.

Because of the tendency to emotional volatility, these Fours tend to vacillate between periods of exceptional productivity and then almost just as intense withdrawal from others as well as work in lack of interest or focus. In maturity and health, and when they find their purpose-filled identity in alignment with their values and skills, they can be charismatic and inspiring. They can paradoxically be demanding of the others they work with, and at the same time empathic, caring, and nurturing. Some identify this subtype as one of the very most effective and productive when their focus and purpose are clear. They often possess many gifts that work well relationally in terms of sensitivity and a desire to connect and collaborate, and with a strong sense of vision they also bring an intensity and drive for efficiency and productivity.

When in stress, these Fours need to notice the signs and get in touch with the sense of inadequacy that may be driving the hard work and ignoring the feelings. The outward expression of their anger can help. They should be discerning about how they choose to release the initial wave of intensity onto someone else who may not respond the way they want.

It should be important for these Fours to recognize that intensity in itself is not necessarily what needs to be brought into equanimity. The intensity may work well for them in many circumstances, perhaps it could be the enthusiasm they bring to parenting, or how hard they are ready to work on a professional project that lines up with their values and purpose. If you drive a Ferrari you don't want to crawl along the road like you're driving a 1969 Beetle. Where these Fours really need to keep an eye on is the intensity of their reactivity.

**Working with Arrows in Growth and Stress**

Much of the theory about basic stances have Fours moving *away from* the action. This comes from the emphasis on how their attention moves inward in their subjective responses to objective happenings. They tend to reflect on their feelings and impressions of reality. When they move too far back, they stand aloof mostly out of fear they will be misunderstood. Or you could say their subjective impressions override their clear focus on outer reality. When this happens they may engage in a strong fantasy life. This really differs between the subtypes in the case of Fours. It would seem this natural disposition to withdrawal is most clearly seen in the behavior of Social Fours. The contrast and the predisposition to moving against can be seen in the behavior patterns of One-to-One/Sexual Fours. And we see an ambivalence in Self-Preservation Fours.

The theory of moving with, against, or towards can be helpful, but it can also be confusing. For instance, we can observe paradoxical patterns of behavior in Fours across the subtypes. For all that is stated above about withdrawal, at the same time, as Naranjo observes, Fours also have strong inclinations of "moving toward." They crave love that they do not (or cannot) give to themselves. They crave care and attention and there is also a commonly observed "helplessness" (114). Fours have long been observed as needing protection and reassurance to maintain their equanimity. Isolation and aloneness, therefore, can be frightening. We include the stances of types because they do give us a broad brushstroke for further understanding, but at the same time we want to point out where more research is needed, or where there are underlying flaws and confusions in the current theory.

We see gentle shifts in growth for Fours as tapping into the high side of their Three and Five wings respectively. The high side of Three takes them into productivity and efficiency, in getting things done and not overanalyzing their emotional purview into stasis and inertia. The high side of the Five encourages connection with the mental center, in growing deeply in knowledge and shifting the balance of over-indexing on the intensity of the feeling center.

To be clear, and just as a reminder, we think of wings as neighbors to our personality type when it comes to the Enneagram of Personality. They are indicators as to where we can go through self-awareness if we want to make gentle conscious decisions in how to move forward and break out of our fixated, sleepwalking behaviors.

Arrow work, by contrast, involves bigger leaps. And while we don't yet have enough evidence to fully prove this theory, we tend to see that when you move to any given type (whether high or low side), you tend to most reflect *the same subtype.* That is, when you go into your wings on either side, if you are self-preservation, that will be the tendency in your other styles. Exceptions do occur, however, especially if you had strong early examples of another subtype in your past.

When Fours do consciously focus on the arrow work and move first to point One, they *move against* the arrow. On the high side of One they recognize what needs to be done assertively and into action. This is a big move in that it places them in the body center and may not seem akin to the creative predisposition of Fours. But we can see how such a move can be exactly what can ground Fours in several ways. For one, they become focused and persistent in their pursuit on what is right. For another, they can connect to what it means to follow through and follow procedures. Further, if they have become too fixated on their specialness and how the rules don't apply to them, getting firmly in touch with the One, will reconnect them to the solidity of rules and why they exist not only for themselves but, perhaps more democratically, for all. Of course it is possible to make an arrow move in stress to the One, which tends to be unconscious. In these cases, they may realize they are moving too much against others, becoming critical, as well as overly righteous about their opinions and judgments.

When Fours make a conscious move with their second arrow to Two, they *move towards* others. They get in touch with how their natural affinity to empathy can be focused on others rather than themselves. On this high side of Two, they lift up and out of themselves and into connection with others.

For all arrow movement, we recommend connecting with your first arrow against in regular and sustained conscious ways before focusing on the second arrow moving away. Generally speaking, the reason for this is that it is unlikely the second arrow work will last if you haven't addressed the first arrow first. You may find yourself there for brief periods of time, but when some of the work has been skipped over, it is not likely to endure. On the low side, when Fours move to Two in stress, unconsciously, or out of one anxiety or another, they overdo their movement towards others. They become too involved with the "other" and lose their boundaries. Also, just as the Twos themselves do in their unconscious games, they give in order to receive affirmation and approval.

### Reactive Impulse Under Stress

The reactive behaviors vary considerably between the subtypes of Fours. However, broadly speaking, you can see how the passion of envy manifests itself in ways that are often blind to Fours. They can be so fixated in their patterns of "what is missing" whether in themselves or circumstantially that they don't even know they are doing it. They may always be sizing up others or their life situation and wishing they had more or that they were more. This has a lot to do with why they are constantly suffering to make themselves feel better by considering themselves "superior" rather than have to accept the "inferiority" they fear and often feel.

Under stress, and in reactivity, Fours can turn a vicious critical examination upon themselves. They can internalize and analyze their emotions with intense scrutiny. They also have a tendency to create a fantasy out of their projections of what actually may have happened (reality). Depending on the subtype, these expressions exhibit themselves in vastly different ways as described above. One important insight for Fours to understand is that just because they will interiorize and wrangle with their emotions, they will also—just like any and every type—avoid certain emotions or realities they don't want to face. That recognition can be keys to the kingdom for growth.

Whether the reactions are toward holding in sadness, expressing it in the form of shame, or in outrage and anger, they are triggered by the same feelings of lack. Fours already feel like they aren't enough so that is why when someone criticizes them, or names the very deficiency they feared or felt, the reaction can be explosive. The first step in growing out of the typical defense mechanisms is to understand how, where, and when it happens. Then, in that clearer understanding, stopping the behavior in its tracks.

Remember the famous sketch played by Bob Newhart? He just has two words for his client who has a lot of issues, starting with the fear of being buried alive in a box. Those two words are: "Stop it!"

"Just stop it?" she asks.

"That's right, stop it," he says.

"So, you're saying I should just stop?"

"That's right, you don't want to go around feeling like

you're going to be buried inside a box, do you? That sounds terrible."

"No," she says. "I don't."

"Then, stop it!" he yells.

We all feel like telling ourselves (and everyone else) the same thing especially when we understand some of the patterns we find ourselves (or others) repeating. So, we get it when we say, "stop the behavior in its tracks." It's all "easier said than done."

But on a cognitive behavioral level, it is true, there really is a component when you've taken the first step to notice yourself in the behavior. The second step is actually not letting it carry on. Stopping the behavior isn't the end. It's actually just the beginning. Beyond that, you can start working on understanding the feelings you're having, why you're having them, and reflect on other ways of expressing how you feel, as well as possibly re-consider whether you're interpreting them in the way they were intended, or if it is just your own "special" interpretation.

### Defining Characteristics in Personality

- → A fundamental desire to stand out and be seen as unique, special, or gifted
- → Big value placed on authenticity of expression and "being real"
- → Unapologetically emotional which can be seen as moody, sensitive, or dramatic
- → Deeply in tune with their own emotions as well as those of others
- → Big value placed on relationships, especially those seen as authentic or that they have a special connection with
- → Motivated by meaningful work, and a hard time staying consistently motivated by work that isn't

## Superpowers

Fours don't just imagine they are uniquely gifted and in touch with their special alignment with their perceptions of reality, they really do see things in an unusual way. Not only do they see things in a different light than most, they tend to be highly verbal and often do find ways of expressing their special flavor. They are extraordinarily adept at picking up on how much they connect (or don't) with you, and how you probably feel toward them. Their impulse to be "real" often pushes them in creative directions, and often in relational ones. They can be great friends who will listen to your troubles, as well as leaders who can put up with some emotional drama when things don't always go as planned. Fours will tell you the truth even if they understand you might not like what they've got to say rather than say something that feels fake. They can be low key or seek to stand out, but they stand out in a way that is intended to represent "who they really are" or "how they really feel," which is in direct contrast to the Threes disposition to shapeshift into the marketing sensibility of what pleases others. At their best, they can be great counselors, coaches, mentors, guides, teachers, poets, and running the full spectrum of artistic expression. They can mediate conflict, and they can lead others in energetic and inspiring ways when their values are lined up with their goals.

### Common Stressors for Fours

→ Not getting recognition or rewards or compensation for their hard work and the time they give of their talents and abilities.

→ Being consistently overlooked or not listened to.

→ People who are fake.

→ People who aren't personable or relatable.

- → Having to do nothing but mundane tasks.
- → When no one else cares about the order or aesthetics of the environment they live or work in.
- → Working for someone who has everything they want and constantly feeling that they will never measure up or have the opportunity to do so.
- → Knowing when and where and how to spend their time and energy, experiencing confusion on exactly what the next best step is for fear it will lead them in the wrong direction.

### Type Four Patterns to Observe to Make More Conscious

- → Staying in melancholy. Learn how to spot it. Fours are good at reading their own emotions and feeling the world around them. Pay attention to how you go into the "sweet sadness" of melancholy, and develop specific strategies to break out of the habitual patterns. One effective and proven way is through a gratitude practice.
- → Recognize what really is special, strong, and positive about you. Focus on how you already possess gifts and talents.
- → Pay attention to how you romanticize the past or get filled with nostalgia with some time when everything was simpler and better. What is good right here and now? And what one small step can you take to make your present and future better today?
- → You are not your emotions. Learn to analyze your feelings and distance yourself from them. What specifically is causing you anxiety or stress? Identify the source. Is it yours to carry?

## Activities To Lower Stress And Practice Self-Development

**Body work:** Exercise is important for Fours. They can build up a lot of anxiety from their feeling-centered world or emotions. Fours also do a lot of mental work when they analyze and interpret the meaning of their feelings or actions. Often they are most disconnected from their bodies. All forms of exercise are on the table here from the intense to the calm. Direct connection with the body is what is important here.

**Breath work:** Pushing emotions outward rather than keeping them in. Practicing breathing and meditation methods that focus on pushing out and releasing the stress and interiorization work well for Fours.

**Tap into the virtue of equanimity:** In short, sweet moments, when you don't compare yourself to everyone else in the room, or everyone else in the world, or your past self or future self, you really realize that we are all on the same level because we are all one. Practice self-observation around your need to be better, or how you feel when you deem yourself inferior. Welcome how it feels to be normal and average and experiencing calm.

**Learn to moderate emotions and self-accept:** Your emotional range is a strength. You should welcome your emotions, but also begin to see the cycles you may run yourself through. You are capable of moderating your emotions, and with the extra energy, you can begin to recognize the gift you can give to others with your ability to relate, handle difficult emotions, and value the strengths and gifts of others, as well as accepting their limitations.

(As Mark Twain once said, "Anyone who expects a friend without flaws, will have no friends.")

**Three good things:** This is a super simple, but highly-effective exercise. It helps you stay top of mind with the things that are going well in your life. Write down three things you're grateful for every day, and why you're grateful for them. This trains your brain to look for new things to be grateful for every day. A boost to your already high sense of well-being, and the development of your overall resilience.

**HEAD**

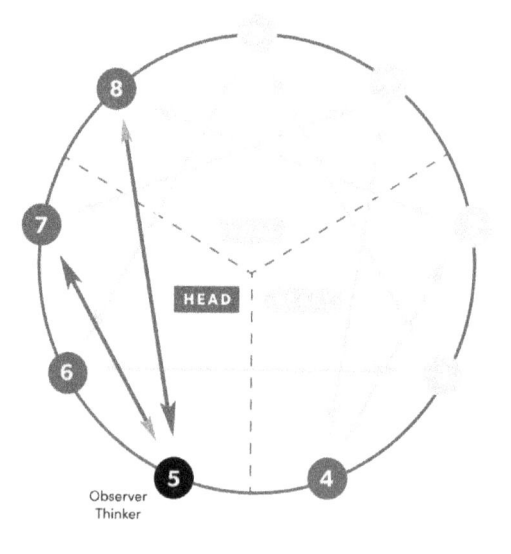

Observer
Thinker

PATH OF ENERGIZING     PATH OF RESOLUTION

# FIVES:
# THE WALLS THAT HOLD YOU INSIDE

*"A person who thinks all the time has nothing to think about except thoughts, so he loses touch with reality and lives in a world of illusions."*
—Alan Watts

**In a single syllable:** Keep
**Persona:** Cap and Gown
**Mantra:** "I am wise. I am perceptive."
**Reactivity defense mechanism:** Isolation
**Passion:** Avarice

### In a Nutshell

Ichazo's Ego-Stinge is termed from the idea that this type controls their boundaries from avoidance and emotional distancing. They want to know, to understand, to figure out how any and everything works and why. Sometimes called the Investigator, the Observer, as well as the Thinker, and the Quiet Specialist. Fives tend to approach the world from a stance of inferiority and so to learn, to know how things work and function, to master whatever it is they believe they should know, is to show up in superiority. They may come across as aloof, calm, even mysterious at first. Fives need time to develop their knowledge, and generally speaking, they love learning and constitutionally are well-suited to it. It doesn't mean they're all bookish and librarians, but it does mean they love their time alone to sort out what they want to learn and understand, or to recognize how they might feel about a situation. They tend to have strong boundaries and are highly sensitive to encroachments. They are actually highly sensitive in general, even though they may not seem like it from an emotional lens.

Knowledge is one of the most valuable human pursuits. In order to grow spiritually, you must reconcile that growth with the intellect. Fives are more prone than any other type to do what is called "spiritual bypass," which happens when "knowing" through learning supersedes knowing through experiential understanding. Fives are happy in the coolness of their heads, and what they need is a little heat from the heart and body.

### Defining Characteristics of the Five Type

Fives report that they are in constant measurement of whether they're going to be engulfed or ignored. They are especially sensitive to others' assessments. Rather than play the game of being overwhelmed by someone's emotional response or their indifference, Fives seek to forgo the game altogether and just wall off. They can be called emotionally insensitive or even controlling, when really they think of their behavior as just preserving their autonomy.

Fives compartmentalize their lives. They show up objective and detached as leaders. Underneath the cool composure the mental workings are flying.

The Fives' ego creates and wants to feel connection, but fears what it may require of them as well, and they live as if in a scarcity mindset that there will not be enough energy to go around. To some extent, from what we know of introverts in general, the idea that they need to "recharge their batteries" is commonplace understanding. But for Fives it is not only about the difference between where you get your energy. It is also about personal independence.

First, we should recognize Fives as the head types they are, the first as we make our way clockwise around the points on the Enneagram of Personality. Podcast panelist, Chris Schoolcraft describes his experience on being a head type as follows:

> It's a disconnection from my heart and body. So it's an overuse of trying to understand and mentalize and conceptualize and frame in my mind the world as a way to understand it to be safe. And to be able to make assumptions about it that helped me navigate without using energy, without overextending myself, without revealing too much of myself. And so really the center of intelligence is in one way a disconnection from the heart and the body. And so navigating the world without my heart being engaged, or without it being walled and protected, and without my body being fully present, and sensing what's happening in the moment. So it just leaves my head. And so that allows me to protect myself.

Fives also love complexity that demands understanding and interpretation. Spiderwebs, fractals, Quantum Physics, the history of the Enneagram, you name it, Fives love the sense that their mind can just be at ease and consumed in the world of ideas, the endless complexity in understanding systems, behavior, or the unexplainable. Fives would call that bliss, to fall into complexity, and absorb it at a really deep and high level. Heart types might want to fall into relationships or feelings and give themselves to that, or body types want to get lost in action, or in the flow of doing. For Fives, anything that can be broad enough and big enough and deep enough for them to lose their mental selves offers a sense of bliss and connection that they believe they miss out when all the centers of intelligence are engaged.

They are attracted to truth because they want to know what is real. Descartes clearly falls into this camp. He walled himself off from the world in order to ascertain reality and what is really real, and he came out with his famous cogito dictum, "I think therefore I am." Behind the desire to understand and the pursuit of truth, is a deeper (if idealized) pursuit that energizes Fives, and that is for wisdom. Wisdom implies something greater than mere intelligence. Wisdom is about putting together all the fractured pieces into a unified whole. It's the Grand Unified Theory of Everything that Fives revel in.

They say Albert Einstein was a five, as well as Emily Dickinson. And from these two disparate personalities in time and space, we can somehow see a similarity. They stand aloof and distracted and yet completely plugged into their pursuits, their synthesis of their particular form of study and apprehension. Dickinson was profoundly creative, but she also has this almost austere, distanced, and controlled perspective. Her poems are these tightly controlled, little intensities or distillations, pointing to a greater and larger whole. As for Einstein, $E=MC^2$ may be the most famous equation ever, and in essence explains how energy and mass are different forms of the same thing.

In his book *Nine Lenses on the World,* Jerry Wagner (a Five himself) tells the story of Bernard Longeran, a Jesuit Philosopher, who was asked what he thought of the problem of pollution. Longeran didn't give them what they may well have expected from such a complex subject.

"The problem with pollution is the principle of the double effect," he said.

Wagner points out how this single sentence summed

up the problem. Industries intend one thing in the manufacturing of their products (the first effect), but they get an unintended consequence in pollution as one of the by-products (the second effect).

Fives are considered the most introverted of the Enneagram types, and often come up as INTP, the introvert who has a predominance of intuition over sensation, thinking over feeling, and perception over judgment. When they emerge as leaders it is usually due to their deep knowledge of a given subject. They limit their interactions with others, and they detach from their emotions as a stress response. Emotions are messy and they'd rather not deal with them either in themselves or with others. They can be quiet when they are in uncomfortable situations or with unfamiliar people, and this reticence can make them appear disinterested, aloof, or arrogant. For the most part, however, they are shy and want to keep the focus off of themselves. The best way to engage them is through discussing an intellectual subject, especially ones that they are interested in. In such cases, you may get them to talk at greater length than anything you would normally expect.

You will also see them delay in taking action because they are being pressed to act before they feel comfortable with their knowledge or understanding. They also don't like the obligations of having to collaborate with others. Intuitively, they neither want to rely on others or depend on the contributions of others. This doesn't only show up in the workplace. You may observe Five behavior in friends who always have their own plans and agendas with what they're going to do with the family.

Even when high-functioning and doing a lot, they are more like lone wolves in their temperament. You are welcome to join them in their activities (sometimes), but they have made them on their own and they already have a plan. Some types need the accountability of others when it comes to forming habits or sticking with routines like exercise or other disciplines. Fives aren't just faking it when they say they will workout sustainably on their own. That can really be how they thrive, especially if their boundaries are already encroached on in other areas of their life.

**The Passion of Fives**

Fives "miss the mark" through the passion of avarice. Avarice here is not meant as the greed associated with Ebeneezer Scrooge in Dickens' *A Christmas Carol*. Rather, as Chaucer captured famously in "The Parson's Tale" from the *Canterbury Tales:* "Avarice consists not only of greed for land and chattels, but sometimes for learning and for glory."

Naranjo (also a Five) observes that if anger is an outward expression of greed, an assertive demandingness, avarice is almost the inverse. It is a holding in, a retentiveness. The grasping is inward, as if they would lose themselves were they not able to hold onto their privacy. He likens it to "an experience of impending impoverishment (66)."

The way out of the castle keep and into a greater understanding of self and personality is through the virtue of nonattachment. In this respect, Fives are open to giving and receiving through life's natural flows and rhythms, not in holding everything pent up inside. But what if Einstein had never worked in the public sphere of ideas, had never shared his ideas but kept himself locked up in an interior world? Dickinson may have had a form of epilepsy, and was fortunate to have family and friends with whom she could live. She did in fact live a fairly short, isolated life, but what if her over 1,800 poems had never been published or shared afterwards? We will examine areas for concerted focus and growth through the work with wing stretches and arrow movements.

### Functional Versus Authentic Personality

We tell a lot of types they need to have better boundaries, but this would not be true for Fives. They are the masters of boundaries. Fives may have been the source of inspiration for Paul Simon's "I Am a Rock." Because, after all, "a rock feels no pain, and an island never cries." Also, whereas with some types you may experience various forms of demandingness, Fives neither demand, nor do they take.

Boundaries are good. It gives you space to focus on your needs, and if you've minimized those needs, then what is the problem, right? You can see the effectiveness of this as a survival strategy. Further, the clear boundaries and the coolness of the emotions allows for all kinds of inner knowledge work. You can become deeply knowledgeable in anything that interests you.

The virtue of nonattachment is the key to the passion of avarice. Fives can begin to see the fundamental difference between holding everything inside to letting go and being willing to receive as well as to give. Also, learning to recognize that you need to connect with others in order to experience a fuller and more invigorating life experience. Connecting with emotions does not have to deplete you. It can also connect you to a clearer and more pronounced sense of joy.

### Psychological Roots and Key Patterns that Create Stress for Fives

Like all head types, the central need for Fives at an early developmental stage is for practicing. The unconscious reaction to this lack is that they don't feel fully protected or reassured by their primary caretakers. Their adaptive strategies focus on detaching from their emotions and the need for connecting with others. They create strong boundaries to protect their precious inner resources. They also minimize their needs, which reduces the chances of them having to interact with others. Fives have a hard time with letting go, but when they do they awaken to a reality that is their true self, and not the false personality lurking behind the walls of the mental personality.

In slightly less clinical terms, we often hear from Fives that boundaries were an issue in early childhood, from either end of the spectrum. Either they report overbearing parents who didn't respect their boundaries, or, by contrast, varying degrees of neglect. It may have well been "benign neglect" in which the child seems to be happy making do on their own and so leave well enough alone. Whatever the case, these young emerging personalities figured out how to get by on their own with what few resources they had at their disposal. Sometimes, too, they found themselves in the middle of intense family drama or trauma, and learned as a coping mechanism that an effective strategy was to withdraw physically and detach emotionally.

We see irritability and some frantic activity when Fives feel stress. They also tend to retreat as soon as they get a chance, and they may aggressively retreat. They may stay in bed. They may become as invisible as possible in their room of choice. They tend to have a danger of staying in stress for too long because of their choice to isolate themselves from others. You could make an argument that Fives need to connect with their bodies more than any other type.

**Self-Preservation Fives: Castle**

This type is easiest to remember if you've ever read (or are familiar with) Franz Kafka's famous short story, "A Hunger Artist," (and Kafka himself is considered to probably have been an SP Five). As the story goes, the man (whose name we never learn) fasts in a cage for forty days at a time, traveling from town to town. He is always dissatisfied at the end, mainly because he knows he can fast longer than the forty days, and that fasting really isn't difficult for him. The impresario who is in charge of his "performances," insists that the fast end at forty days because the audiences grow bored.

Over time, audiences do lose interest in the hunger artist, and he finally gets his chance to break his record as a sideshow at a circus. But the audiences aren't interested, and the managers don't even keep an accurate record of how many days the hunger artist has gone without eating. He eventually withers away saying he only wanted to be admired, but that really he shouldn't be admired because he really had just never found a food that he liked. After he passes away, his cage is replaced by a panther who symbolizes the opposite of what the hunger artist represents, the total embodiment of wildness, hunger, desire, and wanting to be free. Audiences are enthralled by the wild beast, and the story ends.

The Self-Preservation Five is the "most Five" of the Fives. Their passion is for hiddenness, and they literally create a sanctuary, a den, a lair, or what have you. They need to be walled in, protected through a physical boundary. This physical boundary serves as a psychological wall, too. They are self-sufficient behind their walls. The world is a dangerous and needy place. They venture out only when life imposes on them. Jerry Wagner calls this "a womb with a view." They need their own special place to recharge their batteries, and re-energize so they can get back out there into the world.

This subtype is stereotyped as being bookworms or intellectuals, and this isn't always necessarily true. They do have a strong mental predisposition, so you will find them engaged in activities or careers that engage their mind.

And even for all their "walled off" priorities, some can be disarmingly outgoing, at least for short periods of time. They can be funny and creative.

All of this disconnection is a form of control, the motivation of which is to not waste any resources and energy on what takes them away from their interests. This is a control that can be emotionally cold to those near to them. They also have issues with expressing anger. Of course, the general stance of walling yourself away (the poor hunger artist notwithstanding) is that it's not really compatible with an engaged life, or really even meeting basic human needs.

Because of their self-preserving nature, some SP Fives take good care of themselves. They may indulge in excellent food and eating right, or hanging out in comfortable places, as well as engaging in physical activities and exercise. Usually, however, these are viewed as "means to an end," often done reluctantly or out of a sense of necessity. If there is any kind of demandingness from this subtype, it manifests itself as demanding time to meet his or her own needs. Things may fall apart around them: their home, their office, their basic hygiene, their relationships, but so long as no extraneous demands are being made on them, they are safe within their cocoon and the interests that matter most to them.

We can see the embedded and symbolized lessons that Self-Preservation Fives need to learn from an analysis of "A Hunger Artist." We can also see that through their virtue of nonattachment they can learn to ease up on their boundaries, to let others in and be willing to open up to those others. They can also come to recognize that the very thing that is intended to give you energy, may in the end leave you empty and impoverished.

## Social Fives: Totem

Of all the subtype subsets, the differences between the Fives are perhaps the least pronounced. Unlike the intensity of Fours, which shoots them into striking differences between subtypes, the coolness and measured calm of Fives may be one reason for the more subtle differences. With that said, we see the social expression of the Five here in seeking the highest of ideals through knowledge.

Their fundamental fear is less of being intruded on in their "womb with a view," and more of being seen as "the emperor who has no clothes." They fear not knowing something (that they believe they should). The "totem" is usually in the form of a specialized form of knowledge or system of knowledge. Through this specific and deep understanding, Social Fives seek to engage with the world through recognition of their status and mastery. The totem could be anything: from mastering the Enneagram to collecting vinyls. We see it in the butterfly collector who collects and documents more species than we even know of from Encyclopedias and museums. Also, contrary to popular belief, not all these head types place value on knowledge only. They look for the best and brightest anywhere. It could be creative, political, or social groups they strive to be among. They seek outstanding and interesting people in general. When those happen to line up with their interests as well, they seek to dive in. A totem, in effect, is anything that is given privileged status and is idolized in one form or another.

They are more "out there" than the other Fives and they relate to others who are outstanding among people. They seek super value, says Naranjo, the ultimate meaning, to the extent that they become disconnected and disinterested in life, and bypasses empathy and sometimes, too, spiritual growth. This is the subtype most likely to do what is called "spiritual bypass." All types are perfectly capable of this, but Social Fives are especially at risk of this defensive strategy. You have "to do the work" when it comes to spiritual growth, which, at least in part, means engagement in community and connection with the mind, heart, and body. You can't just "know" all there is to know and think that will create growth, maturity, and understanding.

Author of *Man's Search for Meaning,* Viktor Frankl himself may have been this subtype. He documented his experience in the Nazi concentration camps, and created a system of understanding how the system of psychological responses prisoners had to their experience. For the survivors, and for our society and culture at large, he developed a system for finding purpose in life, as well as the recognition of how life is imbued with meaning in every moment. He called his system for analysis logotherapy. We are all interested in purpose and our interpretation of how to live in modern society, but for Social Fives, it can be all-consuming. In fact, as has been documented, the drive to find the ultimate truth, or the "Grand Unified Theory of Everything," often creates a divide between the ultimate and the ordinary.

One way the virtue of nonattachment holds the keys to greater self-understanding and personal growth is to let go of needing social distinction. They don't have to seek community through setting themselves apart. They can learn to broaden their focus from knowledge to connecting to feelings, and rather than having everything needing to line up neatly in their systems of higher ideals and knowledge, they can learn to appreciate the daily, the ordinary, and connecting with people themselves rather than some fantasy projection of who they might be or could be.

### Sexual/One-to-One Fives: (countertype) Confidence

The name given to this subtype has less to do with "being confident," and more with needing the special, trusting confidence of another. It's the kind of confidence in sharing a secret with someone: "No one knows what we have shared."

In a similar way that Social Fives idolize the pursuit of their special blend of knowledge, this subtype seeks the ultimate union. Many times this doesn't work out so well. As you can probably guess, it would be hard to be the amazing muse and not just pretend to be until the spell is broken. But in a general sense, these Fives can find trust in a partner who fulfills certain expectations, like high intelligence or creativity and other valued traits, as well as one who can be relied on. Part of what makes for a great union, after all, is safety.

These Fives are very much like the others in many respects, but the differentiation is their romantic spirit. Their vibrant inner life comes alive with intensity and a broader array of emotions than the other Fives have as accessible when in personality. They promote themselves through demonstrating their rich, fascinating, and possibly even edgy inner world. They are also the most aesthetically inclined of the Fives. They have a focused creativity that comes alive in music, painting, novels, and the exchange of ideas, often of a philosophical bent. Their art can be iconoclastic and transgressive, as well as highly detailed and technical.

They run against the passion of avarice through their stronger desire than other Fives to connect and bond through an intimate relationship. At the same time, they still remain very much Five-ish in their contradictory feelings of both having needs and yet also trying to minimize them, or creating the very conditions of lack that they would seek to avoid by having little demands made upon them. They have a tendency to mentally abstract themselves from their experience, even when it comes to sexual expectations.

This subtype holds others to high expectations as a form of avoiding intimacy. For growth work, they need to learn to relax their need to test others. One way to start is by recognizing the fear that comes from relationships and the expression of emotions. Understanding the fear, and getting closer to the source is a great way for this subtype to begin to break free from their automated, repeating behaviors.

### Working with Arrows in Growth and Stress

Fives' basic stance is to *move away from* people. They step back and assess the big picture. They detach and invoke the virtue of The Beatles' famous song, "let it be, whisper words of wisdom, let it be." They prefer solitude, silence, and space. When they step out of the game, they may forget to step back in. They become rigid, retentively controlling loners, overly protective of their privacy.

Remembering the virtue of nonattachment seeks to reframe the wisdom of "let it be," and rather than letting the world flit and fumble around the walls of their high castle, they open the doors and windows. They even amble out of the keep and engage in other communities and activities. They begin to realize there is nothing that they need to fear when it comes to engaging with others. Masters of boundaries that they are, they can always maintain them if need be. Much more important for their own growth and development, they recognize how much they actually have inside them to share, and how energizing it can be to share these things with others.

Gentle movements for self-awareness and growth

would be to first connect with the high side of their Four neighbors, arguably the most feeling of all types. Growth in this area alone reaps significant rewards for Fives, as it brings warmth and equanimity to their relationships, as well as embracing the higher side of the originality and unique contribution of their work. The lower side of their Four wing may find them even more in their self-absorption or overanalyzing and critiquing the motivations and behaviors of others and being overly sensitive to their own shortcomings and sense of deficiency. Connecting with the high side of their Six neighbors puts them in touch with recognizing a world of possibilities. There are more options available to them than meets the eye and stepping into them with courage is another step in a gentle growth movement. The lower side of their Six wing may find them caught up the whirlwind of their thoughts and ideas, overanalyzing the motivations of the world around them, and feeling frozen. They may lack confidence to do the next right thing.

When Fives have worked on the conscious and high sides of their wings, they are ready for bigger sustained leaps in their personal inner work, and they should first aim for their arrow against, the point Eight. This dramatic move is also a *move against* people with assertive self-assurance and confidence. When Fives do this, they apply their knowledge boldly. They open up rather than conceal themselves. They say what they want and actively work towards their goals free from thought, and in a body stance of action. When Fives move to Eight unconsciously or in stress, they push beyond assertion into aggression, and express anger contemptuously. They may put others down instead of being confrontive.

Once Fives have put in the hard work in consciously remaining in Eight, they are ready to work with the second arrow, and *move towards* people at the point Seven. They become more outgoing, friendly, humorous, and "out there" in their sometimes nerdish, subversive, self-deprecating Five-ish ways. They engage with others and don't even mind when spontaneous surprises emerge. They go with the flow and keep their options open. When Fives find themselves moving to Seven unconsciously or in reactivity, they tend to do so in pleasure-seeking activities, which at its root is pain avoidance. They avoid confrontation or anything that might induce anger by being overly optimistic.

**Reactive Impulse Under Stress**

As we have observed before about all the types under stress, there can be a doubling down on their defining characteristics. Another way of putting it could even be that what makes for a real strength, or a functional part of their personality, becomes distorted because it is overdone or overvalued.

For Fives, if we can boil it down to a single overriding issue, it would be their reluctance to engage with others. This manifests itself as a walled off person, but also means being emotionally distant and distracted, as well as lacking an ability to even communicate well what they do know. For the latter, Naranjo documents the example of a teacher who isn't a good teacher because he is so lost in the content itself that he doesn't even think about how the delivery of the information is a form of teaching as well. They may make for great objective thinkers, and they may be clear-thinking analysts, but sharing that information in a way that also communicates on any kind of emotional level the importance of the given information will be lacking. For stressed Fives or Fives in reactivity, there may be little expression of emotional intelligence.

Stress shows up for a lot of Fives as low-level irritability.

Sometimes Fives stop right in the middle of stress. They defend themselves from everyone's expectations and demands and seek immediate retreat for as long as it may be sustainable. Fives are also known to be able to live in stress for long periods of time. Fives as a rule can endure where most types would wither away or make their needs or demands known.

Fives rarely express direct anger. When they do it is usually because others are encroaching on their boundaries or on one of the very few close relationships they have. Anger isn't always bad (in spite of Seneca's famous systematic treatise against all forms of anger in *De Ira*). Sometimes the expression of anger is a sign that you are feeling disrespected. In such cases, the expression of anger for Fives can be a good thing because it can engage them in emotion, one of the key tasks for their personal growth, especially emotion in the present moment.

Naranjo uses the illustration of King Midas as another key for understanding the Fives' aspiration and its unintended consequences. On its face, there is nothing wrong with "renunciation," with asking less of the world or expressing worldly needs, especially in an effort to be in touch with higher spiritual principles and ideals. But in their wish for the "riches" of the highest ideals and ultimate pursuits, Fives tend to disconnect from all that is human in themselves and others. They break from the body, heart, and even from thinking itself in the idea of constantly striving, grasping, becoming. So, in turn, as Midas's magic touch turns his daughter into gold, he runs into the dehumanization of the ideal. Similarly, this is how the Fives' pursuit of the extraordinary can result in "impoverishment in the capacity to value the ordinary (95)."

### Defining Characteristics in Personality

- → Hypersensitive even while paradoxically communicating detachment
- → Relative indifference to praise or criticism or the feelings of others
- → Lack of warmth and affection toward others
- → Talks at length about intellectual pursuits or complicated problems, but almost never about anything personal
- → Will say little in meetings or in group situations, but always seems to be listening intently and when called upon or asked their opinion may well offer deep insights and summary assessments
- → Tendency to close their door or shut themselves off from outside interference
- → Prefer to go it alone: don't need others and don't want others to need them

**Superpowers**

For all their headiness, their disconnection from emotions, and their general reluctance to dealing with others, you will often find Fives at the pinnacle of their professions. Their desire to "know" combines with a terrific ability to focus, something that few other types possess in such measure. They have a natural tendency to discipline themselves in ways that other types can barely dream of or recognize.

There is also an inherent modesty in not talking until you know something well, there is a wisdom, a recognition that the more you know, the less you realize you really know. Also, Fives may not like to collaborate with others, but that isn't necessarily because they're going to let you down. They may sometimes be deliberate in their methods, but when they have a deadline they are generally resourceful and precise. And collaboration can be messy and difficult for virtually everyone, even those who prefer it. It almost always seems someone else pulls more weight than someone else, or that some kind of drama inevitably shows up to get in the way of someone's ability to follow through. Fives are independent, a value many Westerners cherish. As leaders, they are among the most likely to leave you alone and let you do your job.

When they are in a good space and their batteries are charged up, they can be fun and humorous and self-deprecating. Their humor tends to be of a flavor that is witty and epigrammatic, as well as withering in dry assessments of human behavior and motivations.

**Common Stressors for Fives**

- → Surprises, especially last minute tasks.
- → Intrusion, of physical space or demands on time or in the form of interruptions.
- → People who want to get personal.
- → When forced to collaborate and people don't do what they say they will do on time.
- → Unclear boundaries of any kind, including structures, roles, expectations.

**Type Five Patterns to Observe to Make More Conscious**

- → Pay attention to how you hoard information, as well as your emotional availability from others. If there is no outlet for a body of water it becomes a cesspool. By opening up the boundaries and letting everything you know and feel flow freely through you, you will relax your tight-fisted control. You will actually discover more freedom, not less. You will deepen in your relational joy, both in what you give and receive.
- → Let yourself become more conscious of when you are

shutting down emotionally. When you do reflect or take time to feel, ask yourself what leads you to run from your feelings. Why do you feel like it's not safe to be more open?

→ Similarly, become more conscious of when you are shutting down to your body. How can you reconnect with grounding yourself in the ordinary experience of movement? Recognize that all levels of experience are important, from the transcendent to the ordinary.

→ Are you willing to have a beginner's mind? What would you learn from the humility of not being the expert at everything you discuss?

## Activities To Lower Stress And Practice Self-Development

**Connect with community:** We tend to double down on our defense mechanisms, so "I am a rock, I am an island" can especially emerge for stressed Fives. Fives are also notorious for not joining communities. Recognize your natural stance to move away from people. You've probably been doing it in some form or fashion all your life. Or you've only run into connections with others because you had to. What would it be like to join a community on your terms? Where would it be? What would it mean for you to take such a step? What fears or thoughts immediately come up that make you resist this suggestion?

**Get into your body:** Getting into your body and really getting into exercise can help tremendously. When Fives are focused on activities that get them into their bodies, they tend to prefer individual activities and especially those that "get them out of their heads," although this is broadly true for all head types. Running is the most highly reported activity that is simple enough to begin, but is also a solo endeavor, and repetitive enough to help you break free from your constant mental maneuvering. This works doubly well if you can couple this with other behaviors like meditation and concentrating on your breathing while running (rather than listening to more lectures, books, podcasts, or music).

**Tap into the virtue of nonattachment:** Use your desire for knowledge (through your functional personality) to learn all about what the passion of avarice really means, as well as the antidote with the virtue of nonattachment. Once you've done the learning and feel like you've got a grasp on your intellectual understanding, begin the work. Re-examine the theory of gentle moves to your Four and Six wings, as well as the important but more challenging arrow work. Consider the deep wisdom of the Enneagram of Personality and how it is a dynamic system meant for transformation and growth, not something you can merely inculcate into your intellectual life. What are ways you can begin to break down your walls and begin to flow more freely?

**Do something spontaneous:** One way to move towards others and have a little fun at the same time is to break out of your entrenched routines. What would it be like to do something different? This works better if you try to engage someone else in your spontaneity. Either way, it can be a step out of personality and into a more flexible and relaxed approach to your possibly sleepwalking behaviors.

7

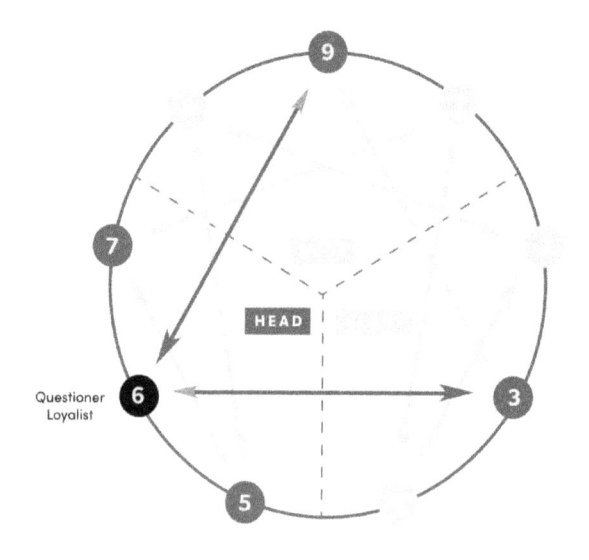

9

HEAD

Questioner
Loyalist  6

5

3

PATH OF ENERGIZING    PATH OF RESOLUTION

# SIXES:
# TRUSTING WITHOUT TESTING

*"Of all the liars in the world, sometimes the worst are your own fears."*
—Rudyard Kipling

**In a single syllable:** Fret
**Persona:** Skeptic
**Mantra:** "I anticipate everything and therefore fear nothing."
**Reactivity defense mechanism:** Projection
**Passion:** Fear

**In a Nutshell**

Ichazo's Ego-Cow, short for cowardice or the passion of fear, is placed in the center of the head types. Perhaps all three of the head types have streaks of rebellion in them. For Sixes the rebellion shows up as stubbornness, obstinance, a refusal to listen to figures of authority. Sixes have an innate contrarian streak. Lacking in trust of themselves, or the opinions of others, they sometimes do the exact opposite of expectations or guidance. Oddly enough, they frequently look for guidance for the very reason that they don't trust themselves. Sixes (like Fours) have amongst the most pronounced differences between subtypes, but for as different as these responses and personality constructs show up, the underlying passion remains fundamentally the same. This is where overarching names like the Loyalist are misleading when it comes to typing. The disposition to moving toward authority is only one of the three ways Sixes show up. The response, however, is always toward an *overvaluation* of authority, whether as a system, individual, or institution. The other two subtype responses may be one of defiance (most well known as the "counter-phobic"), as well as warmth within the structures of safety (so as to remain safe). We prefer names like the Skeptic or the Troubleshooter. Sixes of all subtypes tend to have good interpersonal skills. They are keenly tuned in to who is worthy of trust and who is not. When in the right environment and with some self-awareness, they can galvanize their stubborn streak into right action. In so doing, they move from timidity and anxiety into determined, forthright, often bold directions.

**Defining Characteristics of the Six Type**

Occupied with matters of trust and authority, Sixes experience constant doubt and ambivalence. They also have a tendency of manifesting a self-fulfilling prophecy. They are prone to creating scenarios where what they most fear actually does happen. Ironically enough, the anticipated fears they are always scanning for end up manifesting because of the ensuing paralysis that accompanies the analysis. This is one way they become known for being "sticks in the wheel" in the workplace, or getting in the way of execution, which they don't intend to do.

"I think that my brain is constantly going and always taking in all of the facts," says one Six we've worked with. "And the feelings to me are I do have a side to me that is deep in feelings and very sensitive, but especially in a business way, just really looking and taking in facts and constantly assessing risk, which is a good thing to do in my position. But then it also ends up with me looking very contrarian, right? When there's something that really feels good to others and everyone is like, 'Yes, we should do it', and it's all warm and fuzzy, or it's sexy, or whatever it is. And then I come and I'm showing up to ruin the party with 12 different scenarios of how it can all go wrong."

You could characterize the fear of Sixes as an unpleasant emotional and physiological response to recognize sources of danger. It tends to accompany anxiety, and the reason it turns into anxiety is because it focuses on something that may not even be real. The focus is on the anticipation of danger from an unrecognized or unknown source or even originating in your own mind. No other type projects fear the way Sixes do.

Fear in Sixes is often reported as an all-encompassing anxiety, because it's not like they're always staring at the lion face to face. And instead they come up with all the different directions the lion might come from. And they get busy just taking up mental energy, constantly creating scenarios. They also tend to project a potential fear, constantly scanning for the source of the danger.

"If we could just find it we wouldn't have these feelings," says one Six. "We won't be afraid." For this reason, Naranjo observes that this fear based in insecurity can become "insatiable."

Sixes can be hard on themselves, but in a different way than how the inner critic works in Ones or how "lack" and deficiency shows up in Fours. For Sixes, even if things go well, they are already ahead of it, thinking how it could have been better. They don't fully trust themselves, and they sure don't trust others who might be telling them how well things went.

Sixes overthink. More than their head type neighbors, the Fives and Sevens, they are prone to become unproductive in their mental habits. They can spin out thought after thought in micro-moments with the best of them. They are famous for their tendency to spin around in their thinking.

While they may sometimes come across as the person who quells everyone's initial enthusiasm, they often resent the label. In the workplace especially, their tendency to want to think through scenarios can be valuable. It certainly is better than the "ready, fire, aim" mentality that occurs in groupthink situations and many organizations.

"I like dismantling things in my head," says podcast panelist Marta Gillilan who identifies as a Sexual/One-to-One Six. "And seeing what's going to actually happen. If we were to dismantle the system at church or dismantle something in leadership. It's almost like a drive to figure out in my head, what that would look like. But also, I like to reconstruct things as well. So I think we get blamed a lot for being 'worst case scenario folks', but I really do resonate more with being 'opposite case scenario, or all case scenarios.'"

Sixes say they forget how they first felt about things, especially when it comes to making a decision. Because they go into their heads immediately and start to ruminate. One interesting observation that we've heard from Sixes is that they often characterize their first feelings about things as a "gut reaction" and that they wish they had trusted the original response. However, they also at the same time forget what that initial gut feeling was because they've made so many other decisions in the meantime, and because their minds are often whirling.

"Does it always circle back to the first reaction?" asks Marta rhetorically. "I don't remember. We're on to the next decision."

Sixes are also tuned in to others, but not in the way heart types might be able to "read a room" on an empathic level.

Sixes report that they "get a vibe" from people right away. They also say they have a very real capacity to test people. If they get a quick intuitive sense that they can trust a person then they feel like they are free to be their pleasant selves. If they pick up on something that doesn't feel right, or if the "test" isn't passed, they become guarded.

They often find themselves in either-or territory. Things are going to be terrible, or things are going to be glowing. The truth is, most humans' experience in life is that there are going to be great times and terrible times and in-between times. There are going to be times to step up and times to hold back.

Sixes, you could say, have an odd relationship with authority. They're often called the Loyalist, but some push right back against authority, and most do report that they *really* don't like to be told what to do. Some say they like to put their authority in others' hands, but mostly because they then want that person to say: "I think you really do know what to do." And in many cases, that's how they develop trust with those around them, by being given back their own personal authority. With Sixes it's about "support and space," and building that trust is a long game.

### The Passion of Sixes

Fear is the passion for Sixes. All types fear different things for different reasons, but the key to understanding fear for the Six type is to understand the way they anticipate and project fears that aren't even necessarily real. At face value, the passion is usually a blind spot for the types until you become familiar with what the passion really means, and through self-observation notice how it shows up.

Sixes may not see their fear as fear. They may wonder why everyone doesn't do what they do, which is to scan the horizon for anticipated outcomes. They may think this is just the way you need to operate in the world, especially if you're a good problem solver.

The real problem, however, is the constant anticipation of what might happen leads to a generalized anxiety that is hard to root out because it's hard to recognize the source (since the source may not even exist as anything other than projection). Sixes' constant vigilance makes them often wound up tight and unable to relax. They may also lack the confidence to push ahead in their personal or professional lives in constant hesitation or ambivalence.

For each of the distinct ways that the Six subtypes may look, the virtue of courage remains the same. By becoming aware of the ways that fear takes over and functions within the head, heart, and body, Sixes can begin to work on how they can throttle open the source of their courage. Courage means moving forward even in the face of fear. We will examine areas for concerted focus and growth through the work with wing stretches and arrow movements.

**Functional Versus Authentic Personality**

No doubt asking lots of questions and scanning for what might go wrong can be a smart and strategic way to move through life both as it relates to your environment, as well as interpersonally. Many types jump right into situations they wish they would have thought through a little more deliberately. So many lessons that had to be learned the hard way. Not so for Sixes. Sixes vet those they put their trust in, and try to find good leaders worth serving. When they do find what they're looking for, they are some of the most supportive allies you will find. They are incredibly tuned in to who is worthy of their trust. In part, this means people act in accord with what they say.

When Sixes are open to the feedback from others about

how they may slow down the process through asking too many questions, they can adapt. By modifying their approach, they can show others how looking for good data to support rational decision-making is a valuable asset.

When Sixes relax their grasp on analyzing everything and everyone, they break free from their generalized anxiety. They stop their mental looping behavior patterns and realize that not everything has to be questioned in the style of a flow chart. Not only does this apply to systems, or organizational decision-making, it also applies to people. Not everyone needs to be viewed with a skeptical eye. Sometimes the tests that Sixes put people through are far more stringent than they need to be. Many people are worthy of their trust that they don't even realize. Sixes may well find, when they loosen up the hold of their automated personality patterns, that opportunities and possibilities they never would have otherwise seen open up. Finally, they are also able to realize that the most trusted source is their own inner authority. Trusting themselves is the beginning for growth, as well as the end result of how they can step more courageously into their most authentic selves.

### Psychological Roots and Key Patterns that Create Stress for Sixes

All head types needed more practicing at an early key development stage. In this case, it usually centers around inconsistencies with their primary caretakers. When parental behavior fluctuates between extremes it can lead to an undermining of one's own personal authority. For whatever reason, Sixes develop a wariness to how they approach life because they never felt completely safe in their smaller world growing up. They became on guard for when the next real or perceived attack might be coming from.

In many cases, too, there is an internalization that they were not trusted. It could be as small as not being able to play on their own in the neighborhood. Or an overbearing parent had to make sure what they wore to school met their approval first, or that they didn't trust the child to do their homework (with inconsistent responses to what this did or didn't mean). Or a child perhaps did test limits and were also met with responses ranging from authoritarian and strict to permissive and laissez-faire, or under the guiding principle of "natural consequences."

Sixes respond either by compliance, finding ways around the rules, or aggressively pushing against. In the latter case, what the Six is effectively doing is calling out the fear source so that he or she knows where it may be coming from. In stress, Sixes are doubling down on their fear and anxiety. They are scanning for danger, deception, and betrayal to the point of paralysis. They become indecisive and paranoid. They can either freeze, or they can become aggressive. Either way, they increase their hyper vigilance and either follow the rules or get everyone else to. They become even more stubbornly ensconced in their attitudes and thinking to the point of being dogmatic. They can become openly rebellious, as well as even more dependent on other trusted sources to meet their needs.

Sixes often have an attachment to stress. They don't feel like they're doing their job if they don't feel stress. In these cases, they need to do cognitive work and discern their false beliefs and projections.

### Self-Preservation Sixes: Warmth

These Sixes want to feel family love where there is no enemy. "We are friends," says the SP Six. They show up much more like the rabbit than the bulldog. You might imagine what the Self-Preservation instinct would do with the

Sixes' tendency toward anxiety. The world is a dangerous place. You can't be too careful. As a result, these Sixes seek alliances for security and protection. They provide these few trusted individuals with their own version of friendliness and trustworthiness. They make themselves into allies. Allies aren't cold and prickly, they're warm and amenable.

When they are free from stress and are able to put together an awareness of how anxiety operates within their lives, they are able to understand how well they are (or have been) supported. As a result, they find in a practical sense how easy it can be to part ways with fear. They can be excellent at processing information. They are tuned in to how the parts work with the whole, much more so than their head type neighbors Fives, who are also highly observant but narrower in focus. These Sixes can also be extremely hardworking, and they often care for and feel responsible for the well-being of the people they care about.

They tend to manage their stress and anxieties through systems that work for them. For the very reason they feel chaos, they impose order. They like predictability and for things to stick to a routine. This control may manifest itself in a wide variety of ways, but it can focus on orderliness, cleanliness, calendaring on an hourly basis, dietary needs, etc.

While many of these regulatory and systemic approaches to living keep anxiety at bay and their lives functioning (sometimes at very high levels), it can also result in keeping them stuck, which leads to (usually unconscious) stress. Sometimes they may feel stuck in a job they dislike because they fear what else is out there. The same can be applied to relationships and other environmental contexts. Compounding the potential issue is their ability to see so many different angles and to consider so many different types of questions, they are especially prone to overthinking and analyzing.

Everything is shades of gray, so that there is no good direction, everything is flawed, no position is worth fully embracing. Nothing is black-and-white. This ambivalence coupled with their inherent passion of fear can make them among the most uncertain of the types.

All Sixes can be especially hard on themselves, akin to the inner critic of Ones, but unlike Ones who are in their body, Sixes keep the mental processes whirring in a dizzying array of voices. Some have postulated that the difference may be in Sixes having given up on truly achieving their desired goals through the goodness of others. Naranjo seemed to believe that Sixes were more introverted and inner-directed. Whatever the case, they may feel an inner guilt for not moving forward, but feel equally stuck in their fixated fears of the unpredictable world. When they run in these patterns long enough, they often turn to distractions on the wrong thing. They may shift their point of focus obsessively on virtually anything other than the actual source of their avoidance. This attentional shift in what should really be their point of focus functions as self-deception: they believe they are making some kind of "progress" when really they are not.

Because of their disposition to anxiety and their projected fear of what is really "out there" in the dangerous world, these Sixes are prone to panic attacks. They can run to self-soothing medications like alcohol, CBD or hemp, and other prescription-based medications. When they break free from the tyranny of anxiety and tap into the virtue of courage, they often find they are more than the sum total of their thoughts. They are more than the support systems they require, or the systems they put in place to function. They find they need alone time (more so than the other Sixes), and that they have an quirky creative side, as well as an adventurous side, both of which would put them into a more relaxed space in which they tap into a more complete and integrated sense of identity and selfhood.

**Social Sixes: Duty**

As opposed to warmth, these Sixes are cold. They can be a little like Threes in their efficiency. Ichazo first attributed the name of "Duty" to this subtype. This means less that they perform their duty, and more that they determine what their duty is. This is also the type most closely associated with the popular idea of Sixes as loyalists. Naranjo referred to them as a "Prussian character" referring to the dutiful and authoritarian stereotype of German rigidity.

These Sixes neither completely trust in others (like the Self-Preservation Six), nor in their own self like the Sexual Six). They handle their fear by attempting to placate and please something outside themselves, which manifests in the form of an authority. Like the Bob Dylan song "You Gotta Serve Somebody," these Social Sixes find a frame of reference, some kind of structure or agreed upon set of rules and beliefs, and follow the paint-by-numbers.

We probably see some characteristics of both of the other subtypes mixed into this one. Social Sixes are for sure a "cooler" character than the Self-Preservation. Another difference is their relationship with certainty. Whereas Self-Preservation Sixes see almost only shades of gray, Social Sixes tolerate no uncertainty or ambiguity. To do so would be to invite anxiety. These Sixes overcompensate in the other direction. They hold tight to their ideologies. They find safety in submitting to the prescribed rules of behavior they have come to recognize, accept, and/or believe in.

The rules they follow are not those that the Threes follow, those of popular opinion or trending on the market tastes and values. They tend to be "the rules of present or past authorities, such as the set of implicit inner rules of Don Quixote, who follows the knight errant in his imagination (235)." Political ideologies, religions, and family legacy and loyalty are all possible targets for their rigid adherence.

When the goals are clear and transparent, Social Sixes thrive. They are hard workers who tend to place a lot of pressure on themselves, mostly in assessing what is expected of them and how well they are executing. They tend to be highly skilled interpersonally, and in organizations are generally "in the know." While they can be rigid, especially when they sense that someone isn't in line with their own beliefs or ideals, they can also be non-threatening confidants. Often they see themselves as protectors of the group's dynamics. The way they test has less to do with one-to-one relationships and more to do with whether someone fits into the group.

In stress, many of these positive characteristics can disintegrate into ideologies without also engaging their active minds. Their projections can become life-like paranoidal fantasies and they can turn their anxiety onto blaming others for imagined slights. They might focus obsessively on people who don't fit into their belief group and persecute them. They may struggle with knowing their own identity as separate from their belief system or group loyalty. These Sixes do well to experience more spontaneity and to follow pleasure rather than measuring everything they do through the lens of duty and rule following. Their virtue of courage can lead them to a closer connection with themselves and their true emotions rather than out of fear of displeasing the given authority.

**Sexual/One-to-One Sixes: (countertype) Strength/Beauty**

While the Self-Preservation Six is seen as a doubling-down on the Sixes' anxiety, the mix between the anxiety and the sexual/one-to-one instinct here is more like oil and water. It's a strange mix that sometimes produces unexpected results. The counter-type, also termed the "counter-phobic," is often mis-typed as an Eight. They turn against the fear more like the bulldog than the rabbit, but it is a dog with more bark than bite. The underlying fear is quite different than it is for Eights. When it comes to fight or flight, this is very much the subtype with fight. They go after fear to manage it so that it feels less scary. The lack of "bite" means that they really aren't the in-your-face, nothing-but-body-confidence that Eights tend to be. You can recognize the head type patterns, and the passion of fear lurking not too deep beneath the surface. Another difference is that Eights seek to create order, while these Sixes create chaos and tend to disrupt order. Also, while Eights may mis-read social cues due to their movement against any kind of vulnerability, these Sixes are prone to mis-reading social cues more because they project threats and criticism where none may exist.

While it may be true that they have less bite than bark, their bark is fierce enough (or it wouldn't work). Their aim is to come from a position of strength and readiness, attacking and appearing strong so as not to be attacked. While all Sixes are full of contradictions, these Sixes are especially so. While they may come on strong through their testing and suspicious vigilance, they can switch to charming and assertive on a dime. They are notoriously non-trusting. They will bow up and get aggressive against any dominant position as a defensive strategy, and you can almost tell how strong their fear is based upon the intensity of their contrarian response. They like to work and think for themselves, which on its face may seem strange to the few others in their orbit who know the truth is that they don't actually trust themselves, which is a vulnerability they usually do not want to face.

But for all our descriptions of them as more like the bulldog than the rabbit, they can be friendly, open, and charming. It may be noted here, too, that this subtype has also been named "Strength/Beauty," as it has been theorized that the strength manifests among men and the beauty among women of this subtype. However, we see something of a blend in both genders. We still see the fundamental element of attacking anxiety in women and men, as well as the application of charm in its varieties, which sometimes implies physical beauty.

When they are thriving, they are even seen as outgoing, reaching out and connecting with people they may not know. They may project self-confidence and be high energy. All of this, however, can be viewed through the lens of testing out people and situations.

While they may be testing, they do value the approval of others. Of the three Six subtypes, they are the most likely to actively pursue opportunities. They like to demonstrate their skills and they expect others to do the same. When others fail to meet these expectations, these Sixes may come to distrust them, wondering what their hidden agendas might be.

Unlike their Seven neighbors, who are known as the optimists of the Enneagram, these natural contrarians can easily be mistaken as pessimists. But overall, in most cases, they report seeing the possibilities in ideas, they just believe that others generally are too strong in their support without really thinking things through. It is their incisive mental acuity that they bring as their contribution. When others push back or criticize them along these lines, they can be reactive. In stressful situations, or over prolonged periods of time without self-awareness, they move from supporting others who are on the same team to becoming combative and competitive. Their anger is a reaction to the uncertainty they feel, and it can be helpful for others who work with them to recognize their apparent sudden shifts in behavior.

The virtue of courage here may not seem as relevant since they seem to show courage already. But their courage as it relates to a response to fear means that they are always on guard, always armed (or projecting the need to be). In their case, these Sixes need to recognize the value and importance of putting down their arms.

### Working with Arrows in Growth and Stress

Sixes primary stance tends to *move towards* others. They can be welcoming of others and highly sensitive to how others in their immediate proximity are doing. There is a caretaking in the way Sixes can be loyal and bond with others in spite of what we've observed in the contrasts between subtype styles. One way or another, we see they want to be close to and on the side of authority.

They can move against authority, often in the form of testing. When they move against authority they may take contrarian stances reflexively. People who understand this about them may even play reverse psychological games with them, offering the opposite of what they really think. By contrast, Sixes can also cozy up to authority. When Sixes go too far in their positioning toward others they may become overly compliant and lose their sense of identity or values and what is important to them all in the name of pleasing the right people.

When Sixes move to the high side of their first neighboring wing style, they move into the Five point. Here, they can listen to their own source of inner wisdom. They can begin to trust their own sense of authority and boundaries and recognize within themselves their own autonomy and personal independence. The low side of Five might see them isolate themselves from others, unable or unwilling to move forward on their own for fear of what might happen on the other side of their fortress. Once Sixes have done some conscious work on establishing their Five wing, they are more prepared to focus on their Seven wing. The high side of the Seven wing will see them willing to act more spontaneously, to tap into their own sense of humor, try things out with curiosity and a sense of adventure. The low side of their Seven wing might see them unwilling to look at anything but the positive data at work, home, or in their relationships.

When these gentle moves—both within the head center—have been consciously developed and sustained, Sixes are ready for making the leaps out of the head through arrow work. When Sixes move against their first arrow, and toward the Nine consciously, they *move away from* others and their environment. They step back from their constant mental looping and step into a more embodied way of responding. They relax their fears and go with the flow. They aren't so caught up in what authority figures are or aren't doing. They trust that things will work out. When they go to the Nine in stress or unconsciously, they avoid conflict and fall asleep to themselves. They detach by procrastinating. They may act like they don't care, but they are disconnected more as a form of avoidance than anything else.

When Sixes have grounded themselves in solid and consistent movements into their Nine arrow, they are ready to move to their second arrow into the heart center at point Three. When they do this, they *move against* others and their environment. They express their agenda and take action to bring it about. They get organized, proactive and own their assertive energy instead of projecting their anger or fears onto others and then experiencing the world as a hostile and dangerous place. They get grounded in their personal will and move forthrightly in reasonable and strategic ways. They learn to accept fear, to be with fear, and not run from it. This in turn helps them to be their own inner authority, their own personal ally, from whom they can consult and trust. If they remain loyal to authorities of one kind or another, they do so out of fidelity to what they sense as right and virtuous, not out of the anticipation of what could go wrong if they don't.

Like so many of us when "getting things done" becomes the ideal, Sixes can move to their Three arrow and become busy to the point of distraction instead of in right action, and productive efficiency. They might also become aggressive or dogmatic in defense of their beliefs and become adversarial and perform tasks because it makes them look good or strong. Interestingly for Sixes, just like for Threes and Nines, they find themselves remaining in their primary center of intelligence while they work only on their wings. The arrow work takes them completely out of their primary centers and enters them into each of the other intelligences.

### Reactive Impulse Under Stress

Stress affects all types of course, but Sixes have a special attachment to stress. They often feel like if they're not stressed they're not being vigilant enough. For these head types in stress, they can get really shut down. The prefrontal cortex, the most recently evolved part of our brains, performs higher cognition, abstract thought, working memory, and all the executive functions. It impacts being able to concentrate, multitask, plan, and organize—everything you effectively need to function in our modern world of online activity, bringing up kids, and navigating the workplace.

As we observed in the beginning of this book, a person's perceived ability to control a stressor is a key determinant of its effect on their brain. If someone is overwhelmed by what is being asked of them, believing it to be beyond their capabilities even if it is not, they will view the task as something to be afraid of and the fear will prevail. The stress-signaling pathways engaged will then weaken the prefrontal cortex and strengthen more primitive parts of the brain. For no other type could this function more clearly than in the heads and personality structures of Sixes whose very passion is based in fear.

The whole idea of "fight or flight" is based on survival and adaptation. Most mammals lack what is called a "ventral stream," which means they literally don't see you unless you are moving. This is all to say that the instinct to freeze in paralysis of what you fear is based in our evolutionary DNA. It pays to freeze when you walk up on a bear (who is hopefully turned the other way). But the problem we face persistently today is that the very cause of the stress demands the executive functioning of the prefrontal cortex.

Sixes perhaps more than all other types or subtypes need to find ways to relax their stress while still meeting the requisite demands being made upon them—or that they perceive are being made. Among the first steps on the journey to the virtue of courage is to simply find what the very next good right course of action is, and to take it. Don't put the entire jigsaw puzzle together first in your mind. Simply put the next piece in place.

**Defining Characteristics in Personality**

→ Difficult to trust others and therefore difficult to work with until the others have passed an unspoken test

→ Poking holes in plans as a way to test them for how

strong they are

- → Analytical especially when it comes to processes and thinking through plans and ideas
- → Thinks in terms of optimal and worst case scenarios
- → Tend to be straightforward and trustworthy
- → Credit others even when they are responsible for the work often because they just are not comfortable with the attention focused on them
- → Can be innovative problem solvers and can also get mired down in fretting over all the problems and possibilities

**Superpowers**

For all of their skepticism and anxiety, when Sixes are at their best, they can be great truth tellers and problem solvers. Why? Because of their natural proclivity to workflow all the possibilities. They just have to trust the people they're working with, and the others have to be willing to hear the truth. These head types don't burrow into deep and narrow details without keeping an eye on the bigger picture, nor do they paint a rose-colored picture of how well everything will turn out. Not at all. Instead, they will break things down into their constituent parts and come up with well wrought solutions. And Sixes don't just ask questions for the sake of sounding smart or feigning curiosity. They are usually engaged when they ask their many questions, and they tend to ask the right questions, which, when conducted constructively leads to useful insights and specific and actionable takeaways. It may be hard sometimes to pass their trust test, or to even know that this is what is happening, but when others do pass it, Sixes will be your greatest allies. They are loyal, reliable, and people you can trust—all things they are looking for in others.

**Common Stressors for Sixes**

- → People and organizations who jump into action before thinking things through.
- → People who aren't reliable.
- → When people in positions of authority abuse their power.
- → When others demand decisions before they are ready to be made.

**Type Six Patterns to Observe to Make More Conscious**

- → Handling the anxiety in a direct way can help. Talking about your anxiety is a huge help for Sixes, who live with a lot of anxiety.
- → Working on when you're letting your mental center dominate. You have access to your Nine and Three arrows, which lead to body knowing and emotional intelligence, which can also give you information.
- → Learn when you are getting worked up into an anxiety frenzy, and trust your body's instinct to pull back and slow down.
- → When you cut others out and as a result might be difficult to work with, ask yourself how can you make yourself more open and receptive to what others who you may not know as well?
- → In all respects play a game called, Experiments with Courage. You might be able to envision all the ways it could go wrong, but what are ways you think you can't see that might transform your life experience?

## Activities To Lower Stress And Practice Self-Development

**Wrestling with the angel:** Jacob wrestled with an angel who turned out to be God. He came out with a permanent limp, but he wrestled with God and came out the other side stronger. Wrestle with your fears. Grow in the struggle. If you're not struggling, you're probably not growing. If you're never falling on the ski slopes, you're probably not becoming a better skier. People asked Gurdjieff all the time how long it would take for them to grow and become the transformed person he promised if they engaged in "the work." He constantly repeated that it depends on how hard you are working.

He once used the analogy of learning Russian. "People say Russian is hard to learn," he said. "But if you learn five words a day, you will never learn it. If you learn 200 words a day, you will learn it much faster."

Besides anxiety and fear, Sixes can also shame themselves when it comes to moments when they do feel paralyzed by their fear. Wrestling with fear is a way to grow even if you don't immediately step into that courage. Also, we encourage Sixes to remind themselves of the people they love, the people that love them, and, in some cases, the people who depend on them.

Sixes need to step into their courage in spite of the initial fear. Acknowledging the fear in the first place can be a starting point for efforts in growth. Sometimes also recognizing simply that you really have no other choice. Perhaps it's your business and you see a change coming up ahead. The business is your primary form of income. You don't need to change right now. In some cases, Sixes report the paradox of being scared not to step into their courage.

**Practice "What Would Happen If….?":** Sixes don't want someone to "fix it" for them. They usually want someone to "right-size" the anxiety. Don't minimize the anxiety, but also don't maximize it and be in the anxiety with them. Instead, work through the scenarios. Sixes can do this work on themselves. When you can stop and recognize yourself getting paralyzed by fear and inaction, run through a set of scenarios asking: What would happen if….?

**Do the next right thing:** Find the hardest thing you need to do for yourself right now, whether that's professional or personal and then ask yourself: What is the easiest way for me to do this?

The strong counter-type (Sexual/One-to-One) of this type is actually the opposite. They need to practice the courage to hold back because stepping forward isn't authentic in the first place. This takes some real negotiation for most one-to-one Sixes. How far is too far to step back? How do you assess accurately when you're attacking unnecessarily?

**Slow down and sink into the body:** The kind of body work for Sixes is like the opposite of what Fives need. They need calming exercise to slow down.

Enthusiast
Adventurer

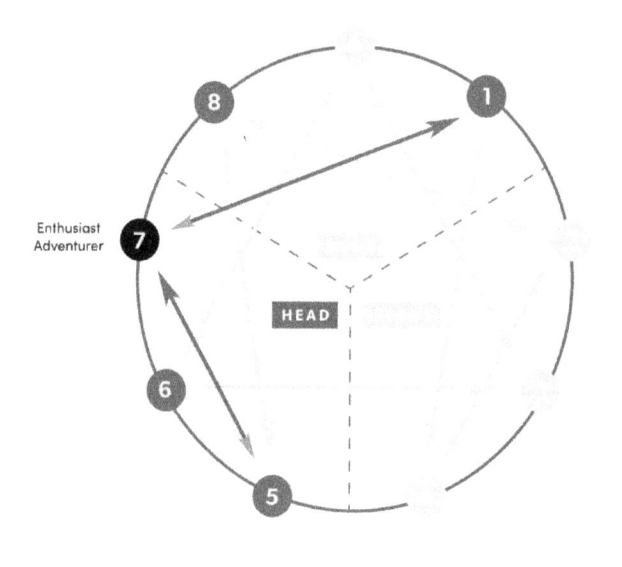

**7**

**HEAD**

**8**  **1**

**6**

**5**

PATH OF ENERGIZING    PATH OF RESOLUTION

# SEVENS: A LITTLE OF THIS, A LITTLE OF THAT (A LOT)

> *"In the time of your life, live—so that in that wondrous time you shall not add to the misery and sorrow of the world, but shall smile to the infinite delight and mystery of it."*
> —William Saroyn (from The Time of Your Life)

**In a single syllable:** More
**Persona:** Dilettante
**Mantra:** "I am not suffering."
**Reactivity defense mechanism:** Rationalization
**Passion:** Gluttony

### In a Nutshell

Ichazo's Ego-Plan focuses the center of egoic attention on making plans for the next big thing and the next. They are the ultimate samplers, never staying with one thing too long because there are so many options and sources of pleasure and gratification at their disposal. Sevens have an infectious enthusiasm for projects and engaging with others. They bring the fun. They are excellent ideators with deep faith in the possibilities ahead. Sevens tend to multitask, and are adept at brainstorming. They can lift the spirits of a group, and with their skills at storytelling they are naturally skilled at giving presentations, as well as marketing, sales, internal communications, and really anything that involves framing a narrative with some optimism. Sevens emphasize the positive data. With a little bit of self-awareness they begin to see how much of their motivation is about avoidance. They want to look at the shiny side of things and can't be bothered with anything that's going to bring them down. They are always looking for the exit doors in case they start feeling limited or trapped. They have a rebellious streak in them, which is masked by charm, as well as the avoidance of confrontation.

**Defining Characteristics of the Seven Type**

People new to the Enneagram sometimes joke that "everyone wants to be a Seven." On its surface, being in your Seven ego fixation can be a real joy ride. People respond so favorably to their optimism, the good vibes they put out, the new fun and interesting things they're always doing. They want to live a boundless life; they certainly don't want to be told what to do, or that they can't have all the things they want. And what do they want? They want options. They want opportunities. It's all good.

In fact, the question for many a Seven is: Why would I want to grow out of this and do a lot of difficult and painful work? The answer to that question is the same—in a sense—as it is for any type. Because the reality you've constructed is false. Because life isn't a rose-colored joy ride. If you avoid others all your life to keep your skewed reality in place as much as possible, you'll still experience painful emotions. You may experience the loneliness of disconnection, or of only having shallow connections for starters. You may still experience illness, the death of family members, or difficulty and stress in your occupation.

You may also experience the reality check that, in fact, there are limits.

Let us consider the incisive wisdom and insight from William James' *Varieties of Religious Experiences*, first published in 1902:

> In many persons happiness is congenital and irreclaimable. 'Cosmic emotion' inevitably takes in them the form of enthusiasm and freedom. I speak not only of those who are animally happy. I mean those who, when unhappiness is offered or proposed to them, positively refuse to feel it, as if it were something mean and wrong…In its involuntary variety, healthy-mindedness is a way of feeling happy about things immediately. In its systematical variety, it is an abstract way of conceiving things as good. Every abstract way of conceiving things selects some aspect of them as the essence for the time being, and disregards the other aspects. Systematic healthy-mindedness, conceiving good as the essential and universal aspect of being, deliberately excludes evil from its field of vision (78, 82).

Without reference to the Enneagram, James seems to have locked in on the Seven type. But for as functional as this optimistic frame of reference may be, what's at stake for Sevens? Why can't we all just look on the "sunny side of life"?

The most obvious answer is that for one thing there is pain in life. Loneliness, anxiety, sadness, any mental or physical health struggle, you name it. And it's not just pain within one's self, it's the pain that others experience in a Seven's life. But it's also about fulfilling a larger life plan. As Self-Preservation Seven, Elle Worsham, has said on our podcast:

> "Unfortunately, the ego of the Seven is so blinded from pain, pain in ourselves, pain that we caused others, because we rationalize our behavior very quickly

to dismiss any sort of pain that we may have caused somebody else. And so it takes quite a bit of courage. And I think you really probably have to have maybe gone through some life event, if something's not working. And you finally realize, maybe it's because you've added too many things to your plate, you keep dropping the ball, and we all live with this deeper knowing if we're honest, that this isn't working. And so, I think there's got to be something pushing you towards that…We're all a fraction of the whole. And if you're interested in becoming more of an integrated and whole version of yourself, then you have to be willing to open up to your slice of the pie and touch other numbers and move along the the map move beyond your type in order to integrate and ultimately that's going to grow you in compassion because you can connect with others more readily. And then, if you are a spiritual person, you are going to have a deeper spiritual life. And that's just the beauty of it."

Wonderfully said. Fear is the core emotion for all three of the head types, experienced in different ways. For Sevens you could say it's a fear of suffering. And so living in the head is almost like just staying there thinking through pleasurable things. You can stay there making plans or managing them or preparing for something fun, then you don't have to dip into that suffering.

We're not here to crash the Sevens' party. We get it. Everyone is in charge of their own experience, and everything should be available to everyone. If there is something out there that you want to experience, why shouldn't you be able to experience it, especially if you're willing to put your mind to it and make it happen? If limits are placed on you, your initial response is anger or irritation. Why should you be limited to something you want, especially when our Western culture especially talks about things like "manifesting your reality" and you "become your thoughts" and the "power of positive thinking" and "anybody can have whatever they want"?

The way you experience the rebellious nature of Sevens will usually not be obvious. Partly because by the time it may become apparent, they may be long gone. Partly too because they tend to befriend and work closely with those who are calling the shots in an effort to head off anything like confrontation or negativity at the pass. Sevens also report that they are not interested in following directions blindly. They want to cognitively understand why you're asking them to do something. They need to know why they need to do a specific activity, and what is the intended outcome. When they feel clear about their marching orders, then they feel free and possibly enthusiastic about doing a really good job. Otherwise, they're going to resist.

No doubt, any and all types get fixated in their functional personalities and stay there in the relative safety of those early adopted strategies all the days of their lives. We're not saying it's any easier or harder for any type. But we do agree with Elle's statement that for many Sevens, it may take some serious life challenges before they begin to step back and self-assess.

**The Passion of Seven**

On its face, much like the passion of avarice or lust, if we take "gluttony" literally then a preponderant love for food doesn't measure up to passions such as pride or self-deceit. But when we broaden our interpretation just as we do with avarice and lust and sloth, we can see immediately that the constant pursuit of pleasure (related to hedonism) is serious indeed. Such a hold on the psychology of an individual has the potential to pervade one's entire being. It certainly is an obstacle to reaching what we've mentioned above, which is a greater sense of self-knowledge and a fuller way of being and operating in the world.

C.S. Lewis touches on the subject in his 1942 book, *The Screwtape Letters*. The demon Screwtape is writing to his student who is actively working on taking hold of the soul of a "patient." He tells him (in the 17th Letter) that for a century they have made great strides in getting humans to think of gluttony of Delicacy, not gluttony of Excess. In other words, people who run around focused on trying a little of this and a little of that as if it were a virtue, but all the while they are totally consumed by trying the next thing and the next.

Gluttony is similar to lust in its insatiable nature. The difference, as pointed out by Naranjo and Ichazo, is that gluttony tends to seek variety in its search for pleasure. The glutton might stay with the same thing, but characteristically they are dreamers, aspirants of the next thing and the next. They don't want the same thing, but tend to like the "remote and the bizarre, adventure, and surprise." Naranjo also observes that gluttony, just like envy, seeks something outside that it "dimly perceives" it lacks within. The difference between the two is that envy has a "pronounced awareness" of the insufficiency, whereas gluttony covers it up with a "false abundance comparable to that of pride (172-173)."

Sobriety is a path towards seriousness, and going toward contentment over pleasure. It's hard to accept at first—it really does sound like we're here to crash the Sevens' party—but liking what you're doing, instead of doing what you like is the path. It's a reclaiming of proportion, and using just the energy needed to get a job done, and responding just to what life is bringing you in this moment. Sobriety doesn't translate as, "Have no fun." It means having a deeper satisfaction focusing on the one thing. Stick with an experience all the way to the end. It also means reducing the exaggerated need for stimulation and constant movement. We will examine areas for concerted focus and growth through the work with wing stretches and arrow movements.

**Functional Versus Authentic Personality**

We often say that the hard work of the Enneagram as a tool for growth is not for everyone. Gurdjieff said it again and again in no uncertain terms. It's not easy for anyone for a wide variety of reasons, not only because of the perception of favorable ego falseness like optimism, joy, and boundlessness. Also because, as we have stated now several times, our ego serves a purpose. We just want to be more than an automated pattern of behaviors. We want to be more than conditioned responses, most of which occurred at early life stages and we've been recreating ever since. This is what Gurdjieff meant when he said your personality is "not you" and to practice self-remembering.

Authentic personality for Sevens begins in a rooted wisdom, recognizing boundaries, and being willing to go deep where once the shallow banks had flooded over. It means getting grounded in your body, too. The head isn't the only place to habituate. Specifically, in authentic Sevens, we see a more relaxed approach to life. There is less of a need to charm others for fear of limitation, and more of a stability in the mundane or in activities that might have once seemed stultifying. They realize nothing outrageous and wild needs to happen for them to experience pure, unadulterated satisfaction. Another way of thinking about the pursuit of pleasure is that pleasure itself isn't to be feared or avoided, it's your relationship with it or your understanding of what pleasure really is.

**Psychological Roots and Key Patterns that Create Stress for Sevens**

As children, Sevens have a central need to feel a sense of safety and security during a period in which they need "practicing." When this isn't met for whatever reason, Sevens react to this by developing strategies and defenses for protection by idealizing the future and dreaming of options. They deal with anxieties and painful feelings by devaluing the boring and idealizing the stimulating or pleasurable.

In Sevens we see that the pleasure-seeking becomes equated with love equaling the indulgence of their wishes. The search for love becomes a striving for demonstrating their charm and superiority often through wit. Oftentimes they are celebrated for having a certain strength or giftedness. Naranjo also found that in many instances their fathers were fearful types, and in the majority of cases were head types (5, 6, or 7).

What many people don't realize is that Sevens are actually quite hard on themselves. They tend to hold in a lot of anxiety as well (although their level of awareness varies depending on subtype). What happens is they increase their activity and move faster and sometimes charm others. All of these actions serve to hide the anxiety. What's really important, of course, isn't the pleasure they're seeking, which can often just carry the stress and anxiety along with them. What they need to do is address it, and become more aware of it. It's never advisable to keep running from stress.

**Self-Preservation Seven: Keepers of the Castle**

Self-Preservation Sevens tend to arrange their lifestyle around practical choices, which in turn opens up the possibilities for pursuing the experience and interests that drive them. To that end, they tend to be the most materialistic of the three subtypes. They can be more grounded than the Sexual/One-to-Ones who tend to be more dreamers and idealistic, as well as the counter-type Socials who are more other-referencing and choose an anti-gluttony approach as a form of being good (more on them in a moment).

These Sevens tend to express their gluttony as a pursuit of the necessary resources that will maximize their well-being, their pursuit of pleasure, and their quest for an interesting life. This makes them adept at things like networking. They tend to always have their radars tuned in for tantalizing opportunities, and can be self-interested in the connections they do make (although this is not always conscious). They don't just make any alliances, however. They tend to band together with a select few whom they can rely on and trust. Especially when they've met their needs and are established with the band of friends or family they have chosen, they can be generous, giving every bit as much as they receive.

Because of their pragmatism, and their more self-focused nature, these Sevens are likely to recognize the limits of their gluttony and do something about it. Panelist and self-described Self-Preservation Seven, Justin Sainton says:

> I feel like sometimes I'm just enthusiastic and easily distractible. Which is why sometimes I have a hard time understanding why I am kind of internally so analytically driven about things. And I surprise myself and other people with that all the time. Like most people who know me they see me as fun and vivacious and whatever, but then they see the amount of spreadsheets that I run my life with, and the amount of detail and analysis that goes into every decision, and the amount of consideration of every potential perspective, before executing a plan.

Self-Preservation Sevens may at first struggle to know in

what direction to first turn when it comes to skill-building, or where to put roots down, but it doesn't tend to slow them down too much. It's possible for these Sevens, like any other type, to get stuck in roles they are expected to play rather than pursuing passions and ideals of their own. When this happens, it's perfectly possible to remain stuck, to keep looping in doubt from time to time, and maybe push back here and there to life circumstances, but never emerge into what they truly want to do. Most of the time, however, Self-Preservation Sevens find they are pretty good at a lot of things, and can learn skills quickly. Between their mental agility, and the sheer force of their upbeat attitude and often charismatic personalities, they are adept at trying things out until they do find what suits them.

When they do find what suits them they can be very hardworking, and even perfectionistic. They make To Do lists with the best of them, but paradoxically, if they spend too much time on a project, they become frustrated. Another apparently contradictory part of Self-Preservation Sevens is their desire for order and processes, but then resisting and possibly resenting them at the same time. While they are personable and potentially charismatic, we also observe that they tend to like to work on their own and on their own time frame.

What does suit them is generally things that leverage the most money for their time, and that grants them the independence they need so as not to feel confined or trapped. This subtype was originally called "family" by Naranjo and "defender" by Ichazo, which placed an emphasis on the need to form close relationships and alliances in order to meet their objectives. While the more current name is broader in application of how we define family, it still emphasizes the need of this subtype for taking care of each other through close bonds, as well as the intuitive need for boundaries in which to pursue the hunger for all the other possibilities life presents.

### Social Seven: (countertype) Sacrifice

You may know some Sevens by their sheer optimism if nothing else (see William James' quote in the general description for Sevens), but not so the Social Seven. You might even think that the Social Seven would be a "doubling-down" on Seven because of their general affability and good-natured spirit. But you would be mistaken. These Sevens can be hard to pin down (like many countertypes). The main reason is that Sevens work in "sacrifice" to their innate passion of gluttony, and they instead tend to submerge it in service to others. Naranjo calls them a type that wants to be "pure."

The altruistic behavior we often see in these Sevens saves them from the guilt of their attraction to pleasure or what they might view as selfish. When in personality, they very much want to be seen for their sacrifice. They want to be seen as "good" in whatever way it is defined culturally or socially. They may in fact do lots of good, but they also want to be seen as good. They want to be recognized and appreciated for what they do.

We often see this subtype in helping professions. We see them in ministry, nonprofits, and in the medical field, especially when it comes to reducing pain, such as with anesthetists, chiropractors, and physical therapists. In this respect, they can often look like Twos, who often like to be of service to others. One way to distinguish between them is that Twos are other-referencing while Sevens are self-referencing. Both, you could say, help for its own rewards. We have seen this type look a lot like Ones as well, especially in men who might have issues with anger or irritability. Ones, however, resist giving in to joy and excitement for fear of losing control. They can also be rigid and have an especially intense inner critic. Overall, you have to be able to recognize the mental operations going on in these Sevens and recognize them for the head types they are.

Panelist, Erin Maslowski, details her experience of learning how she wasn't the Self-Preservation Seven she tested as, and learned later how she was a Social.

> I didn't realize I was sort of a pain avoider. And then I came to one of the CP Enneagram workshops, not knowing my type for sure, I just knew Self-Preservation didn't really seem right. So I went to the workshop not knowing. And I went up to Beatrice [Chestnut] after a session, and said, 'Well, if you worry about your kids, like all the time, what's that? Is that Self-Preservation? Or is that Social?' She said it could be Social. And she had mentioned earlier that a lot of Social Sevens go into fields in which they take away pain. And that's just crazy because that's literally my job. I do a ton of back injections and send people to rehab therapies and guide them through various painful processes and stuff.

We also see in Social Sevens that they are future directed like the other Sevens. Their aspiration for social ideals are in service to a future in which they belong, or receive the social acceptance they never felt before. This insatiable thirst shows up as a longing for ease in social contexts, a release from any insecurities they feel. To the end, they are constantly envisioning how the larger world (and the smaller one they are locally entrenched in) could be made better, and they are playing their part.

They have an ability to be more down to earth than their subtype neighbors, often being able to work with people at any given level of an organization. Their aspirational ideals may frustrate those they work with when they are in leadership roles, but a good administrative team can help to keep them grounded. In general, whether in leadership or otherwise, they make for collaborative team members. They like to be recognized, but generally are modest about their accomplishments and contributions.

**Sexual/One-to-One Seven: Suggestibility**

Sexual/One-to-One Sevens are among the most high energy and apparently extroverted of all the subtypes in the Enneagram. They are constantly searching for ways to be entertained, as well as to entertain others. They are the visionaries, the dreamers, the ones who tend to see the world through rose-colored glasses. Their thoughts and imaginations are likely to take over their connection to their feelings or their body center. The "suggestibility" has to do with their susceptibility to other people's ideas. They may get readily excited about the latest and greatest idea or band or cool person at work or vacation possibilities. Because of their instinct to connect or relate to others, the focus of their attention (and therefore what they are most likely to be influenced by) are people they are attracted to.

These Sevens can be intense in their creativity, their approach to problem solving, and in their constant search for the next big thing. While all their excitement and enthusiasm and living in their head can generate a great deal of positive energy, it can also cloud their sense of reality. Sometimes, it may well be true that living on dreams can feed us more than facts, but those fantasies always have to come home to roost one way or another.

For all their visionary ability and willingness to work hard at solving problems, they are easily distracted. They are especially prone to the shiny new object. In work situations this can mean a quick mind packed with loads of curiosity about "what could be." In personal life, it can make it very difficult to settle down with a single partner.

They can be the ultimate "life of the party" type, the neighbors where everyone goes to party, the *bon vivant* who attends all the summer music festivals, and who will jump at any occasion to "run with bulls" or "paint the town red." As a colleague this can be fun to a point, but without self-awareness and maturity, the act wears thin to many. Not all the data is always positive. Every sales quarter isn't the best. Every fish you catch wasn't the biggest. Every event you attended wasn't the coolest.

They tend to exaggerate and to pull out the positive even in the most dismal situations. On the surface, they are fun and everyone wants to be around them. But most types begin to see through the act when there isn't more depth, and an act is exactly what it is when we function in personality and are not more conscious of our behaviors and the motivations behind them.

The virtue of sobriety can ground this subtype from living not only in their heads, but also in their fantasies. They can also learn to self-observe why they tend to exaggerate and why every story they tell has to focus on how it was "the best" or the "the brightest." Through the first steps of self-awareness and deepened self-understanding, they can begin to connect also with their feelings.

### Working with Arrows in Growth and Stress

Sevens primary stance tends to *move towards* others. Sevens are sociable and gregarious and enjoy being with people. They want to cheer people up and show others a good time. When they overdo their moving towards, they want all their encounters to be nice. They don't want any discomfort and don't want to be alone or bored.

We can observe differing levels of nuance in these behavior patterns, however, depending on the subtype, which may impact the degree to which these Sevens find themselves moving against, away, or toward. Much like with Fives, however, Sevens don't vary nearly as much from subtype to subtype in their basic stance of moving, in their case, *toward* the world, as most other types. Some minor variations can be observed.

We see a pragmatism in the self-preservation subtype, which keeps close and generally tight-knit alliances in friends and family and may have more of a materialistic appetite than the other two. With these preserving Sevens it is reasonable to assess they tend to *move away* unless there is a more practical reason for engagement. The countertype of the social Sevens demonstrates an unconscious move away from the passion of gluttony, but you could say they do tend to *move toward* others in a "doing good" or virtuous manner. They tend to make more of a show of doing good than perhaps we see in the basic motivations of Ones, but generally speaking their stance remains in step with the other Sevens. Finally, too, in the sexual/one-to-one subtypes, we find them dreaming of a perfect world in "sunshine daydreams" that once were and—with their future-oriented focus—of what could still be. In some cases and ways, then, they may at times *move away* from the world as well.

When it comes to working with the small growth movements involving wings, we see that Sevens share a neighboring head center at point Six, and move out of the head and into the body center at point Eight. Connecting first with the gentle movement of wing work, when they move to the high side of their Six neighbors, they see the possibilities but with a more grounded lens. They recognize that not all plans will work out just because they sound good right at first. They use the workflow and spreadsheet style of ideating to think through ideas and possibly the impact on others before spontaneously running them down. The lower side of their Six wing may find them caught up in the whirlwind of their thoughts and ideas, overanalyzing the motivations of the world around them, and feeling frozen. They may lack confidence to recognize what the next right thing to do really is.

When they become familiar with consciously stepping into their neighboring Eight wing and move more into their body they can experience the strength of putting their work and thoughts into action. They don't even need to think, they just do. They become their action, they know what to do even if it means a few ruffled feathers. Stepping into their Eight wing unconsciously or under stress may show up as aggression rather than assertiveness. They may find themselves doing more harm than good and others may see this as an irritable or angry side and feel less trustful of what they're going to get.

When Sevens have done the conscious work with their neighboring wings, they are ready to focus on the more dramatic shifts in their conscious personality work with arrows. When they move first to Five, they find themselves consciously *moving away from* others. Often in the form of meditation and breath work they take ownership of what they have been unconsciously consuming. They practice "transmuting internalization." They internalize and do for themselves what their external environment has been doing for them. Sevens who do this learn to detach and counteract their gluttonous impulses. Of course, when they move too far back in stress or unconsciously, Sevens can get overly intellectual and distanced from their feelings and body responses. They become walled within the castle rather than freely coming and going.

When Sevens feel grounded and ready for the next arrow move, they move to the One. In this way, they *move against* others and the world. Again they move to the body, but this time rather than in challenge and raw strength, it is more in procedure, process, and following through. They discriminate, critique, and chew on what they are offered rather than swallowing everything whole without so much as tasting. Their idealism keeps them actively engaged in their endeavors and are willing to engage even though the work becomes painful. When Sevens move too far into their stance against situations, they become overly critical and even angry that their exciting or exotic plans aren't panning out. Their anger can seep out as contempt or they might become piqued that they're not getting what they want when they want it.

**Reactive Impulse Under Stress**

Most Sevens are actually hard on themselves, but they tend to hide it. They don't tend to communicate the stress at first. When they become more acutely stressed it does show. Sevens avoid the stress by doing something fun and getting distracted rather than deal with it. They quicken their pace, becoming even less grounded and not slowing down to listen to feedback or especially to face difficult realities.

Sevens do have a lot of anxiety, but some of the subtypes are more inclined to being aware of it. Sometimes their pace quickens when under stress. They might do more, charm more, find other fun activities. And for a while this may look like it will produce great results, but they do tend to carry their anxiety with them.

A lot of time we may see a doubling-down of personality under stress, or a reactivity that is very much in the definition of a personality but just more acutely clear. While this is also true for Sevens, when the stress becomes more acute we often see them acting "out of character." They may become controlling, perfectionististic, difficult to work with, and cut down communication. They will also seek the quickest possible exit if they don't (unconsciously) sabotage and are asked to leave first.

**Defining Characteristics in Personality**

→ Like to make friends with everyone and nearly everyone likes them

→ Love talking about plans and rationalizing what they want to do over what they may be expected to do

→ Attracted to new opportunities and possibilities

→ Usually expresses positivity, happy and upbeat

→ Easily bored in meetings or anything dull or heavy and looking for the exit

→ Jump into new projects or relationships that excite them without slowing down to examine potential problems or self-assess

**Superpowers**

It's hard not to appreciate the gifts that Sevens bring to our lives. They make us laugh, they make us feel better about ourselves and the teams we work with. They are democratic in who they befriend, and tend to treat everyone as a peer (even in leadership positions). They are diplomatic and friendly. Their interest in you isn't fake, either. Most of the time they are sincerely interested in others. They also want to see others do their best. Rather than focusing on what isn't working, they will want to plow ahead and solve problems. Sevens tend to keep things moving along. They keep life interesting and upbeat. If you are prone to anything like melancholy, negativity, or criticality, Sevens can be your antidote. We all can use some Seven energy in our personal lives and on our teams.

### Common Stressors for Sevens

- → When people slow things down due to overanalysis or pessimism or simply not following through.
- → Confrontation, especially about what isn't going well or a difficult situation.
- → When anyone tries to control or manage them.
- → When everyone around them is morose or negative or serious.
- → When they are forced to do anything that is boring or pointless, from meetings to busywork to paperwork to unnecessary or difficult processes that don't yield tangible results.
- → When others don't take them seriously because they like to have fun.

### Type Seven Patterns to Observe to Make More Conscious

- → Ask yourself why it is so important to focus on the future. What is it about the current experiences you're having that you are avoiding and why?
- → Why is it so terrible to have limits? Why do you run at the first sign of constraint?
- → Most important of all, your avoidance of feelings. In your relentless pursuit of fun and positivity, do you ever think about what it is you're running from? Regardless of type, our emotions are the foundation of telling us the truth. Emotions tell us the "What?" that is going on inside. Your arrow work may point you to the Five point and then the One point, both of which will ground you. But don't overlook the work of integrating all of your centers of intelligence into your life. Doing work on letting yourself be available to your feelings may be one of the biggest leaps in your growth and development.

## Activities To Lower Stress And Practice Self-Development

**Give yourself structure:** Oftentimes we hide our pain even from ourselves. That can be really difficult for some Sevens to seek order because their external world is a reflection of what's going on inside. If you can remember that, maybe you can have some more compassion and help yourself by adding structure to your life that will eventually lead you to a greater freedom. Choose one thing, from the smallest to the larger depending on where you self-assess.

**Meditation:** Slow down. Ask yourself questions about how you're really doing. Develop a meditation practice. A common theme is to stop and assess. Consult with the heart and give space for emotions.

**Develop your three advisors with decision-making:** Before making a decision, start with your head. Ask yourself: What do I need to know about this decision? Then, move to your heart. Ask yourself: What should I pay attention to regarding feelings and value with this decision? Finally, go to your body. Ask yourself: What action should I be taking or not about this decision? Write each of these answers down. Why write them down? It helps to clarify your positions. If your advisors are in alignment with each other, this is usually a good sign that you are integrating all your centers into a sound decision. If they are not, this is a good sign that you are in conflict. You may need to reflect on the differences and consider which advisor is speaking with the most clarity and truth.

**Boundary tracker:** Sevens can have trouble with recognizing the need for boundaries. They also like to turn potentially difficult things into fun challenges. So, here's one: Pay attention to where you feel agitation and dissatisfaction in your life. Keep a stress tracker and check in with yourself three times every day to examine where you are. Keep a scale of 1 (I'm cool as a cucumber) to 10 (I'm at Defcon 1, about to explode.)

Peel back the mental layers of what's going on around you and how *you're interpreting it.* Once you are aware of where your stress is coming from and why it's happening, you can begin to shift your interpretations to something more useful.

# A FINAL WORD ON BURNOUT AND DEALING WITH DANGEROUS PEOPLE

By Dr. Shelley Prevost

*"Before you diagnose yourself with depression or low self-esteem, make sure you are not, in fact, surrounded by assholes."*
—William Gibson

We are social creatures and not only live in relationships with others, we know ourselves in relationships with others. It's not accurate to assume that we don't affect each other in both negative and positive ways.

We are all dangerous. Each of us has patterns of behaving and reacting in the world and when those patterns get disturbed or distorted, the result is a stressful encounter. If you exist in close and ongoing proximity to this person, you will perpetually be stressed.

I am a naturally empathic and emotional person. I have been this way since I entered the world. I explain it like I have emotional tentacles protruding from my body and they voluntarily and unconsciously sync up with other people's emotions, whether I want them to or not. This is a skill I believe I was born with. I can enter a room or speak to someone and instantly know the emotional climate of the room or the person. This is something a lot of heart types can relate to. I also didn't even know I was doing it for the longest time. I figured everyone else was filtering their reality in very much the same way. You don't know what you don't know.

Strong personalities can take advantage of this. They don't mean to, but it can be like a bug drawn to the light. If they don't have the empathy gene or the ability to deeply feel, they may siphon it from others who have it in spades.

It became clear that this was happening to me when, at one point not too long ago, I looked around and noticed that most of my professional relationships were with people who sucked me dry emotionally. I think this quickened my burnout episode.

There is a psychological phenomenon known as *narcissistic supply*, which we can think of as the emotional siphoning and adoration that a narcissist requires in order to feed his ego and retain power in the relationship. When you feed a narcissist for too long, it begins to drain you. Like a parasite, you give and give, feel and feel, until you realize you've given too much.

And then there's a reckoning with yourself. What in me needed to give so much?

And not all people are dangerous *to you*. You will have certain patterns of behavior (often unconscious) that attract dangerous people to you. And when you remain unaware, it will gradually lead to your undoing.

What makes someone dangerous to *you*?

→ Reinforces your false story for their own gratification
→ Low level of awareness—heightened reactions
→ Reinforces your unhealthy habits and patterns

We can all be dangerous to each other. If you operate from a low level of awareness, you too can be someone's "dangerous person." Identify the dangerous people in your life.

These are the people who reinforce your false stories and whose very survival depends on you staying stuck. And just as you are in a cage, so too is everyone else that hasn't done their inner work.

It can be tricky to talk about burnout. On the one hand it is an individual "work condition" brought about by unrelenting stress. And, on the other hand, this unrelenting stress is the result of both individual stressors *and* social forces that keep some people up and some people down. Both are true. And both deserve our attention and a deeper conversation.

Healthy systems are an upward spiral of positive exchanges where new ideas can be birthed. They are collaborative and resilient.

Unhealthy systems are ego-stoking, self-interested, and emotionally charged. Everything in the air and water feel toxic and to anyone who cares to notice, they are not psychologically safe. These systems exist and become a special sort of breeding ground for varying degrees of burnout. To do the hard work of understanding and recovering from our burnout, we have to wrestle with the fact that we may be steeping every day in a highly toxic and sick system.

### What To Do About It?

→ Get support—get a weekly shot in the arm from people who care about your well-being. This isn't sustainably the best route, but it may be enough to help you persist until you can exit. Some of the best support we can get is from deep listening.

→ What can be fixed? Who can you talk to?

→ If all options are exhausted, can you leave? Or, at the very least, can you create a plan for leaving? Truth bomb, company cultures are often a behemoth and changing them is slow change at best. If they change at all. Your life and health and relationships can be sacrificed on the altar of a job that no longer serves you.

In addition, we have a litany of hierarchical systems that keep some people up and some people down. I don't think we can talk about burnout in its entirety until and unless we deal with our imbalances as a society. It will never be perfect and stress will always exist, but if we can rebalance systems in such a way that stress is contained and not inflamed then we will be further along in the pursuit of an equal, just and healthy society.

**Acknowledgments**

Thank you to our teachers, mentors, and coaches.

Thank you to those who participated on panels on the Big Self Podcast and/or who volunteered to participate on panels to offer their personal experiences, insights, and expertise on types and subtypes. In no particular order, we thank you for the wealth of inner work, vulnerability, and humility you offer. We count you among the brave and generous:

Julie Baumann Rieth, Jared Byas, Angie Mabry Liskey, Jim Gum, Steph Barron-Hall, Jonathan Bow, Shay Bocks, Gene Jeffrey, Kirsten Barker, Mindy Klein, Chris Schoolcraft, Kristi Rider, Justin Ridley, Anne Frances Trusler, Linda Moore Graham, Matt Lesser, Stacey Ruff, Jessica Denise Dickson, Suzanna Cooper, Lesley Scearce, Vicki Hickenbottom, Randa Hinton, Carolyn Swora, Ashton Whitmoyer-Ober, Denise Cali DeAngelo, Kathy Turner Bryant, Richie Daigle, Suzy Anthony, Marta Gillilan, Roger Coles, Justin Sainton, Elle Worsham, Erin Maslowski

# BIBLIOGRAPHY OF BOOKS REFERRED TO OR CITED

### On Burnout

Davis, Paula. (2021) *Beating Burnout at Work: Why Teams Hold the Secret to Well-Being and Resilience.* Wharton School Press, Philadelphia.

Malesic, Jonathan. (2022) *The End of Burnout: Why Work Drains Us and How to Build Better Lives.* University of California Press.

Moss, Jennifer. (2021) *The Burnout Epidemic: The Rise of Chronic Stress and How We Can Fix it.* Harvard Business Review Press. Boston, Massachusetts.

Nagoski, Emily and Amelia Nagoski. (2020) *Burnout: The Secret to Unlocking the Stress Cycle.* Ballantine Books, New York.

### On Culture and Philosophy

Bateson, G., Jackson, D. D., Haley, J. & Weakland, J., 1956, "Toward a theory of schizophrenia." *Behavioral Science,* Vol. 1, 251-264.

Ichazo, Oscar. (2021) *The Religious Consciousness.* The Oscar Ichazo Foundation.

## On the Enneagram

Almaas, A.H. (1998) *Facets of Unity: The Enneagram of Holy Ideas.* Shambhala, Boulder, Colorado.

Almaas, A.H. (2021) *Keys to the Enneagram: How to Unlock the Highest Potential of Every Personality Type.* Shambhala, Boulder, Colorado.

Blake, A.G.E. (1996) *The Intelligent Enneagram.* Shambhala, Boulder, Colorado.

Chestnut, Beatrice. (2013) *The Complete Enneagram: 27 Paths to Greater Knowledge.* She Writes Press. Berkeley, California.

Chestnut, Beatrice and Uranio Paes. (2021) *The Enneagram Guide to Waking Up: Find Your Path, Face Your Shadow, Discover Your True Self.* Hampton Roads Publishing, Charlottesville, Virginia.

Christlieb, Fatima Fernandez. (2016) *Where on Earth Did the Enneagram Come From?* Self-Published.

Lapid-Bogda, Ginger. (2004) *Bringing out the Best in Yourself at Work: How to Use the Enneagram System for Success.* McGraw Hill Books. New York.

Maitri, Sandra. (2005) *The Enneagram of Passions and Virtues: Finding the Way Home.* Penguin, New York.

*Naranjo, Claudio. (1994) *Character and Neurosis: An Integrative View.* Gateways Books. Nevada City, California. *primary source

Naranjo, Claudio. (1996) *Ennea-Type Structures: Self-Analysis for the Seeker.* Gateways Books. Nevada City, California.

Riso, D.R. and Hudson, R. (1996) *Personality Types: Using the*

*Enneagram for Self-Discovery*. Houghton Mifflin, New York.

Sikora, Mario and Maria Jose Munita (2020) *Instinctual Leadership: Working with the 27 Subtypes of the Awareness to Action Enneagram*. Self-Published.

Wagner, Jerome. (2010) *Nine Lenses on the World: The Enneagram Perspective*. NineLens Press. Evanston, Illinois.

## On General Psychology

Bargh, John A. (2017) *Before You Know It: The Unconscious Reasons We Do What We Do*. Touchstone. New York.

Brown, Jenny. (2012) *Growing Yourself Up: How to Bring Your Best to All of Life's Relationships*. Exisle Publishing. New Zealand.

Hillman, James. (1996) *The Soul's Code: In Search of Character and Calling*. Warner Books. New York.

Van Kaam, Adrian. (1972) *Envy and Originality*. Doubleday, New York. (in reprint from Epiphany Books, Pittsburgh, Pennsylvania.)

Usatynski, Theodore J. (2009) *Instinctual Intelligence: The Primal Wisdom of the Nervous System and the Evolution of Human Nature*. Flying Cedar Press. Worley, Idaho.

## Gurdjieff

Ouspensky, P.D. (1949) *In Search of the Miraculous: The Teachings of G.I. Gurdjieff*. Harcourt, New York.

Ouspensky, P.D. (1957). *The Fourth Way: An Arrangement of Subject of Verbatim Extracts from the Records of Ouspensky's Meetings in London and New York, 1921-1946*. Vintage Books, New York.

**On Stress in the Body**

Hari, Johann. (2018) *Lost Connections: Why You're Depressed and How to Find Hope*. Bloomsbury, USA.

Mate, Gabor. (2003) *When the Body Says No: Exploring the Stress-Disease Connection*. Turner Publishing Company, Nashville, Tennessee.

Van Der Kolk, Bessel A. (2014) *The Body Keeps the Score: Brain, Mind, and Body in the Healing of Trauma*. Penguin, New York.

**On Time, Sleep, and Boundaries**

Pink, Daniel H. (2018) *When: The Scientific Secrets of Perfect Timing*. Riverhead Books. New York.

Roenneberg, Till. (2012) *Internal Time: Chronotypes, Social Jet Lag, and Why You're So Tired*. Harvard, UP. Cambridge, Massachusetts.

Sanok, Joe. (2021) *Thursday is the New Friday: How to Work Fewer Hours, Make More Money, and Spend Time Doing What You Want*. HarperCollins Leadership. New York.

**Further Reading on Gurdjieff**

Lachman, Gary. (2004) *In Search of P.D. Ouspensky: The Genius in the Shadow of Gurdjieff*. Quest Books. Wheaton, Illinois.

Lipsey, Roger. (2019) *Gurdjieff Reconsidered: The Life, the Teachings, the Legacy*. Shambhala, Boulder, Colorado.

Wertenbaker, Christian. (2017) *The Enneagram of Gurdjieff: Mathematics, Metaphysics, Music, and Meaning*. Codhill Press. New Paltz, New York.

Wilson, Colin. (1986) *G.I. Gurdjieff: The War Against Sleep.* Aeon Books, London.